ABOUT THE SIXTH EDITION

This 2021 edition of *Freedom in the 50 States* presents a completely revised and updated ranking of the American states on the basis of how their policies promote freedom in the fiscal, regulatory, and personal realms.

This edition again improves on the methodology for weighting and combining state and local policies to create a comprehensive index. Authors William Ruger and Jason Sorens introduce many new policy variables suggested by readers and changes in the broader policy environment (for example, vaping regulations). More than 230 policy variables and their sources remain available to the public on our website for the study (www.freedominthe50states.org).

In the 2021 edition, the authors have updated their findings to

- Provide the most up-to-date freedom index yet, including scores as of January 1, 2020.

- Add a new section analyzing how state COVID-19 responses have affected freedom since the pandemic began. This section also discusses significant policy changes and trends since the data cutoff, ensuring that readers have a strong sense of the state of freedom in the states today.

- Refresh their analysis of how the policies driving income growth and interstate migration have changed pre– and post–Great Recession.

In addition to providing the latest rankings as of the beginning of 2020, the 2021 edition provides annual data on economic and personal freedoms and their components back to 2000 (and for some variables, back to 1937 and up through the start of 2021).

Published by the Cato Institute and accompanied by demographic and economic data on each state, *Freedom in the 50 States* is an essential desk reference for anyone interested in state policy and in advancing a better understanding of a free society.

www.freedominthe50states.org

Where liberty dwells, there is my country.

—Benjamin Franklin

FREEDOM IN THE 50 STATES

An Index of Personal and
Economic Freedom

Sixth Edition

William P. Ruger
Jason Sorens

Cover design and art direction by Jon Meyers.
Book design by Melina Yingling Enterline.
Printed in the United States of America.

To reach the authors of this publication or ask questions about state and local
policy, please contact the Cato Institute at 202-789-5200 or pr@cato.org.

ISBN: 978-1-952223-26-6 (paperback)
ISBN: 978-1-952223-27-3 (ebook)

Library of Congress Cataloging-in-Publication Data available.

Cato Institute
1000 Massachusetts Avenue, NW
Washington, DC 20001
www.cato.org

CONTENTS

INTRODUCTION

his study ranks the American states according to how their public policies affect individual freedoms in the economic, social, and personal
spheres. Updating, expanding, and improving on the five previous editions of *Freedom in the 50 States*, the 2021 edition examines state and local
government intervention across a wide range of policy categories—from
taxation to debt, from eminent domain laws to occupational licensing, and
from drug policy to educational choice.

For this new edition, we have added several more policy variables while
improving the way we measure land-use regulation, minimum-wage regulation, and (for the alternative indexes) abortion policy. Our time series now
covers the 20 years in the period 2000–2019. Finally, we continue to investigate the causes and consequences of freedom with detailed, up-to-date
methods.

We began this project to fill a need: *Freedom in the 50 States* was the first
index at any level to measure both economic and personal freedoms and
remains the only index to do so at the state level. We also strive to make it the
most comprehensive and definitive source for economic freedom data on
the American states.

Measuring freedom is important because freedom is valuable to people. It
is both a means to their flourishing or "life projects" and an end in itself. At
the very least, it is valuable to those whose choices are restricted by public
policy. Although the United States has made great strides toward respecting each individual's rights regardless of race, sex, age, or sexual preference,
some individuals face growing threats to their interests in some jurisdictions. Those facing more limits today include smokers, builders and buyers
of affordable housing, aspiring professionals wanting to ply a trade without

paying onerous examination and education costs, and less-skilled workers priced out of the market by minimum-wage laws. Moreover, although the rights of some have increased significantly in certain areas, for the average American, freedom has declined generally because of federal policy that includes encroachment on policies that states controlled 20 years ago.

In the American system, even "benefit to others" cannot justify trampling on certain freedoms. Books may not be banned simply because the ideas and arguments they present offend some readers. Racial segregation would be unjustified even in the unlikely event it was somehow considered efficient. Likewise, state and local governments ought to respect basic rights and liberties, such as the right to practice an honest trade or the right to make lifetime partnership contracts, whether or not respecting these rights "maximizes utility." Some infringements on these rights may seem relatively small, almost harmless, or only symbolically significant, such as laws that allow police to build automated license plate databases that track drivers, or laws that authorize DNA collection from nonviolent arrestees without a court hearing. Nevertheless, even minor infringements on freedom can erode the respect for fundamental principles that underlie our liberties. The idea of respecting the moral dignity of individuals through the legal protection of their rights is underrated, and its erosion by thinking of people abstractly or primarily as members of groups underappreciated. This index measures the extent to which states respect or disrespect these basic rights and liberties; in doing so, it captures a range of policies that threaten to chip away at the liberties we enjoy.

Our index encompasses both economic and personal freedoms because the two sets of freedoms are complementary. A state scoring high in economic freedom but not in personal freedom—a hypothetical American Singapore—would not be a really free state in the way the liberal tradition understands it. Nor would a state high in personal freedom but low in economic freedom—an American Argentina—provide the liberal conditions necessary for human flourishing in the broadest sense.

Even to economist Milton Friedman, a mere "economic freedom index" would not be a real freedom index. In his 1962 book *Capitalism and Freedom,* Friedman explores the connection between economic and political freedoms, finding that political freedom in the absence of economic freedom is unlikely to last. He writes, "It is a mark of the political freedom of a capitalist society that men can openly advocate and work for socialism,"[1] while a socialist society does not permit the reverse.

Similarly, at the state level, Americans will derive more value from their

1.   Milton Friedman, "The Relation Between Economic Freedom and Political Freedom," chapter 1 in *Capitalism and Freedom* (Chicago: University of Chicago Press, 1962), p. 16.

economic freedom the more extensive are their personal freedoms, and vice versa. That does not mean that states scoring high on a particular dimension of freedom—fiscal, regulatory, or personal—will also score high on the others, but Friedman's work suggests that the different dimensions of freedom are most valuable in combination.

Several different audiences have found the information and analysis in this book useful. We believe this book will continue to be valuable to the following readers:

- State legislators and governors, their staffs, and local policymakers interested in liberty can use the data and rankings to see where their states stand relative to other states and to determine where real improvements can be made. Although policymakers are better situated than we are to make precise judgments about the benefits of specific legislation, this book does offer reform ideas tailored to each state. These ideas are contained in the state profiles located at the end of the study.
- Scholars can use the index to model politics and policy outcomes in areas such as economic growth and migration. These data are also a valuable resource for teachers and students, providing easy access to information that can be used for policy analysis or statistical projects.[2]
- Businesses considering new investment opportunities or relocation can use the data to analyze state tax and regulatory regimes and the relative openness and toleration that attract highly productive employees.
- Reporters can use the data to understand their states' policy debates in a national context. They could also use them to hold elected officials accountable for infringements on freedoms and state performance.
- Individual citizens can use the data to better understand what their state governments are doing and thus be better-informed participants in the democratic process. The data are also useful to those seeking to move to a freer state, something we have observed anecdotally as happening more and more.

This book scores all 50 states on their overall respect for individual freedom, and also on their respect for three dimensions of freedom considered separately: fiscal policy, regulatory policy, and personal freedom. To calculate these scores, we weight public policies according to the estimated costs

---

2.   See our State Policy Database at http://www.statepolicyindex.com or footnote 18 in this book for citations of research using the data.

that individuals suffer when government restricts their freedoms. However, we happily concede that different people value aspects of freedom differently. Hence, our website provides the raw data and weightings so that interested readers can construct their own freedom rankings; this information is available at www.freedominthe50states.org.

DEFINING FREEDOM

"Freedom" is a moral concept. What most people mean by freedom is the ability to pursue one's ends without unjust interference from others. Of course, reasonable people can disagree about what counts as unjust interference, and it is also controversial whether freedom in this sense ought to trump other desiderata, such as social welfare, equality of outcome, or equity. These questions cannot be answered in a value-neutral way, but citizens and policymakers must try to answer them nonetheless. We are forthright about our moral philosophy so that we can be precise about what counts as "freedom" for us, but we recognize that others may define freedom differently. We have made the data and weights available online so that people can alter our index to fit their own conceptions of freedom. We consider it an open, but interesting, question whether freedom is in any way related to indicators of aggregate social welfare, such as income growth and migration. Part 2 takes up this question in more detail.

We ground our conception of freedom on an individual rights framework. In our view, individuals should not be forcibly prevented from ordering their lives, liberties, and property as they see fit, as long as they do not infringe on the rights of others.[3] This understanding of freedom follows from the natural-rights liberal thought of John Locke, Immanuel Kant, and Robert Nozick, but it is also consistent with the rights-generating rule utilitarianism of Herbert Spencer and others.[4] From the Declaration of Independence, through the struggles for the abolition of slavery, and up to the 20th century, this conception of freedom was the traditional one in the United States. As Justice Louis Brandeis wrote in his 1928 dissent in *Olmstead v. United States,* "The makers of our Constitution . . . conferred, as against the government, the right to be let alone—the most comprehensive of rights and the right most valued by civilized men."[5] In the context of the modern state, this philosophy engenders a set of normative policy prescriptions that political theorist Norman Barry

---

3. We recognize that children and the mentally incompetent must be treated differently from mentally competent adults, and also that some rights may not be alienated even by consenting adults.

4. See John Locke, *Second Treatise of Civil Government;* Immanuel Kant, *Foundations of the Metaphysics of Morals;* Robert Nozick, *Anarchy, State, and Utopia* (New York: Basic Books, 1974); and Herbert Spencer, *Social Statics, or the Conditions Essential to Happiness Specified, and the First of Them Developed* (London: John Chapman, 1851).

5. *Olmstead v. United States,* 277 U.S. 438 (1928).

characterized as "a belief in the efficiency and morality of unhampered markets, the system of private property, and individual rights—and a deep distrust of taxation, egalitarianism, compulsory welfare, and the power of the state."[6]

In essence, this index attempts to measure the extent to which state and local public policies conform to this ideal regime of maximum, equal freedom.[7] For us, the fundamental problem with state intervention in consensual acts is that it violates people's rights. To paraphrase Nozick, in a free society the government permits and protects both capitalist and noncapitalist acts between consenting adults.[8] Should individuals desire to "tie their own hands" and require themselves to participate in social insurance, redistributive, or paternalist projects, they should form voluntary communities for these purposes.[9]

Those who endorse the "law of equal freedom" at the heart of classical liberalism and the political order espoused in this index do not necessarily reject the notion of "constraints." Neither the liberal order nor even the libertarian approach requires that one take an ethically or normatively neutral stance about how people use their freedom. For instance, it is perfectly consistent to reject "libertinism" ("do whatever you want so long as you do not hurt anyone else, whether it be snorting cocaine or engaging in casual sex") and even make strong moral claims about the proper way to live a virtuous, flourishing life without sacrificing one's credentials as a friend of liberty.[10] Libertarianism does not imply libertinism, and the two may even stand in some tension, if Steven Pinker is correct that the "civilizing process" has encouraged the adoption of new moral and mannerly constraints to allow people to interact more peacefully with each other without Leviathan.[11] Supporting the right of consenting adults to use drugs or of bakers to contract with bakeries to employ them more than 60 hours a week does not require judging those behaviors to be wise or even morally justified. Therefore, the freedom index makes no claim about the wisdom or morality of the behaviors that states should allow adults to pursue freely. It is left to philosophers, theologians, and all of us as

---

6. Norman Barry, "The Concept of 'Nature' in Liberal Political Thought," *Journal of Libertarian Studies* 8, no. 1 (1986): 16n2.

7. The "equal freedom" that persons enjoy in a free society is, for us, equality of rights and equality before the law, not equality of opportunities or "positive freedom." On positive freedom, see Isaiah Berlin, "Two Concepts of Liberty," in *Four Essays on Liberty* (Oxford: Oxford University Press, 1969).

8. Nozick, *Anarchy, State, and Utopia*, p. 163.

9. Almost all real-world governments do not constitute voluntary communities because their constitutions do not enjoy the unanimous consent of the governed. Homeowners' associations, by contrast, do in theory fit into this category.

10. Elsewhere we define libertinism more specifically as "radically indifferent to the choices that people make with their freedom. This line of thinking holds that as long as an act is consensual and respects at least one truth—the inviolability of the person's fundamental right to choose how to use his or her person and property—not only should the law not get involved, but there is also no ground for moral criticism of the act." See William Ruger and Jason Sorens, "The Case for 'Virtue Libertarianism' Over Libertinism," Reason.com, June 9, 2016.

11. Steven Pinker, *The Better Angels of Our Nature: Why Violence Has Declined* (New York: Viking, 2011).

moral agents to make arguments about the legitimacy of particular moral constraints.[12] However, we think the evidence of human experience strongly suggests that freedom is more likely to survive if there is a supportive moral ecology that emphasizes respect for the moral dignity of all people, the importance of personal responsibility (including an active concern about minimizing negative externalities), thrift, probity, temperance, benevolence, courage (which in this world might mean opposing "safetyism" and the "precautionary principle"), humility, and other traditional and bourgeois virtues.

Although our belief in limited government and a free society is based on the moral dignity of each human being, empirical evidence suggests that the protection of individual rights tends to foster economic growth and the coinciding improvements in people's living standards. Economist Robert Lawson explains the relationship between economic freedom and economic growth:

> Numerous studies have shown that countries with more economic freedom grow more rapidly and achieve higher levels of per-capita income than those that are less free. Similarly, there is a positive relationship between changes in economic freedom and the growth of per-capita income. Given the sources of growth and prosperity, it is not surprising that increases in economic freedom and improvements in quality of life have gone hand in hand during the past quarter of a century.[13]

We also recognize that freedom, properly understood, can be threatened as much by the weakness of the state as by overbearing state intervention. Individuals are less free when they have reason to fear private assaults and depredations, and a just government punishes private aggression vigorously. However, this book focuses on threats to individual liberty originating in the state. Therefore, we do not code the effectiveness of state governments in reducing rights violations. For instance, we do not calculate measures of the efficacy of state police and courts or of violent and property crime rates.[14] Thus, our "freedom index" does not in theory capture all aspects of

---

12. We consider ourselves to be "virtue libertarians" (a term we have adopted as the result of many conversations over the years about our particular "conservative libertarian" brand of ethical and political thinking)—espousing strong support for a libertarian political order but also strong convictions about what a flourishing, moral life demands and how we ought to use our freedom (with proper humility, of course, about our ability to know with any certainty what the best life is for any individual or for people in general). We also think that certain behaviors are more consistent than others with the preservation and security of a free society. Our approach owes much to the work of Frank Meyer, Albert J. Nock, and Walter Block.

13. Robert A. Lawson, "Economic Freedom and the Wealth and Well-Being of Nations," in *The Annual Proceedings of the Wealth and Well-Being of Nations*, 2009–2010, vol. 2, ed. Emily Chamlee-Wright and Jennifer Kodl (Beloit, WI: Beloit College Press, 2010), pp. 65–80.

14. Measuring the efficacy and justice of criminal penalties, arrest procedures, and so forth with regard to deterrence, proportionality, retribution, rehabilitation, and the like is an extremely complex endeavor that deserves a lengthy treatment on its own. See Richard A. Posner, *The Economics of Justice* (Cambridge, MA: Harvard University Press, 1981). See, for example, the CIRI Human Rights Dataset, http://ciri.binghamton.edu.

freedom, and we encourage readers to use our scores in conjunction with other indicators when assessing government effectiveness or quality of life. At the same time, we do attempt to capture the extent of "overcriminalization" by states, as well as the extent to which state civil liability systems put property rights at risk.

Our definition of freedom presents specific challenges on some high-profile issues. Abortion is a critical example. According to one view, a fetus is a rights-bearing person, and abortion is therefore almost always an aggressive violation of individual rights that ought to be punished by law. The opposite view holds a fetus does not have rights, and abortion is a permissible exercise of an individual liberty, which entails that legal regulation of abortion is an unjust violation of a woman's rights. A third view holds that a fetus gains personhood and rights at some threshold during its development, and at that point legal regulation is pro tanto justified. Rather than take a stand on one pole or the other (or anywhere between), we have not included the policy in the main freedom index. We have coded the data on state abortion restrictions and made them available online at http://www.statepolicyindex.com, and *Freedom in the 50 States* has a section that includes alternative indexes based on three of many possible state abortion regimes.

Another example is the death penalty. Some argue that murderers forfeit their own right to life, and therefore state execution of a murderer does not violate a basic right to life. Others contend that the right to life can never be forfeited, or that the state should never risk taking away all the rights of innocent individuals by falsely convicting them. State sentencing policies short of the death penalty could also be debated, such as lengthy periods of solitary confinement. We personally have serious reservations about some of these punishments, but we do not include them in the freedom index, although we have coded the death penalty data and made them available online at http://www.statepolicyindex.com.

It is important to note that the freedom index stands within the mainstream tradition in social science of measuring normatively desired phenomena, such as democracy,[15] civil liberties,[16] and human rights.[17] Clearly, our index will have intrinsic interest for classical liberals and libertarians. However, nonlibertarian social scientists will also benefit from the index because it is an open question how individual liberty relates to phenomena such as economic growth, migration, and partisan politics in the American states. In the same way, political scientists may value democracy for its own sake; however, they can also research empirically what causes democracy and

---

15. See, for example, the Polity IV Project, http://www.systemicpeace.org/polity/polity4.htm.

16. See, for example, the Freedom House indicators, http://www.freedomhouse.org.

17. See, for example, the CIRI Human Rights Dataset, http://www.humanrightsdata.com/p/data-documentation.html.

how democracy affects other phenomena. In fact, a broad range of social scientists and policy analysts have already used this index to investigate a range of interesting questions, including the effects on growth, migration, corruption, entrepreneurship, accident death rates, veterans' earnings, and state bond ratings.[18]

CREATING THE INDEX

We started this project by collecting data on more than 230 state and local public policies affecting individual freedom as previously defined. For data other than taxes and debt, we code laws enacted as of January 1, 2020 (even if they come into force later). We also code these variables for 2000–2019 and, in some cases, for prior years. For taxes and debt, the latest available data covering states come from fiscal year (FY) 2020 and for local governments from FY 2019, which for most states ran from July 2019 to June 2020. To create a fiscal policy index, we assume that FY 2020 local debt, assets, and taxes are equal to FY 2019 local debt, assets, and taxes, whereas we have actual FY 2020 data for the state level. For each year's freedom index, we use tax and debt data from the subsequent fiscal year because state budgets are enacted in the year before. Thus, the most recent fiscal year featured in the index is FY 2020, because it represents the budget that had been enacted as of December 31, 2019, in each state.

For a few variables in the index that we do not have available for every year, we have to carry forward or back or interpolate the data for these policies to include them. The master spreadsheet available at http://freedominthe50states.org includes comment fields explaining exactly what was done in each of these cases.

The index also includes variables that do not differ across states for particular years. Usually, this lack of variation is a result of policies being nationalized at the federal level. Sometimes, this centralizing process occurs in a pro-freedom direction, as when the Supreme Court struck down Chicago's

18.   Noel D. Johnson et al., "Corruption, Regulation, and Growth: An Empirical Study of the United States," *Economics of Governance* 15, no. 1 (2014): 51–69; Richard J. Cebula, "The Impact of Economic Freedom and Personal Freedom on Net In-Migration in the US: A State-Level Empirical Analysis, 2000 to 2010," *Journal of Labor Research* 35, no. 1 (2014): 88–103; Nicholas Apergis, Oguzhan C. Dincer, and James E. Payne, "Live Free or Bribe: On the Causal Dynamics between Economic Freedom and Corruption in US States," *European Journal of Political Economy* 28, no. 2 (2012): 215–26; Rick Weber and Benjamin Powell, "Economic Freedom and Entrepreneurship: A Panel Study of the United States," *American Journal of Entrepreneurship* 6, no. 1 (2013): 67–87; Leland K. Ackerson and S. V. Subramanian, "Negative Freedom and Death in the United States," *American Journal of Public Health* 100, no. 11 (2010): 2163–64; Alberto Dávila and Marie T. Mora, "Terrorism and Patriotism: On the Earnings of US Veterans Following September 11, 2001," *American Economic Review* 102, no. 3 (2012), 261–66; Ariel R. Belasen, Rik W. Hafer, and Shrikant P. Jategaonkar, "Economic Freedom and State Bond Ratings," *Contemporary Economic Policy* 33, no. 4 (2015): 668–77; Wenchi Wei, "Fiscal Slack, Rule Constraints, and Government Corruption," *Public Administration Review* (2021); Joshua C. Hall, Donald J. Lacombe, and Timothy M. Shaughnessy, "Economic Freedom and Income Levels across U.S. States: A Spatial Panel Data Analysis," *Contemporary Economic Policy* 37, no. 1 (2019): 40–49; Dean Stansel and Meg Tuszynski, "Sub-National Economic Freedom: A Review and Analysis of the Literature," *Journal of Regional Analysis and Policy* 48, no. 1 (2017): 61–71.

gun ban and several states' sodomy laws, but more often it occurs in an anti-freedom direction, as when the Patient Protection and Affordable Care Act (PPACA) legislated health insurance community rating, guaranteed issue, prior approval of premiums, and an individual health insurance mandate nationwide. The last policy, the individual mandate, has since been ended by Congress. This is the only example in our data set in which Congress explicitly decentralized a policy to the states and increased freedom. Federalization of state policies has now happened frequently enough over our time series that we continue to include for the second time in the history of this study alternative freedom indexes that exclude all policies that were federalized at any point (see Appendix B). These indexes are particularly useful for investigating the freedom impact of state-level policymakers, rather than the freedom environment enjoyed by state residents.

The top-level data used for creating the index are available in a downloadable spreadsheet at http://freedominthe50states.org. However, to obtain details on data sources and the construction of indexes (such as the eminent domain reform and renewable fuels standards indexes), interested readers should navigate to http://statepolicyindex.com and download the policy category spreadsheets. Each variable in the top-level spreadsheet has a code, such as "adebtpia" (state and local debt divided by adjusted personal income). The first letter of that code corresponds to the particular spreadsheet where its details may be found. Thus, "adebtpia" comes from the "a_fiscal_20.xls" spreadsheet for fiscal policies. Quite often, these spreadsheets contain additional policies not included in the freedom index, as well as data for additional years when available. Some state and local tax and spending data are available annually back to FY 1977 and quinquennially back to FY 1957. Some alcohol policies are available from 1937.

Because we want to score states on composite indexes of freedom, we need a way to weight and aggregate individual policies. One popular method for aggregating policies is "factor" or "principal component" analysis, which weights variables according to how much they contribute to the common variance—that is, how well they correlate with other variables.

Factor analysis is equivalent to letting politicians weight the variables, because correlations among variables across states will reflect the ways that lawmakers systematically prioritize certain policies. Partisan politics is not always consistent with freedom (e.g., states with more marijuana freedom offer less tobacco freedom; indeed, the correlation between tobacco freedom and marijuana freedom is −0.56, which is quite strong). The index resulting from factor analysis would be an index of "policy ideology," not freedom.[19]

19. Jason Sorens, Fait Muedini, and William P. Ruger, "U.S. State and Local Public Policies in 2006: A New Database," *State Politics and Policy Quarterly* 8, no. 3 (2008): 309–26.

Factor analysis is also not justified if important variables do not line up with a clear ideological position but have a major effect on freedom. That is in fact the case. Occupational licensing is neither more nor less prevalent in conservative versus progressive states. The lawsuit environment is also only weakly related to state ideology. In a factor-analysis approach, these variables would be discounted, but they are important variables in our study because of their economic impact.

Another approach, used in the Fraser Institute's "Economic Freedom of North America," is to weight each category equally, and then to weight variables within each category equally.[20] This approach assumes that the variance observed within each category and each variable is equally important. In the large data set used for the freedom index, such an assumption would be wildly implausible. We feel confident that, for instance, tax burden should be weighted more heavily than court decisions mandating that private malls or universities allow political speech.

To create the freedom index, we weight variables according to the value of the freedom affected by a particular policy to those people whose freedoms are at stake. Each variable receives a dollar estimate, representing the financial, psychological, and welfare benefits of a standardized shift of the variable in a pro-freedom direction to those people who enjoy more freedom. We base these values on estimates derived from the scholarly literature in economics and public policy that quantifies the effects of policies on behavior.

The "freedom value" of each variable represents the benefits only to those people whose freedoms have been respected. We do not include the benefits to those who wish to take away freedoms. For instance, private companies may benefit from receiving eminent domain transfers, but we count only the costs to those whose property has been taken away.

We do so because we do not want to create a utilitarian calculus. An index of social welfare is not the same as an index of freedom. We leave it an open question whether deprivations of freedom have net social benefits or costs. Of course, the costs of these deprivations to their victims would be *part* of a utilitarian calculus, but we do not want to foreclose future empirical research on whether government intervention that classical liberals consider unjust might nevertheless have some beneficial social consequences.

Our approach shares something in common with John Rawls's famous criticism of utilitarianism:

> As an interpretation of the basis of the principles of justice, classical utilitarianism is mistaken. It *permits* one to argue, for example, that slavery is unjust on the grounds that the

---

20.   "Economic Freedom of North America: 2020," Fraser Institute, 2021.

advantages to the slaveholder as slaveholder do not counterbalance the disadvantages to the slave and to society at large burdened by a comparatively inefficient system of labor. Now the conception of justice as fairness, when applied to the practice of slavery with its offices of slaveholder and slave, would not allow one to consider the advantages of the slaveholder in the first place. . . . The gains accruing to the slaveholder, assuming them to exist, cannot be counted as in any way mitigating the injustice of the practice.[21]

That is precisely our position, not only with regard to the extreme example of slavery, but also to the more mundane but equally systematic deprivations of freedom in contemporary American society. Therefore, we count only the disadvantages to victims of government action.

In addition, we have techniques for including second-order victims in our calculations, who may not lose property or freedom directly, but who can be expected to suffer fear of having their rights violated in the future ("if they can do that to X, they can do that to me"). We discuss some of these techniques in the relevant sections that follow. Our raw data contain comments describing in detail the justification for each variable's weight and citing relevant sources.

Consistent with the method used in the fifth edition of the index, the value of the freedom affected by a given policy represents the dollar-terms value of the freedom to potential victims if a one-standard-deviation change in that variable were imposed nationwide. That common standard allows us to compare variables with each other and sum their costs. When we discuss the values of a particular freedom or, equivalently, the victim costs of restrictions on that freedom, we are referring to that metric. The following two equations express how each variable is standardized and then compiled to build the freedom index.

$$(1) \quad z_i = (-) \frac{(x_i - \bar{x})}{s_x}$$

$$(2) \quad f_i = \sum_{z=1}^{Z} z_i \frac{v_z}{\Sigma V}$$

The standardized variables $z \in Z$ represent the standard deviations freer than the mean of the raw variable x that each state i is. The negative operator applies when higher values on the raw variable (for instance, cigarette

---

21.   John Rawls, "Justice as Fairness," *The Philosophical Review* 67, no. 2 (1958): 187–88 (emphasis in original).

taxes per pack) represent less freedom. The freedom score for each state f_i is a weighted sum of values on the standardized policy variables, where the share of each variable's freedom value $v \in V$ in the sum of all variables' freedom values is the weight.

Again, the value of a freedom represents not just financial benefits, but consumer surplus, psychological benefits, and so on. These estimates are based on economic and policy research, but admittedly that research does not always allow very precise, certain estimates. We lack the resources to conduct in-depth statistical analysis on the social and economic consequences of each of the 178 top-level variables in the data set. Absent that capability for precision, our aim in this edition was to construct weights that are accurate within an order of magnitude. Using dollar values derived from the literature imposes greater discipline on our weighting choices than a rougher, more qualitative assessment of individual policies' significance like that used in the first two editions of this index.

With plausible variable weights, quantifying freedom permits researchers to investigate the relationship between freedom and other desiderata quantitatively and to judge changes in freedom over time objectively, rather than anecdotally. Measurements of freedom will improve as scientific estimates of the relative values of different freedoms improve, but taking the first step toward an objective assessment of different freedoms' values is essential to the social-scientific enterprise.

Thus, our index of freedom should be understood to represent each state's relative respect for freedom, as reflected in the value enjoyed by the "average" person who would otherwise be deprived of the freedoms we measure. However, each individual will value different policies differently, and for that reason, again, we encourage readers to apply their own weights and personalize the freedom index at http://www.freedominthe50states.org. Readers can download the master spreadsheet to create their own weights for each variable. We have used Excel's "comment" function to annotate important information about how variables were coded and weighted and what particular columns and rows mean. To investigate how any particular variable was created or coded, anyone can download the constellation of policy category spreadsheets at http://statepolicyindex.com. Variables and the policy category spreadsheets are named with an initial letter so as to make their location clear. For instance, debt as a percentage of income, "adebtpia," is found in the fiscal policy spreadsheet, "a_fiscal_20.xls." The individual policy category spreadsheets contain a "metadata" worksheet with detailed information on data sources.

PART I
DIMENSIONS OF FREEDOM

F or the purposes of the freedom index, this book identifies three overarching "dimensions" of freedom and further divides each dimension into categories composed of one or more of the variables used to generate the state scores and rankings. Following our objective weighting system described in the Introduction, variables in the fiscal policy dimension end up with 30.4 percent of the summed freedom values of all variables for the average state, variables in the regulatory policy dimension with 34.9 percent, and variables in the personal freedom dimension with 33.2 percent.[22] Taken individually, the categories may interest readers on core topics of concern, such as taxation, state debt, health insurance regulations, restrictions on alcohol sales, and so on. The following sections explain how each category was constructed and earned its respective weight within the index. Together, these categories make up the overall rankings, found in the section, "Overall Freedom Ranking."

22. Because of the way we weight local taxation, the weights for the fiscal dimension vary by state. They range from 29.0 percent (for the state with the most competing jurisdictions) to 31.1 percent (for the state with the fewest competing jurisdictions). For further explanation, see the section titled "Local Taxation."

FISCAL POLICY

The fiscal policy dimension (Figure 1) consists of six variables: (a) state tax revenues, (b) government consumption, (c) local tax revenues, (d) government employment, (e) government debt, and (f) cash and security assets, each of which earns a significant weight because of its importance. The tax, debt, and assets variables are measured for each fiscal year, whereas the employment and consumption variables come from different sources and are available for the calendar year.

In the first three editions, we included fiscal decentralization (ratio of local to state taxation) as a separate variable. In the past three editions, we have done something more sophisticated. We have separated state and local taxation and assigned different weights to the two. See the following section for details.

FIGURE 1 Fiscal Policy Weights

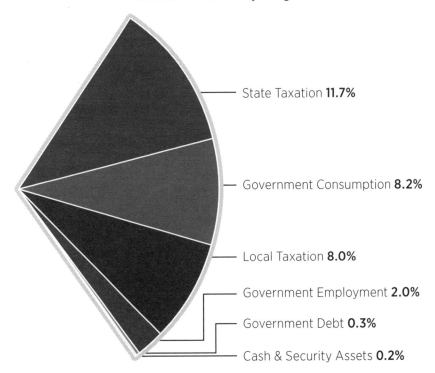

State Taxation **11.7%**

Government Consumption **8.2%**

Local Taxation **8.0%**

Government Employment **2.0%**

Government Debt **0.3%**

Cash & Security Assets **0.2%**

STATE TAXATION

11.7% State and local tax burdens are measured by calculating state and local tax revenues as a percentage of each state's adjusted personal income, excluding taxes on motor fuel, mineral severance, alcohol sales, and tobacco sales.[23] Gas taxes are excluded because their freedom impact is contestable. To some extent, these taxes approximate user fees that are paid roughly in proportion to road use by the user, unlike other taxes.[24] Some states have higher gas tax revenues simply because their residents drive more, which is appropriate in a "user pays" system. Gas taxes could also represent a policy choice by states separable from simply paying for the roads. We take no stand here on the question of the optimal gas tax. Severance taxes on natural resources such as hydrocarbons, minerals, and timber are excluded because they are paid by energy, mining, and timber companies that pass the costs on to consumers worldwide, not just to residents of the state where they operate. Alcohol and tobacco sales taxes are excluded because they are included in the personal freedom dimension. Personal income is the denominator because it represents the size of each state's economy: it statistically correlates better with state and local revenues and expenditures than any other commonly used measure of economic size, such as gross domestic product (GDP).[25]

Adjusted personal income—which is personal income plus capital gains plus taxable pensions and annuities minus supplements to wages and salaries—is used to make our denominator as close as possible to the popular but infrequently updated tax burden measure from the Tax Foundation.[26] The taxation variables therefore roughly represent the average tax burden that state taxpayers face.

We weight tax burden under the assumption that some taxpayers would consent to pay their full tax burden conditional on others doing the same, and some of what those taxes pay for does not diminish and may even enhance freedom (e.g., protection of rights). Some even advocate a higher tax burden, to pay for services they value.

To adjust for consented-to taxation, we take the following steps. First, we assume that the current tax burden in each state represents the ideal point of the median voter. Positive theories of democracy suggest that this

---

23. The Census Bureau taxation measures used here exclude user fees (such as state university tuition) from the tax category, but include business, motor vehicle license, and alcohol license fees, which is appropriate for the freedom index.

24. Some people would argue that gas taxes that merely pay for roads are too low, because a higher gas tax could discourage pollution, a negative externality. Others would argue that some states' existing gas taxes are too high, because state governments often divert them to nonroad uses.

25. When total spending and total taxes are regressed on personal income, gross domestic product, and earnings by place of work, only the first correlates positively with the fiscal variables.

26. Liz Malm and Gerald Prante, "Annual State-Local Tax Burden Ranking FY 2011," Tax Foundation, April 2, 2014.

is as good a guess as any about where public opinion lies.[27] Then, half of the voters would prefer a higher tax burden (and the services it would finance), and half would prefer a lower tax burden. Right away, we can slash the tax burden weight in half, because half of the voters nationally would not see the taxes they currently pay as any diminution of their freedom at all.

Now, this move assumes that the median-dollar taxpayer is the same as the median voter. That is unlikely to be the case. In fact, the median-dollar taxpayer is likely to be somewhat wealthier than the median voter and thus more ideologically conservative and more hostile to taxation. Thus, if anything, slashing the tax burden in half on these grounds is slightly too aggressive. We discuss our solution to this problem in the following section.

Before we solve for that issue, we continue with the exposition. Of at least half of the taxpayers who would prefer a lower tax burden, most would not see all of the taxes they pay as a diminution of their freedom. That is, conditional on others doing the same (absent the collective action problem), they would be fully willing to pay a lower tax burden that is greater than zero. To illustrate the logic, assume a normal probability density function over possible tax burdens, as seen in Figure 2.

On the x-axis of Figure 2 is tax burden, and on the y-axis is the proportion of the population corresponding to a particular view on tax burden. Fifty percent of the curve lies to the left or right of the mean of the tax burden distribution, which is 9.5, the actual national mean of state plus local tax burden. (We have drawn the curve under the assumption of a standard deviation of 2.375, a fourth of the mean, but nothing that follows hinges on this assumption. Note that the standard deviation of voters' views on taxation should be significantly greater than the standard deviation of actual state tax burdens, because each state tax burden roughly represents a median of a distribution.)

This means more simply that, we guess, half of the voters are satisfied with tax burdens of 9.5 percent or higher, while half of the voters prefer tax burdens below 9.5 percent. Taxes take away the freedom of only the second group. Also, the vast majority of the second group does not want to get rid of all taxes. Only part of their tax burden reduces their freedom.

How much of their tax burden is a loss of freedom? We could imagine a "loss curve" that looks like a mirror image of the left side of the normal density function. In other words, those who want zero taxation will see all 9.5 percent of income taxed away as a loss of freedom; those who want taxation of 2.5 percent of income will see 7.0 percent of income taxed away as a loss of freedom, and so on. Half of all the taxes that people who prefer lower taxes pay does not take away their freedom, if we assume a normal distribu-

---

27.   Anthony Downs, *An Economic Theory of Democracy* (New York: Harper, 1957).

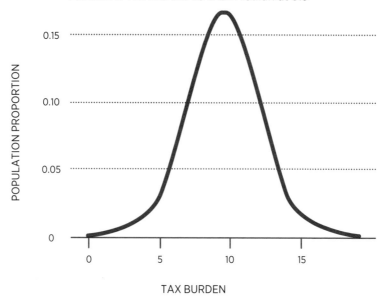

FIGURE 2 Normal Curve with Median at 9.5

tion of preferences over taxes. (The area under the loss curve is 0.5, like the area under the left side of the normal curve.) So only 4.75 percent of personal income, in total, is a loss to those who prefer lower taxation. We can divide the tax burden's weight by 2 again, or by 4 in total. Then, we multiply by 1.1 to account for the fact that the median taxpayer is richer than, and likely more anti-tax than, the median voter. Finally, we multiply by 0.94 because the federal deduction for state and local taxes returned before the Tax Cuts and Jobs Act of 2017, on average, 6.0 percent of state and local taxes paid to taxpayers. When data become available on the impact of that legislation on the value of the state and local tax deduction from 2019 forward (when the change in the deductibility went into effect), we will weight the tax variables higher because of the reduction of federal deductibility in the act.

The values in Table 1 represent the number of standard deviations better (lower tax) than the 2000–2019, 50-state average. Vermont looks abnormally poor on state taxes and good on local taxes because the state classifies all of the property tax as a state tax, even though towns do have some control over the local rate. Because we reward states for fiscal decentralization, the net effect is to depress Vermont's fiscal policy and overall freedom score somewhat.

TABLE 1

Rank	State	State Tax Burden Score, 2019		Rank	State	State Tax Burden Score, 2019
1.	Alaska	2.83		26.	Nevada	0.05
2.	New Hampshire	1.95		27.	Michigan	−0.10
3.	Texas	1.61		28.	Maryland	−0.13
4.	Florida	1.60		29.	Indiana	−0.16
5.	South Dakota	1.52		30.	Massachusetts	−0.27
6.	Wyoming	1.52		31.	Oregon	−0.28
7.	Tennessee	1.15		32.	Rhode Island	−0.31
8.	Colorado	1.04		33.	Kentucky	−0.33
9.	Missouri	0.97		34.	Connecticut	−0.37
10.	Georgia	0.80		35.	Utah	−0.37
11.	South Carolina	0.80		36.	New Jersey	−0.38
12.	Oklahoma	0.71		37.	Kansas	−0.40
13.	Ohio	0.64		38.	Wisconsin	−0.42
14.	Louisiana	0.55		39.	Iowa	−0.45
15.	Montana	0.52		40.	New Mexico	−0.48
16.	Virginia	0.48		41.	Maine	−0.63
17.	Alabama	0.43		42.	New York	−0.64
18.	Arizona	0.36		43.	West Virginia	−0.71
19.	North Dakota	0.33		44.	Mississippi	−0.85
20.	Washington	0.28		45.	California	−0.94
21.	Pennsylvania	0.26		46.	Arkansas	−1.05
22.	Nebraska	0.25		47.	Minnesota	−1.95
23.	Illinois	0.12		48.	Delaware	−2.05
24.	North Carolina	0.11		49.	Vermont	−2.92
25.	Idaho	0.08		50.	Hawaii	−3.46

Note: States with the same rank are tied. States with different scores may appear identical due to rounding.

GOVERNMENT CONSUMPTION

8.2% The government consumption variable (Table 3) represents spending on government operations (wages and salaries and goods and services for the state's own use). We use this variable because new research suggests that government consumption crowds out private-sector income growth, even when it is funded by rents, such as federal grants or mineral revenues, rather than by taxation or debt.

A large literature exists on the size of government and economic growth. Bergh and Henrekson survey the literature and find a robust association of government spending with subsequent growth in rich countries: for every additional percentage point of GDP in government spending, annual average growth declines by at least 0.05 percentage points.[28] This correlation is in addition to the effects of taxation. We look at the effects of a standard-deviation increase in government consumption and investment as a share of personal income over 10 years, assuming the 0.05-percentage-point relationship. We calculate the discounted forgone growth over 10 years assuming a social discount rate of 5 percent. (Using a finite time horizon is necessary to impose finiteness on the number, but endogenous growth theory also suggests that the growth rate benefit of any exogenous variable dissipates eventually when per capita income reaches a new steady state—this is likely to happen over the course of a business cycle.) Then, we divide by two because government employment presumably captures some of the same effects that other studies find via government spending, and we want to avoid double-counting.

28.   A. Bergh and M. Henrekson, 2011, "Government Size and Growth: A Survey and Interpretation of the Evidence," *Journal of Economic Surveys* 25, no. 5 (2011): 872–97.

TABLE 2

Rank	State	Government Consumption Score	Rank	State	Government Consumption Score
1.	Florida	1.89	26.	Arizona	0.61
2.	Pennsylvania	1.87	27.	Kentucky	0.55
3.	Connecticut	1.86	28.	Louisiana	0.44
4.	New Hampshire	1.85	29.	California	0.44
5.	Massachusetts	1.74	30.	Wisconsin	0.42
6.	Maryland	1.50	31.	Utah	0.38
7.	Virginia	1.23	32.	Vermont	0.31
8.	New Jersey	1.22	33.	Kansas	0.20
9.	Nevada	1.18	34.	Hawaii	0.17
10.	Tennessee	1.18	35.	North Carolina	0.04
11.	Indiana	1.11	36.	Washington	0.00
12.	Illinois	1.08	37.	Alabama	−0.04
13.	Maine	1.06	38.	North Dakota	−0.10
14.	Minnesota	1.05	39.	New York	−0.23
15.	South Dakota	1.04	40.	West Virginia	−0.27
16.	Colorado	1.04	41.	Oregon	−0.50
17.	Michigan	1.04	42.	Iowa	−0.54
18.	Georgia	1.02	43.	Delaware	−0.62
19.	Missouri	0.97	44.	South Carolina	−0.68
20.	Rhode Island	0.93	45.	Nebraska	−0.85
21.	Texas	0.80	46.	Oklahoma	−0.88
22.	Idaho	0.77	47.	Mississippi	−0.89
23.	Arkansas	0.70	48.	New Mexico	−1.68
24.	Montana	0.67	49.	Wyoming	−2.00
25.	Ohio	0.64	50.	Alaska	−2.48

Note: States with the same rank are tied. States with different scores may appear identical due to rounding.

LOCAL TAX

8.0% We separate local taxation to take account of fiscal decentralization. Fiscal decentralization affects freedom in that when more taxes are raised at the local level, residents may have more choice over their tax burden and public services. They can more easily vote with their feet—that is, move to a jurisdiction with their preferred policy mix—at the local level than the state level.

But that very ability to foot-vote varies not just by how much revenue is raised at the local level, but by the number of local jurisdictions. If local governments are spatially large, it is difficult for residents to exercise choice. When a city like Houston annexes other independent municipalities, it becomes more difficult for movers to the area to choose a jurisdiction to their liking. Hawaii's single statewide school district prevents parents from moving to a district where they think the schools are better run. Because the relevant decision for a homeowner is typically over local jurisdictions within driving distance to a place of employment, the metric for variety of choice that we use is the effective number of local jurisdictions per square mile of privately owned land (we exclude publicly owned land because it is presumably not developable), in log points (the natural log is taken to deal with skewness and to capture diminishing marginal effects).

"Effective number of local jurisdictions" counts up the weighted sum of general-purpose local governments in each state, where the weights are the percentage of local tax revenue raised by each local government tier. For instance, if a state has 10 counties and 100 municipalities, and counties raise 40 percent of local taxes while municipalities raise 60 percent, then the state's effective number of local jurisdictions is 10*0.4+100*0.6=64. We then divide that number by the number of square miles of private land in the state, then take the natural logarithm to reduce skew in the distribution. (This also helps large states like Nevada and Texas relative to the New England states.)

The variable for the effective number of local jurisdictions per square mile determines the weight on the local taxation variable, which therefore varies by state. It is the only variable in the index with a weight that varies by state. (The weight for local taxation reported in Figure 1 is the average for all 50 states over the 2000–2019 period.) The idea here is that high decentralization (high local taxation relative to state taxation) matters less when there are fewer jurisdictions per square mile and matters more when there are more. Specifically, we multiply the standard taxation weight by 0.75 for the state with the most jurisdictions per square mile (New Jersey) and give a hypothetical state with no local governments the full taxation weight, then arrange the other states linearly according to their effective number of jurisdictions per square mile. In New Jersey, we are assuming that local taxation is only three-quarters the restriction on freedom that state taxation is. In Hawaii, the most territorially centralized state, local taxation is almost the same as state taxation—the prospective homeowner has virtually no local exit option, so local taxes are only a little more likely than state taxes to reflect distinctive local preferences.

Local tax collections come from the most recent fiscal year data released by the Census Bureau (FY 2019). The numbers here represent the combined formula incorporating both the level of local taxation and the weight as determined by the number of competing local jurisdictions. As a result, the numbers in Table 2 are not directly comparable to the figures for state-level taxation already given.

TABLE 3

Rank	State	Local tax burden score incorporating decentralization		Rank	State	Local tax burden score incorporating decentralization
1.	Vermont	0.161		26.	New Mexico	0.009
2.	Arkansas	0.144		27.	North Dakota	0.004
3.	Delaware	0.134		28.	Arizona	0.003
4.	Tennessee	0.103		29.	Washington	−0.003
5.	Idaho	0.101		30.	South Carolina	−0.008
6.	Indiana	0.098		31.	California	−0.009
7.	Michigan	0.077		32.	Missouri	−0.010
8.	West Virginia	0.069		33.	Kansas	−0.011
9.	Alabama	0.068		34.	Oregon	−0.013
10.	Minnesota	0.066		35.	South Dakota	−0.014
11.	Kentucky	0.063		36.	Virginia	−0.015
12.	North Carolina	0.055		37.	Iowa	−0.019
13.	Mississippi	0.054		38.	Rhode Island	−0.019
14.	Massachusetts	0.052		39.	New Jersey	−0.028
15.	Oklahoma	0.047		40.	Ohio	−0.040
16.	Nevada	0.045		41.	Maine	−0.054
17.	Montana	0.040		42.	Louisiana	−0.056
18.	Wyoming	0.040		43.	New Hampshire	−0.060
19.	Wisconsin	0.040		44.	Illinois	−0.066
20.	Florida	0.035		45.	Colorado	−0.069
21.	Pennsylvania	0.024		46.	Maryland	−0.070
22.	Utah	0.021		47.	Alaska	−0.073
23.	Connecticut	0.016		48.	Texas	−0.094
24.	Georgia	0.010		49.	Nebraska	−0.115
25.	Hawaii	0.010		50.	New York	−0.227

Note: States with the same rank are tied. States with different scores may appear identical due to rounding.

GOVERNMENT EMPLOYMENT

2.0% We also include government employment, which can crowd out employment in the private sector (see Table 4). To the extent that government-run enterprises are less efficient than private ones, government employment costs the local economy. Economists Jim Malley and Thomas Moutos use a cointegration framework on time-series data from Sweden and find that a 1 percent increase in government employment is associated with a 0.43 percent decrease in private employment. Economist Evi Pappa uses U.S. state data and also finds that aggregate employment does not increase at moments when government employment does, implying substantial crowding out in the short run and presumably in the long run as well.[29]

According to the Malley-Moutos elasticity estimate applied to state data from 2009, an aggregate disemployment effect occurred from an increase in government employment that year. Although that might be true, it seems like an aggressive assumption. After all, government employment is very high in Sweden; thus, its marginal effect there might be more negative than its marginal effect just about anywhere else.

Instead, following Pappa's results, the freedom index assumes a net-zero effect on total employment from an increase in state and local employment. The private disemployment effect of a one-standard-deviation increase in the ratio of government to private employment, as of 2015, would be 3.81 million nationwide. Average wage per job in the United States in early 2016 was $49,630. The index assumes that compensation equals marginal productivity and that government jobs are only 90 percent as productive as private jobs. The victim cost of a nationwide, one-standard-deviation increase in the government employment ratio is therefore 3.81 million times $49,630 divided by 10, or $18.9 billion. We divide that figure by 2 because government consumption presumably captures some of the same dynamics, and we want to avoid double-counting.

Government employment is available on a calendar-year basis from the Bureau of Economic Analysis.

29.   Jim Malley and Thomas Moutos, "Does Government Employment 'Crowd Out' Private Employment? Evidence from Sweden," *Scandinavian Journal of Economics* 98, no. 2 (1996): 289–302; Evi Pappa, "The Effects of Fiscal Shocks on Employment and the Real Wage," *International Economic Review* 50, no. 1 (2009): 217–44.

TABLE 4

Rank	State	Government Employment Score	Rank	State	Government Employment Score
1.	Nevada	2.17	26.	Colorado	0.63
2.	Florida	2.13	27.	Wisconsin	0.62
3.	Pennsylvania	1.83	28.	Virginia	0.41
4.	Massachusetts	1.83	29.	Vermont	0.41
5.	Rhode Island	1.54	30.	Idaho	0.40
6.	New Hampshire	1.34	31.	Louisiana	0.39
7.	Tennessee	1.30	32.	Kentucky	0.37
8.	Georgia	1.20	33.	Hawaii	0.35
9.	Arizona	1.19	34.	North Carolina	0.31
10.	Illinois	1.13	35.	Montana	0.30
11.	Connecticut	1.12	36.	Nebraska	0.29
12.	Michigan	1.11	37.	South Dakota	0.19
13.	Texas	1.07	38.	Washington	0.12
14.	New Jersey	1.07	39.	Arkansas	0.02
15.	Maryland	1.06	40.	South Carolina	−0.02
16.	Indiana	0.99	41.	Iowa	−0.06
17.	California	0.98	42.	North Dakota	−0.19
18.	Ohio	0.94	43.	Alabama	−0.36
19.	Oregon	0.94	44.	Kansas	−0.66
20.	Minnesota	0.90	45.	Oklahoma	−0.68
21.	Missouri	0.84	46.	Mississippi	−1.32
22.	Utah	0.80	47.	West Virginia	−1.36
23.	Delaware	0.78	48.	Alaska	−1.78
24.	Maine	0.74	49.	New Mexico	−1.86
25.	New York	0.64	50.	Wyoming	−2.21

Note: States with the same rank are tied. States with different scores may appear identical due to rounding.

GOVERNMENT DEBT

0.3% The problem with state and local debt, above a modest level, is that it worsens credit ratings and increases yields paid on government bonds.[30] Current interest payments are already included in the state taxation variable. The problem with additional interest paid because of default risk is that it does not provide any additional services, and therefore we do not imagine that any taxpayers can consent to it, unlike interest paid that reflects pure time preference.

James Poterba and Kim Rueben give readily interpretable coefficient estimates for our purposes. They find that a percentage-point increase in state debt as a share of personal income is associated with roughly a 100-basis-point increase in bond yield. The annual value of the additional interest payments generated by this increase in interest rate on the debt is therefore $-(0.01 \times debt)$. Like state and local taxes, we adjust this figure for federal deductibility.

For debt, we use the latest fiscal year data from the Census Bureau (FY 2019).

30. James M. Poterba and Kim Rueben, "State Fiscal Institutions and the U.S. Municipal Bond Market," in *Fiscal Institutions and Fiscal Performance*, ed. James M. Poterba (Chicago: University of Chicago Press, 1999), pp. 181–208; Craig L. Johnson and Kenneth A. Kriz, "Fiscal Institutions, Credit Ratings, and Borrowing Costs," *Public Budgeting and Finance* (2005): 84–103.

TABLE 5

Rank	State	Government Debt Score		Rank	State	Government Debt Score
1.	Wyoming	2.69		26.	Wisconsin	0.47
2.	Idaho	2.19		27.	Missouri	0.43
3.	North Carolina	1.80		28.	Indiana	0.43
4.	Montana	1.54		29.	Colorado	0.39
5.	Oklahoma	1.52		30.	South Carolina	0.39
6.	Florida	1.49		31.	West Virginia	0.35
7.	Georgia	1.32		32.	Minnesota	0.29
8.	New Hampshire	1.30		33.	Kansas	0.23
9.	Iowa	1.23		34.	Louisiana	0.16
10.	Mississippi	1.20		35.	Nevada	0.11
11.	Maine	1.17		36.	Pennsylvania	0.09
12.	Tennessee	0.97		37.	Oregon	0.07
13.	Virginia	0.92		38.	New Mexico	0.04
14.	Maryland	0.89		39.	Connecticut	−0.07
15.	South Dakota	0.88		40.	Massachusetts	−0.22
16.	Vermont	0.84		41.	California	−0.24
17.	Arizona	0.83		42.	Washington	−0.25
18.	Arkansas	0.80		43.	Texas	−0.36
19.	Alabama	0.78		44.	Rhode Island	−0.39
20.	Nebraska	0.72		45.	North Dakota	−0.50
21.	Delaware	0.70		46.	Hawaii	−0.75
22.	Michigan	0.66		47.	Alaska	−0.77
23.	New Jersey	0.57		48.	Illinois	−0.86
24.	Utah	0.56		49.	Kentucky	−1.54
25.	Ohio	0.48		50.	New York	−1.59

Note: States with the same rank are tied. States with different scores may appear identical due to rounding.

CASH AND SECURITY ASSETS

0.2% Including state and local debt in the freedom index gives an incomplete picture without data on state and local financial assets. To weight this variable, which is also measured as a share of adjusted personal income, we estimate the coefficients on debt and cash and security assets in a time-series cross-sectional regression model of Standard and Poor's credit ratings of state governments. Both coefficients were statistically significant in the expected direction. A one-unit increase in state and local debt was associated with a 6.4-point increase in riskiness on a 0 to 9 scale, while a one-unit increase in cash and security assets was associated with a 0.76-point decrease (improvement). Cash and security assets are less valuable for credit rating than debt is harmful because these assets are often illiquid, tied up in trusts. We use these relative coefficient estimates to weight cash and security assets relative to debt.

TABLE 6

Rank	State	Cash and Security Assets Score		Rank	State	Score
1.	Alaska	7.24		26.	Iowa	−0.24
2.	North Dakota	2.73		27.	Utah	−0.25
3.	Wyoming	1.99		28.	Pennsylvania	−0.25
4.	New Mexico	0.99		29.	Kansas	−0.26
5.	Montana	0.00		30.	Florida	−0.26
6.	Texas	−0.01		31.	Tennessee	−0.28
7.	Ohio	−0.04		32.	Arizona	−0.28
8.	South Dakota	−0.08		33.	Illinois	−0.28
9.	Oregon	−0.08		34.	Arkansas	−0.28
10.	Louisiana	−0.09		35.	New York	−0.30
11.	Rhode Island	−0.09		36.	Michigan	−0.30
12.	Nebraska	−0.13		37.	Maine	−0.31
13.	Hawaii	−0.17		38.	Nevada	−0.32
14.	Indiana	−0.18		39.	Alabama	−0.33
15.	Missouri	−0.18		40.	Mississippi	−0.34
16.	Delaware	−0.18		41.	Washington	−0.34
17.	West Virginia	−0.19		42.	Virginia	−0.35
18.	Colorado	−0.19		43.	New Hampshire	−0.37
19.	Idaho	−0.19		44.	Massachusetts	−0.40
20.	Vermont	−0.20		45.	New Jersey	−0.41
21.	Kentucky	−0.21		46.	Wisconsin	−0.43
22.	Minnesota	−0.21		47.	Georgia	−0.44
23.	South Carolina	−0.22		48.	Connecticut	−0.47
24.	California	−0.22		49.	North Carolina	−0.48
25.	Oklahoma	−0.22		50.	Maryland	−0.51

Note: States with the same rank are tied. States with different scores may appear identical due to rounding.

OVERALL FISCAL POLICY RANKING

30.4% The fiscal policy ranking is available in Table 7. Although the former number-one state New Hampshire continues to improve gradually on fiscal policy, Florida and Tennessee have leapfrogged it with some truly eye-popping improvements. Time will tell whether data revisions will adjust this picture, but for now it seems that government consumption in Florida has fallen from 10.8 percent in 2009 to 7.9 percent of income in Florida in just 10 years, while state and local taxes have also fallen, and the government employment ratio has fallen by close to 3 percentage points. Some of this improvement is likely a result of Florida's rapidly rebounding economy since the Great Recession and Florida's fiscal discipline. Tennessee's improvement is less significant, but the state has brought down its debt ratio quite a bit.

Because the two taxation variables make up a large share of fiscal policy's weight, it is unsurprising that low-tax states dominate the top of the fiscal policy rankings, while high-tax states fall at the bottom. In Table 7, the numbers represent the number of weighted standard deviations each state is above the average. For instance, New York's 2019 score of −0.307 means that even if New York were exactly average on regulatory policy and personal freedom (garnering a total score of 0 on them), it would still be, on average, a third of a standard deviation less free than the average for every policy.

A state that is one standard deviation better than average on every single policy will end up with an overall freedom score of 1.0, and a state that is one standard deviation worse than average on every single policy will end up with an overall freedom score of −1.0. Since fiscal policy represents less than a third of the overall index, New York's score of −0.307 means that it is on average more than a standard deviation worse than average on every fiscal policy.

TABLE 7

Rank **State** **Overall Fiscal Policy Score, 2019**

Rank	State	Score	Rank	State	Score
1.	Florida	0.430	26.	Louisiana	0.060
2.	Tennessee	0.370	27.	Rhode Island	0.059
3.	New Hampshire	0.357	28.	New Jersey	0.058
4.	South Dakota	0.263	29.	Oklahoma	0.054
5.	Pennsylvania	0.251	30.	Wisconsin	0.046
6.	Georgia	0.222	31.	North Dakota	0.041
7.	Missouri	0.208	32.	Washington	0.039
8.	Massachusetts	0.206	33.	South Carolina	0.038
9.	Indiana	0.199	34.	Alaska	0.036
10.	Nevada	0.198	35.	Utah	0.034
11.	Idaho	0.195	36.	Wyoming	0.028
12.	Texas	0.187	37.	Maine	−0.015
13.	Michigan	0.182	38.	Kansas	−0.047
14.	Montana	0.174	39.	Minnesota	−0.049
15.	Virginia	0.159	40.	West Virginia	−0.056
16.	Colorado	0.158	41.	California	−0.056
17.	Connecticut	0.155	42.	Oregon	−0.060
18.	Arizona	0.128	43.	Iowa	−0.106
19.	Alabama	0.116	44.	Delaware	−0.131
20.	Ohio	0.114	45.	Mississippi	−0.134
21.	North Carolina	0.089	46.	Vermont	−0.136
22.	Arkansas	0.088	47.	Nebraska	−0.142
23.	Kentucky	0.079	48.	New Mexico	−0.214
24.	Maryland	0.068	49.	New York	−0.307
25.	Illinois	0.063	50.	Hawaii	−0.369

Note: States with the same rank are tied. States with different scores may appear identical due to rounding.

Figure 3 shows how the average fiscal policy score has changed for all 50 states since 2000. It appears that states' fiscal policies have improved since the Great Recession, mostly because of declining tax burdens and spending cuts.

FIGURE 3 State Average Fiscal Policy Scores over Time

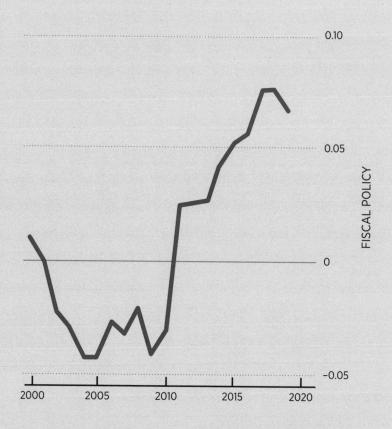

REGULATORY POLICY

The regulatory policy dimension includes categories for (a) land-use freedom and environmental policy, (b) health insurance freedom, (c) labor-market freedom, (d) lawsuit freedom, (e) occupational freedom, (f) miscellaneous regulations that do not fit under another category (such as certificate-of-need requirements), and (g) cable and telecommunications freedom. Figure 4 shows the weights for health insurance policies now controlled by the federal government (8.1 percent) and for only those health insurance policies that states can still control after the PPACA (0.8 percent), altogether summing to 8.9 percent of the index.

FIGURE 4 Regulatory Policy Weights

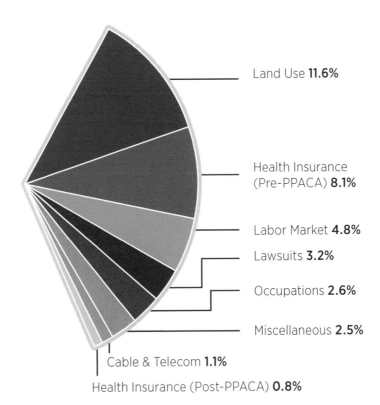

Land Use **11.6%**

Health Insurance
(Pre-PPACA) **8.1%**

Labor Market **4.8%**

Lawsuits **3.2%**

Occupations **2.6%**

Miscellaneous **2.5%**

Cable & Telecom **1.1%**

Health Insurance (Post-PPACA) **0.8%**

The calculated freedom scores do not allow weights to vary by year, even when variation across states disappears. In other words, a variable continues to contribute to the weights even in years when it no longer contributes to differences across states because every state has the same policy. Including this type of variable allows for intertemporal comparisons. That happened when the PPACA passed, and states could no longer choose whether to have community rating, guaranteed issue, and the individual mandate. As a result of our methodological choice, the data show the PPACA as a large negative shock to all states' regulatory policy. However, for the second time, this edition of the study also develops an alternative, chain-linked index in the downloadable data that includes only policies that have never at any time been federalized. We do not put this ranking in the text because it is really for comparisons over time rather than across states, and the 2019 values on this chain-linked index correlate perfectly with the 2019 values on the regular index.

This regulatory policy dimension does not include regulations with a mainly paternalistic justification; those regulations are placed under the personal freedom dimension. They include laws such as private and home-school regulations and smoking bans.

To take into account the wider, unmeasured costs of insecure rights, this index increases the weights on variables representing policies encoded in state constitutions or the federal Constitution. It does so because the fact that a policy has been encoded within a constitution is prima facie evidence that the policy is widely considered to affect a "fundamental" freedom—a freedom with consequences for the security of the citizenry that extend beyond citizens under its immediate purview.

Within the regulatory policy dimension, the weights of certain variables are boosted as follows:

1. The victim cost/freedom value is multiplied by 2 if a closely related policy is encoded in the U.S. Constitution, or has been recognized by at least some courts as relating to a fundamental right. Examples of such policies include eminent domain reform, rent control, regulatory taking restrictions, and mandatory permission of political speech on private property, which we view as compelled speech implicating the First Amendment.

2. The victim cost/freedom value is multiplied by 1.5 if the policy is encoded in state constitutions but not the federal Constitution and has not otherwise been recognized judicially as a fundamental right. Right-to-work laws are the only such policies in the regulatory dimension.

We believe this sort of boost is necessary to capture the particular importance Americans have attached to certain fundamental freedoms, even if it necessarily involves an element of judgment. Freedoms are more fundamental the more widely people consider them part of their flourishing and autonomy, and policies potentially infringing on them are therefore subject to stricter judicial scrutiny than policies that would restrict freedoms that, while potentially valuable, are not as fundamental.[31] By relying on existing judicial interpretations of fundamental rights, the freedom index avoids at least one possible source of subjectivity as it "upgrades" these policies.

31.   Legal Information Institute, "Fundamental Right," Cornell University Law School, August 19, 2010.

LAND-USE FREEDOM AND ENVIRONMENTAL POLICY

11.6% The category for land-use freedom and environmental policy includes eminent domain rules, land-use regulations, renewable portfolio standards, and regulations requiring employers to let their employees bring guns onto company-owned parking lots. Most of its weight comes from three variables: local rent control laws (5.3 percent of the overall index) and two indexes of residential land-use regulations, also known as zoning (together 5.0 percent of the index). One of the zoning indexes is derived from an index built by researchers at the Wharton School of Business.[32] Their original index is available for only two years. We use changes in state cost of living, Partisan Voting Index, accommodation GDP, and effective number of local jurisdictions to impute values for this variable over the entire time series. The other zoning index derives from two Harvard economists, is based on appellate court rulings, and does vary over time but is a "noisier" (more specifically, the same mean and expectation but a larger variance) measure of zoning.[33] According to the best evidence, a one-standard-deviation increase in residential zoning restrictions would directly cost victims more than $13 billion a year, if imposed nationwide.[34] Rather than impose such costs, states should allow property owners to solve most land-use externalities with various contractual arrangements, such as homeowners associations, or at most what Dartmouth economist William Fischel calls "good housekeeping" zoning.[35]

Renewable portfolio standards (RPS), which mandate that power companies buy certain proportions of their energy from (usually) wind and solar sources, are worth 1.0 percent of the overall index. Our variable tracks the stringency of these requirements. The average RPS raises electricity prices by 0.8–0.9 percent, with bigger effects likely for more stringent programs.[36] To promote cleaner electric generation, states could help limit pollution that creates significant, direct, negative externalities through means other than command-and-control regulations.

32. Joseph Gyourko, Albert Saiz, and Anita Summers, "A New Measure of the Local Regulatory Environment for Housing Markets: The Wharton Residential Land Use Regulatory Index," *Urban Studies* 45, no. 3 (2008): 693–729.

33. Peter Ganong and Daniel Shoag, "Why Has Regional Income Convergence in the US Declined?," *Journal of Urban Economics* 102 (2017): 76–90.

34. Edward L. Glaeser, Joseph Gyourko, and Raven Saks, "Why Is Manhattan So Expensive? Regulation and the Rise in Housing Prices," *Journal of Law and Economics* 48, no. 2 (2005): 331–69; Stephen Malpezzi, "Housing Prices, Externalities, and Regulation in US Metropolitan Areas," *Journal of Housing Research* 7, no. 2 (1996): 209–41.

35. William A. Fischel, *Zoning Rules!* (Cambridge, MA: Lincoln Institute of Land Policy, 2015).

36. Cliff Chen, Ryan Riser, and Mark Bollinger, "Weighing the Costs and Benefits of State Renewables Portfolio Standards in the United States: A Comparative Analysis of State-Level Policy Impact Projections," *Renewable & Sustainable Energy Reviews* 13 (2009): 552–66; Jenny Heeter et al., "A Survey of State-Level Cost and Benefit Estimates of Renewable Portfolio Standards," technical report, National Renewable Energy Laboratory, Golden, CO, May 2014.

The remainder of this category takes into account whether compensation or an economic assessment is required before a regulatory taking, an index of eminent domain reform; whether companies must allow employees' guns on their property; and whether free speech is mandated on private property. (The federal courts require compensation for regulatory takings only when they destroy the value of the affected land; therefore, states were coded only for having protections stronger than the federal one.) It may surprise readers that eminent domain reform comprises only 0.1 percent of the freedom index, given that it affects a fundamental right, and given how salient the issue was—especially among property rights advocates—following the Supreme Court's *Kelo* decision.[37] However, the estimated victim cost of eminent domain abuse is relatively low, at roughly $1 billion a year ($500 million without the "constitutional weight" boost), though admittedly this may underestimate losses due to insecurity of tenure, attorneys' fees, opportunity costs of legal challenges, and so on.[38] It is worth noting that most states that have reformed eminent domain have kept open a wide "blight loophole" that could still allow public takings for private interests. Therefore, the eminent domain index has been coded to take blight reform into account, as well as the incorporation of eminent domain restrictions into the state constitution.

Both of the final two variables have to do with property rights: laws banning employers from banning guns from certain company property such as parking lots, and laws mandating free speech on private property. We hold that businesses may permissibly require employees to leave guns at home, just as we defend the right of malls and community associations to prohibit any or all political messages. That view might perplex some gun rights advocates. However, the only consistent property rights–respecting position is that gun rights stop at the boundary of someone else's property; to think otherwise is to impose one's own view on others without their consent. Although symbolically significant, however, these policies do not generally cause severe inconvenience to their victims and therefore are not worth much in the index.

37.   See *Kelo v. City of New London,* 545 U.S. 469 (2005).
38.   "Building Empires, Destroying Homes: Eminent Domain Abuse in New York," Institute for Justice, October 2009.

TABLE 8

Rank	State	Land-Use Freedom and Environmental Policy Score		Rank	State	Land-Use Freedom and Environmental Policy Score
1.	Alabama	0.050		26.	Wisconsin	0.007
2.	Georgia	0.046		27.	Illinois	0.005
3.	Oklahoma	0.046		28.	Alaska	0.004
4.	Virginia	0.042		29.	Utah	0.004
5.	Arkansas	0.042		30.	Idaho	−0.001
6.	Kentucky	0.039		31.	Colorado	−0.006
7.	Iowa	0.038		32.	Pennsylvania	−0.007
8.	Nebraska	0.038		33.	New Mexico	−0.007
9.	Kansas	0.038		34.	Massachusetts	−0.016
10.	North Dakota	0.037		35.	Nevada	−0.017
11.	West Virginia	0.036		36.	Minnesota	−0.020
12.	Texas	0.033		37.	Delaware	−0.023
13.	Louisiana	0.031		38.	Montana	−0.039
14.	South Dakota	0.031		39.	Washington	−0.045
15.	Missouri	0.031		40.	New Hampshire	−0.047
16.	Tennessee	0.030		41.	Connecticut	−0.061
17.	South Carolina	0.030		42.	Rhode Island	−0.061
18.	Indiana	0.026		43.	Maine	−0.090
19.	Ohio	0.024		44.	Hawaii	−0.145
20.	Michigan	0.021		45.	Vermont	−0.173
21.	Florida	0.021		46.	New York	−0.224
22.	North Carolina	0.015		47.	California	−0.257
23.	Mississippi	0.014		48.	Maryland	−0.265
24.	Wyoming	0.013		49.	New Jersey	−0.292
25.	Arizona	0.010		50.	Oregon	−0.293

Note: States with the same rank are tied. States with different scores may appear identical due to rounding.

HEALTH INSURANCE FREEDOM

8.1% The PPACA (Obamacare) nationalized most health insurance regulation. In our "headline" index, we treat such nationalizations of policies that states formerly controlled as changes in state policies. We do so because our primary purpose is to measure freedom as citizens experience it, not as state legislators enact it. This choice allows us to compare the state of freedom over time, using the same policies. We do the same thing with certain gun laws and with sodomy laws, which have also been nationalized (in a pro-freedom direction).

All states are now required to have a small-group-adjusted community rating (2.3 percent of the index), individual market-adjusted community rating (0.4 percent), individual market-guaranteed issue (0.6 percent), bans on elimination riders (<0.1 percent), mandated external review of grievances (<0.1 percent), small-group prior approval of rates (0.5 percent), nongroup prior approval of rates (0.1 percent), and certain "essential benefits" mandates (1.8 percent). States are still able to vary somewhat on the extent of mandated benefits (0.5 percent), standing referrals to specialists (<0.1 percent), direct access to specialists (0.3 percent), and bans on financial incentives to providers from insurers (<0.1 percent). The individual health insurance mandate (2.4 percent) was federalized but then, in a rare exception to the historical norm, was returned to the states. Some states (California, Massachusetts, New Jersey, and Rhode Island) have enacted their own individual mandates since that time.

Community rating and the individual mandate get the highest weights because they represent a large transfer of wealth from the healthy to the unhealthy, approximately $10 billion a year.[39] State-level mandated coverages raise premium costs for consumers. In this edition, we have extensively reviewed statutes to determine the onset of all the particularly costly mandated benefits, such as in vitro fertilization and occupational therapy, by state. The HMO regulations have low victim costs because public backlash against particular practices, such as financial incentives to providers, drove them from the marketplace even before laws were passed.[40] In this case, public opinion drove both market practice and state law. Nevertheless, research suggests that public opinion on this issue may be misinformed. In their heyday in the 1990s, when many of the now widely banned practices were widespread, HMOs successfully suppressed health care costs.[41]

39. These numbers are derived from estimates in Mark V. Pauly and Bradley Herring, "Risk Pooling and Regulation: Policy and Reality in Today's Individual Health Insurance Market," *Health Affairs* 26, no. 3 (2007): 770–79.

40. Mark A. Hall, "The Death of Managed Care: A Regulatory Autopsy," *Journal of Health Politics, Policy, and Law* 30, no. 3 (2005): 427–52.

41. Maxim L. Pinkovskiy, "The Impact of the Managed Care Backlash on Health Care Costs: Evidence from State Regulation of Managed Care Cost Containment Practices," October 17, 2013.

TABLE 9

Rank	State	Health Insurance Freedom Score		Rank	State	Health Insurance Freedom Score
1.	Idaho	−0.028		23.	Tennessee	−0.039
1.	Nebraska	−0.028		23.	Washington	−0.039
1.	North Dakota	−0.028		28.	Arizona	−0.039
4.	Delaware	−0.029		28.	Florida	−0.039
4.	Kansas	−0.029		28.	Missouri	−0.039
6.	Mississippi	−0.032		28.	New York	−0.039
6.	South Dakota	−0.032		28.	North Carolina	−0.039
6.	Wyoming	−0.032		28.	Pennsylvania	−0.039
9.	Iowa	−0.032		34.	Virginia	−0.041
10.	Oklahoma	−0.033		35.	Ohio	−0.041
10.	South Carolina	−0.033		36.	Alaska	−0.043
10.	Wisconsin	−0.033		37.	Colorado	−0.043
13.	Vermont	−0.033		38.	Maine	−0.043
14.	Michigan	−0.035		38.	New Mexico	−0.043
15.	Nevada	−0.037		40.	Utah	−0.045
16.	Hawaii	−0.037		41.	Maryland	−0.045
17.	Illinois	−0.037		42.	Arkansas	−0.047
17.	Minnesota	−0.037		42.	Connecticut	−0.047
19.	Georgia	−0.039		44.	West Virginia	−0.048
19.	Indiana	−0.039		45.	Montana	−0.051
19.	Louisiana	−0.039		45.	Texas	−0.051
19.	New Hampshire	−0.039		47.	California	−0.079
23.	Alabama	−0.039		48.	Rhode Island	−0.087
23.	Kentucky	−0.039		49.	Massachusetts	−0.091
23.	Oregon	−0.039		50.	New Jersey	−0.097

Note: States with the same rank are tied. States with different scores may appear identical due to rounding.

LABOR-MARKET FREEDOM

4.8%   Right-to-work laws make up nearly half of the labor regulation category and more than 2 percent of the entire freedom index. They are valued at over $10 billion a year.[42] Right-to-work laws are controversial among libertarians because they override collective bargaining contracts reached between employers and employee unions, allowing employers to hire workers who do not pay agency fees to a union. Then again, right-to-work laws can be justified as a means of employer and employee self-defense against the mechanisms of the Wagner Act (the National Labor Relations Act), which essentially allows an "agency shop" to form if a majority of workers votes in favor of this action.

From the libertarian point of view, the Wagner Act violates the fundamental freedom of association and basic property rights, and right-to-work laws somewhat restore those freedoms, because few employers would voluntarily agree to an agency shop in the absence of the Wagner Act. Although right-to-work laws violate the rights of some workers and employers, they restore freedom of association to a far greater number. In an ideal world, both the National Labor Relations Act and right-to-work laws would be repealed, and employees and employers would be free to negotiate as they saw fit, collectively or individually.

For those who disagree with our logic, we have produced alternative indexes to the freedom index that exclude right-to-work laws (see Appendix B).

Other policy variables in this category, in descending order of importance, are short-term disability insurance requirements (costs being lower labor productivity[43] and administrative expenses for businesses[44]), the legalization and enforcement of worker noncompete agreements (costs being the transfer of income from stockholders to top executives and firms' underinvestment in worker productivity[45]), state minimum-wage laws (Kaitz index adjusted for median wages), policies dealing with workers' compensation (funding mechanisms and mandated coverages), requirements for employer verification of legal resident status, stricter-than-federal private employment discrimination laws (smoker status, marital status, age, and others), and mandated paid family leave.

---

42.   Steven E. Abraham and Paula B. Voos, "Right-to-Work Laws: New Evidence from the Stock Market," *Southern Economic Journal* 67, no. 2 (2000): 345–62; David T. Ellwood and Glenn Fine, "The Impact of Right-to-Work Laws on Union Organizing," *Journal of Political Economy* 95, no. 2 (1987): 250–73; William J. Moore, "The Determinants and Effects of Right-to-Work Laws: A Review of the Recent Literature," *Journal of Labor Research* 19, no. 3 (1998): 445–69; Robert Krol and Shirley Svorny, "Unions and Employment Growth: Evidence from State Economic Recoveries," *Journal of Labor Research* 28 (2007): 525–35.

43.   John Bound et al., "The Welfare Implications of Increasing Disability Insurance Benefit Generosity," *Journal of Public Economics* 88 (2004): 2487–514.

44.   In other words, the funding mechanism (taxation) does not count here; it counts as part of the tax burden.

45.   Mark J. Garmaise, "Ties That Truly Bind: Noncompetition Agreements, Executive Compensation, and Firm Investment," *Journal of Law, Economics, and Organization* 27, 2 (2011): 376–425.

TABLE 10

Rank	State	Labor-Market Freedom Score	Rank	State	Labor-Market Freedom Score
1.	Texas	0.048	26.	Oklahoma	−0.002
2.	Virginia	0.041	27.	New Hampshire	−0.010
3.	Kansas	0.039	28.	North Dakota	−0.016
3.	Iowa	0.039	29.	Pennsylvania	−0.017
3.	Wisconsin	0.039	30.	Minnesota	−0.019
3.	Indiana	0.039	31.	Delaware	−0.021
7.	Mississippi	0.038	32.	Illinois	−0.024
7.	Alabama	0.038	33.	Montana	−0.025
9.	Tennessee	0.038	34.	Alaska	−0.025
10.	Georgia	0.036	35.	New Mexico	−0.026
11.	North Carolina	0.036	36.	Missouri	−0.026
12.	Utah	0.034	37.	Vermont	−0.030
13.	Florida	0.034	38.	Ohio	−0.032
14.	Kentucky	0.032	39.	Connecticut	−0.032
15.	Idaho	0.032	40.	Maryland	−0.034
16.	South Carolina	0.030	41.	Massachusetts	−0.035
17.	Louisiana	0.030	42.	Maine	−0.037
18.	Nebraska	0.029	43.	Colorado	−0.040
19.	Nevada	0.028	44.	Oregon	−0.043
20.	South Dakota	0.027	45.	Washington	−0.055
21.	Michigan	0.026	46.	New Jersey	−0.057
22.	Arkansas	0.023	47.	Hawaii	−0.062
23.	West Virginia	0.023	48.	Rhode Island	−0.069
24.	Wyoming	0.018	49.	New York	−0.070
25.	Arizona	0.005	50.	California	−0.105

Note: States with the same rank are tied. States with different scores may appear identical due to rounding.

LAWSUIT FREEDOM

3.2% Deciding tort claims among private parties is an important function of a decentralized legal system that provides justice to victims of the unjust, harmful acts of others. In an efficient civil liability system, the costs that defendants have to pay are merely compensation for wrongs and not a limitation on their freedom. Moreover, the liability insurance costs that businesses have to pay reflect, in an efficient system, the likelihood that they will impose harms on others.

In practice, however, the United States' civil liability system imposes vastly higher costs on everyone than every other developed country's system does.[46] Moreover, the costs of the system vary widely by state. In fact, it is more appropriate to think of there being 50 separate civil liability systems in the United States than one national system, and "bad" state systems can impose significant costs above those necessary to remedy wrongs. That is especially the case when defendants are from another state.[47]

The civil liability index captures risks and costs to property and contract freedoms that businesses must pass on to consumers as higher prices. Unfortunately for consumers—and that means everyone—tort abuse's overall cost to the economy is quite high. In fact, according to policy analysts Lawrence McQuillan, Hovannes Abramyan, and Anthony Archie, the nationwide "tort tax" amounts to $328 billion annually in direct costs and $537 billion annually in indirect costs.[48] Not all of those indirect costs are relevant to this variable in our index: administration costs show up in state spending and taxation, and the costs of lost innovation (42 percent of all tort costs according to McQuillan, Abramyan, and Archie) seem too higher-order to be included here. That is consistent with our overall approach, since we do not include the cost of economic growth forgone for any other regulatory variable.

One of the most significant improvements to the index we made in the fourth edition has to do with state civil liability systems. The freedom index includes a single variable, an index of how plaintiff-friendly each state's civil liability system is, which depends in turn on eight variables. We use principal component analysis to find the common variance among each of those: (a) ratings of lawsuit climate by businesses,[49] (b) partisan

---

46. For a good overview, see the contributions to F. H. Buckley (ed.), *The American Illness: Essays on the Rule of Law* (New Haven, CT: Yale University Press, 2013).

47. For evidence, see Alexander Tabarrok and Eric Helland, "Court Politics: The Political Economy of Tort Awards," *Journal of Law and Economics* 42, no. 1 (1999): 157–88.

48. Lawrence J. McQuillan, Hovannes Abramyan, and Anthony P. Archie, *Jackpot Justice: The True Cost of America's Tort System* (San Francisco: Pacific Research Institute, 2007).

49. See *Ranking the States: A Survey of the Fairness and Reasonableness of State Liability Systems,* U.S. Chamber Institute for Legal Reform.

elections for the supreme court, (c) partisan elections for trial courts, (d) lawyer concentration index, (e) legal services share of GDP, (f) blanket punitive or noneconomic damages cap, (g) burden of proof for conduct justifying punitive damages, and (h) joint and several liability abolition.

Even though the U.S. tort system is largely at the state level, certain nationwide features affect the tort environment in every state. Even the "best" state will have a "tort tax" of some kind. Moreover, a state's poor tort environment affects out-of-state defendants, creating an interjurisdictional externality.[50] Nevertheless, Nicole Crain and others find that adopting all recommended tort reforms could reduce a state's tort losses by 49 percent and annual insurance premiums by 16 percent.[51] Using an econometric model of insurance costs and tort system perceptions, Paul Hinton, David McKnight, and Ronald Miller find a potential reduction in tort costs ranging from $20 million in Vermont to $5.3 billion in California, due to comprehensive tort reform.[52] We use their estimates to come up with an estimate of how nationwide tort reform amounting to a standard-deviation change on our variable would affect liability insurance premiums. Then, we divide by 0.55 to take into account deadweight loss and costs of legal representation, which are 45 percent of the tort tax (excluding administration and lost innovation costs) according to McQuillan, Abramyan, and Archie.

50. Tabarrok and Helland, "Court Politics."
51. Nicole V. Crain et al., "Tort Law Tally: How State Tort Reforms Affect Tort Losses and Tort Insurance Premiums," Pacific Research Institute (April 2009).
52. Paul J. Hinton, David McKnight, and Ronald I. Miller, "Determinants of State Tort Costs: The Predictive Power of the Harris State Liability Systems Ranking Study," NERA Economic Consulting (October 2012).

TABLE II

Rank	State	Lawsuit Freedom Score		Rank	State	Lawsuit Freedom Score
1.	New Hampshire	0.063		26.	Kentucky	0.014
2.	Nebraska	0.053		27.	Montana	0.012
3.	North Dakota	0.051		28.	Georgia	0.011
4.	Alaska	0.047		29.	Washington	0.007
5.	South Dakota	0.041		30.	Vermont	0.004
6.	Idaho	0.040		31.	Florida	0.002
7.	Iowa	0.038		32.	Virginia	0.001
8.	Oklahoma	0.035		33.	New Jersey	0.000
9.	South Carolina	0.035		34.	Texas	−0.001
10.	Michigan	0.034		35.	Rhode Island	−0.003
11.	Utah	0.033		36.	West Virginia	−0.004
12.	Arkansas	0.032		37.	California	−0.004
13.	Kansas	0.031		38.	Maryland	−0.006
14.	Wyoming	0.030		39.	Connecticut	−0.007
15.	Colorado	0.028		40.	Ohio	−0.008
16.	Mississippi	0.028		41.	Massachusetts	−0.009
17.	Tennessee	0.028		42.	Delaware	−0.010
18.	Indiana	0.027		43.	Minnesota	−0.012
19.	Arizona	0.025		44.	New Mexico	−0.018
20.	Oregon	0.024		45.	Alabama	−0.024
21.	Nevada	0.023		46.	Missouri	−0.028
22.	Wisconsin	0.021		47.	Pennsylvania	−0.050
23.	Maine	0.016		48.	Louisiana	−0.053
24.	Hawaii	0.015		49.	New York	−0.073
25.	North Carolina	0.015		50.	Illinois	−0.077

Note: States with the same rank are tied. States with different scores may appear identical due to rounding.

OCCUPATIONAL FREEDOM

2.6% The prevalence of occupational licensing is difficult to measure. Some of the literature uses listings of licensed occupations by state at America's Career InfoNet,[53] but we have found those listings to be highly unreliable, often excluding certain licensed occupations or including others that are privately certified, not regulated by the government. We use two redundant measures of the prevalence of licensure to reduce measurement error.

Our first measure of licensure prevalence is a weighted sum for 64 occupations, where each occupation's weight is its proportion of the total employment in those 64 occupations. A second measure is available only for 2014, 2016, 2017, and 2019, and it is carried back and interpolated to other years. It counts the number of mentions of certain phrases in each state's statutes, such as "shall not practice." We do find that these two variables correlate together modestly ($r=0.30$). These two variables together are worth about 1.6 percent of the index, with each apportioned half of the weight.

We also include sunrise and sunset provisions for occupational licensing. But because of a lack of evidence regarding their effectiveness, they are worth less than 0.1 percent of the index. (*Sunrise* refers to independent review requirements before a new licensing board is created; *sunset* refers to automatic expiration of licensing boards after several years so that the legislature must reauthorize them.)

The remaining occupational freedom variables have to do with medical scope of practice. Nurse practitioner scope of practice is the most important, making up 0.8 percent of the index. Dental hygienist independent practice is worth 0.1 percent of the index, followed by two more minor variables: membership in the Nurse Licensure Compact and physician assistant prescription authority.

---

53. For instance, Morris M. Kleiner and Alan B. Krueger, "The Prevalence and Effects of Occupational Licensing," *British Journal of Industrial Relations* 48 (4) (2010): 676–87.

TABLE 12

Rank	State	Occupational Freedom Score		Rank	State	Occupational Freedom Score
1.	Idaho	0.026		26.	West Virginia	−0.004
2.	Wyoming	0.021		27.	Kentucky	−0.005
3.	Colorado	0.021		28.	Washington	−0.006
4.	Rhode Island	0.019		29.	Indiana	−0.007
5.	Vermont	0.019		30.	Michigan	−0.008
6.	Hawaii	0.018		31.	Georgia	−0.009
7.	New Hampshire	0.014		32.	Nevada	−0.010
8.	Nebraska	0.014		33.	South Carolina	−0.010
9.	Kansas	0.014		34.	Pennsylvania	−0.010
10.	Alaska	0.012		35.	Oklahoma	−0.011
11.	Missouri	0.008		36.	Oregon	−0.011
12.	Maine	0.007		37.	Arkansas	−0.012
13.	Montana	0.007		38.	Tennessee	−0.012
14.	Connecticut	0.006		39.	Alabama	−0.012
15.	Utah	0.006		40.	North Carolina	−0.015
16.	Minnesota	0.006		41.	New York	−0.016
17.	Arizona	0.005		42.	Louisiana	−0.017
18.	New Mexico	0.005		43.	Florida	−0.018
19.	Delaware	0.004		44.	New Jersey	−0.019
20.	Iowa	0.003		45.	Ohio	−0.020
21.	Mississippi	0.000		46.	Maryland	−0.021
22.	South Dakota	−0.001		47.	Virginia	−0.023
23.	Massachusetts	−0.001		48.	Illinois	−0.024
24.	North Dakota	−0.003		49.	California	−0.041
25.	Wisconsin	−0.003		50.	Texas	−0.048

Note: States with the same rank are tied. States with different scores may appear identical due to rounding.

MISCELLANEOUS REGULATORY FREEDOM

2.5%   Miscellaneous regulations include, in declining order of importance, certificate-of-need requirements for new hospital construction, auto insurance rate filing requirements, homeowner's insurance rate filing requirements, general unfair-pricing and sales-below-cost laws, price-gouging laws, rate classification prohibitions for some classes of insurance, membership in the Interstate Insurance Product Regulation Compact, direct-to-consumer auto sales, minimum markup and sales-below-cost laws for gasoline, moving company entry regulations, and mandatory product labeling laws.

Certificate-of-need regulations land their first-place slot in this category on the basis of the over $3 billion in extra costs they impose on hospitals, customers, and potential market entrants.[54] Next come state personal auto insurance rate filing requirements. These regimes range from Massachusetts's old "fixed and established" system (scrapped in 2008), in which all car insurance premiums were dictated by law, to no rate-filing requirement whatsoever in Wyoming. A one-standard-deviation change on this −1 to 4 scale, about 1.2 points, would be worth $2 billion nationwide. The main problem with strict rate regulation regimes is that they encourage insurers to stop insuring some drivers altogether, forcing those drivers to find coverage in a state-guaranteed, "residual" market.[55]

Homeowner's insurance rate filing regulations range from "prior approval" to "no file." A one-standard-deviation shift on this variable would be worth $1.3 billion nationwide. The Interstate Insurance Product Regulation Compact makes it easier to sell the same life insurance policy or annuity across state lines. Prohibitions on the use of certain criteria for insurance rating purposes—such as age, gender, territory, and credit rating—redistribute wealth from low risks to high risks and drive some consumers out of the market altogether.

Price-gouging laws, which have gained in popularity recently, try to repeal the laws of supply and demand. They impose price controls on necessary products after disasters, making them even scarcer by disincentivizing supply and incentivizing demand.[56] According to W. David Montgomery, Robert Baron, and Mary Weisskopf, a price-gouging law on gasoline could be expected to reduce economic welfare by at least $1.9 billion in the wake of a

---

54.   Christopher J. Conover and Frank A. Sloan, "Does Removing Certificate-of-Need Regulations Lead to a Surge in Health Care Spending?," *Journal of Health Politics, Policy, and Law* 23, no. 3 (1998): 455–81; Jon M. Ford and David L. Kaserman, "Certificate-of-Need Regulation and Entry: Evidence from the Dialysis Industry," *Southern Economic Journal* 59, no. 4 (1993): 783–91; Patrick A. Rivers, Myron D. Fottler, and Mustafa Zeedan Younis, "Does Certificate of Need Really Contain Hospital Costs in the United States?," *Health Education Journal* 66, no. 3 (2007): 229–44.

55.   Scott E. Harrington and Helen I. Doerpinghaus, "The Economics and Politics of Automobile Insurance Rate Classification," *Journal of Risk and Insurance* 60, no. 1 (1993): 59–84.

56.   Michael Giberson, "The Problem with Price Gouging Laws," *Regulation*, Spring 2011: pp. 48–53.

major disaster on the scale of Hurricanes Rita and Katrina.[57]

Mandatory product-labeling laws include (a) genetically modified organism (GMO) labeling requirements on food (now federalized) and (b) California's unique law mandating disclosure of potential carcinogens, which has a much bigger impact than GMO labeling (about $17 million per year in settlement costs alone[58]). We exclude this mandatory labeling law variable from our chain-linked index because of the federal preemption law on GMO labeling requirements.

57. W. David Montgomery, Robert A. Baron, and Mary K. Weisskopf, "Potential Effects of Proposed Price Gouging Legislation on the Cost and Severity of Gasoline Supply Interruptions," *Journal of Competition Law and Economics* 3, no. 3 (2007): 357–97.

58. Michael L. Marlow, "Too Much (Questionable) Information?," *Regulation*, Winter 2013–14: pp. 20–28.

TABLE 13

Rank	State	Miscellaneous Regulatory Freedom Score
1.	Arizona	0.031
2.	Wyoming	0.030
3.	Idaho	0.026
4.	Utah	0.024
5.	New Mexico	0.021
6.	New Hampshire	0.020
7.	Kansas	0.017
7.	Texas	0.017
9.	Wisconsin	0.017
10.	Illinois	0.016
11.	Minnesota	0.014
12.	Colorado	0.012
13.	Nevada	0.008
14.	Kentucky	0.007
14.	Vermont	0.007
16.	Iowa	0.007
17.	Nebraska	0.005
17.	Ohio	0.005
19.	Missouri	0.004
20.	Georgia	0.004
20.	Oregon	0.004
20.	Virginia	0.004
23.	Oklahoma	0.003
24.	South Dakota	0.003
25.	Florida	0.003

Rank	State	Miscellaneous Regulatory Freedom Score
26.	Alaska	0.002
27.	Indiana	0.001
28.	North Dakota	0.000
29.	Delaware	−0.001
30.	Rhode Island	−0.003
31.	Connecticut	−0.003
32.	Montana	−0.005
33.	Maine	−0.005
34.	Pennsylvania	−0.005
35.	California	−0.005
36.	Arkansas	−0.006
37.	Washington	−0.007
38.	Mississippi	−0.008
39.	Michigan	−0.010
40.	Alabama	−0.013
41.	New Jersey	−0.014
42.	Maryland	−0.014
43.	Tennessee	−0.015
44.	Louisiana	−0.017
45.	West Virginia	−0.017
46.	South Carolina	−0.018
47.	New York	−0.018
48.	Hawaii	−0.019
49.	Massachusetts	−0.020
50.	North Carolina	−0.020

Note: States with the same rank are tied. States with different scores may appear identical due to rounding.

CABLE AND TELECOM FREEDOM

1.1% The least important category in the regulatory policy dimension is cable and telecommunications market freedom. It is important to note that these are the only public utility regulation areas included in the freedom index, because some utility "deregulation" is not truly deregulatory, as in the case of pro-competitive "reregulation" that has restructured electricity and natural gas markets in certain states. Although these services are important for household budgets, it is not at all clear that "deregulation" results in a net increase in individual freedom. The utilities are all characterized by physical connections to the consumer. Because of the monopoly element in transmission (parallel connections are judged infeasible), even under deregulation governments maintain "common carrier" regulations that require the regulated owner of the transmission grid to allow open access to competing providers at a regulated price. The transmission grid then becomes a "commons" with no profit incentive for the owner to expand, upgrade, or maintain the network. In many cases, retail competition is tightly managed by state governments to prevent anticompetitive manipulation of the market. For these reasons, many analysts insist on the term *restructuring* as opposed to *deregulation* for these industries.[59]

Telecommunications deregulation accounts for roughly two-thirds of the weight for this category, and the remainder is accounted for by statewide cable franchising, which eases the entry of telecom firms into the video cable market.[60]

---

59. Peter Van Doren and Jerry Taylor, "Rethinking Electricity Restructuring," Cato Institute Policy Analysis no. 530, November 30, 2004, https://www.cato.org/policy-analysis/rethinking-electricity-restructuring.

60. Adam Summers, "Cable Franchise Reform: Deregulation or Just New Regulators?," *Freeman* 57, no. 3 (2007): 31–34; Cecil Bohanon and Michael Hicks, "Statewide Cable Franchising and Broadband Connections," Digital Policy Institute, Ball State University, 2010.

TABLE 14

Rank	State	Cable and Telecom Freedom Score		Rank	State	Cable and Telecom Freedom Score
1.	Kansas	0.016		20.	Montana	0.009
1.	Texas	0.016		20.	Maine	0.009
1.	Wisconsin	0.016		20.	Pennsylvania	0.009
1.	Illinois	0.016		20.	Mississippi	0.009
1.	Nevada	0.016		20.	Alabama	0.009
1.	Iowa	0.016		31.	Idaho	0.008
1.	Ohio	0.016		31.	Rhode Island	0.008
1.	Missouri	0.016		31.	California	0.008
1.	Georgia	0.016		34.	Wyoming	0.000
1.	Virginia	0.016		34.	New Mexico	0.000
1.	Florida	0.016		34.	Minnesota	0.000
1.	Indiana	0.016		34.	South Dakota	0.000
1.	Delaware	0.016		34.	Alaska	0.000
1.	Arkansas	0.016		39.	Arizona	−0.001
1.	Michigan	0.016		39.	Vermont	−0.001
1.	Tennessee	0.016		39.	Connecticut	−0.001
1.	Louisiana	0.016		39.	New Jersey	−0.001
1.	South Carolina	0.016		39.	Hawaii	−0.001
1.	North Carolina	0.016		44.	Oregon	−0.008
20.	Utah	0.009		44.	Oklahoma	−0.008
20.	New Hampshire	0.009		44.	Washington	−0.008
20.	Colorado	0.009		44.	Maryland	−0.008
20.	Kentucky	0.009		44.	West Virginia	−0.008
20.	Nebraska	0.009		44.	New York	−0.008
20.	North Dakota	0.009		44.	Massachusetts	−0.008

Note: States with the same rank are tied. States with different scores may appear identical due to rounding.

OVERALL REGULATORY POLICY RANKING

34.9% As with fiscal policy, states that rank highest on regulatory policy are mostly conservative, but they tilt toward midwestern more than southern. In general, these are "good-government" states that score well on variables such as the liability system variable. Regulatory policy remains a key element in economic growth, as Part II, "Politics of Freedom," later in the book will show. But both fiscal and regulatory policy are highly correlated; thus, it is hard to disentangle which policy variable is doing most of the work to explain economic growth in the states.

We validate our regulatory policy measure by examining its correlation to small businesses' ratings of their states' regulatory environments. Thumbtack.com conducts an annual survey of independent businesses in each state, funded by the Kauffman Foundation.[61] We average each state's rank out of 45 for 2012, 2013, and 2014 (5 states lack data). Smaller numbers are better, indicating a higher rank. The correlation between the 2014 regulatory index score and Thumbtack.com's regulatory survey rank is -0.70, a strong negative correlation that suggests that our index captures most of what small businesses think about when it comes to regulations that affect their business.

61.   The survey is available at https://www.thumbtack.com/survey.

TABLE 15

Rank	State	Overall Regulatory Policy Score		Rank	State	Overall Regulatory Policy Score
1.	Kansas	0.126		26.	North Carolina	0.007
2.	Nebraska	0.120		27.	Alaska	−0.002
3.	Iowa	0.110		28.	Colorado	−0.019
4.	Idaho	0.103		29.	West Virginia	−0.022
5.	Wyoming	0.080		30.	Missouri	−0.034
6.	South Dakota	0.069		31.	Louisiana	−0.049
7.	Georgia	0.066		32.	Ohio	−0.056
8.	Utah	0.066		33.	Delaware	−0.064
9.	Wisconsin	0.064		34.	Minnesota	−0.068
10.	Indiana	0.064		35.	New Mexico	−0.068
11.	Kentucky	0.058		36.	Montana	−0.093
12.	North Dakota	0.051		37.	Pennsylvania	−0.120
13.	South Carolina	0.050		38.	Illinois	−0.126
14.	Arkansas	0.049		39.	Maine	−0.143
15.	Mississippi	0.048		40.	Connecticut	−0.145
16.	Tennessee	0.047		41.	Washington	−0.155
17.	Michigan	0.044		42.	Massachusetts	−0.181
18.	Virginia	0.041		43.	Rhode Island	−0.197
19.	Arizona	0.037		44.	Vermont	−0.207
20.	Oklahoma	0.031		45.	Hawaii	−0.232
21.	Florida	0.018		46.	Oregon	−0.368
22.	Texas	0.013		47.	Maryland	−0.395
23.	Nevada	0.012		48.	New York	−0.450
24.	New Hampshire	0.011		49.	New Jersey	−0.482
25.	Alabama	0.009		50.	California	−0.486

Note: States with the same rank are tied. States with different scores may appear identical due to rounding.

Figure 5 shows how average regulatory policy has changed over time, when federalized policies such as the PPACA are excluded. Unlike with fiscal policy, states' have not sustained their gains on regulatory policy since the Great Recession. Occupational freedom, land-use freedom, and labor-market freedom have declined since 2016, whereas lawsuit freedom and cable and telecom freedom have improved. Minimum-wage increases were particularly problematic. Were we to include federalized policies, the drop would be even larger in 2012 when the PPACA took effect, more than wiping out even the temporary gains at the state level.

FIGURE 5 State Average Regulatory Policy Scores Over Time

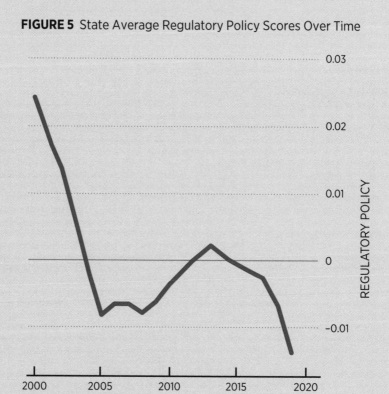

OVERALL ECONOMIC FREEDOM RANKING

Although we believe that a composite freedom index that includes both economic and personal freedoms is most valuable and best represents the actual state of freedom in the states, readers may wish to compare and contrast the states solely on their overall economic freedom, particularly for the purposes of empirical analysis of income growth. We invite researchers to use the economic freedom variable as a tool for investigating income growth and related phenomena. Economic freedom is calculated as the sum of the fiscal and regulatory freedom indexes.

We validate our economic freedom index by correlating it to state scores for taxes and regulations as rated by chief executives of for-profit companies for *Chief Executive* magazine.[62] We use the average Chief Executive scores for 2013 and 2014 for all 50 states. The correlation between our economic freedom index and chief executives' ratings is 0.74, indicating an extremely strong relationship between what we measure as economic freedom and what entrepreneurs are concerned about when it comes to state policy.[63]

---

62. The rankings were announced on *Chief Executive's* website, http://chiefexecutive.net, but are no longer available.

63. We also correlated chief executives' ratings to the Economic Freedom of North America (EFNA) index, as measured in 2012 (latest available year) for the subnational level. That correlation is 0.67, strong but not as strong as the correlation between our index and chief executives' ratings. EFNA also has a weaker correlation with the Thumbtack.com survey results than our index. EFNA and our economic freedom index correlate at a moderately strong 0.59.

TABLE 16

Rank	State	Overall Economic Freedom Score	Rank	State	Overall Economic Freedom Score
1.	Florida	0.449	26.	Montana	0.081
2.	Tennessee	0.417	27.	Kansas	0.079
3.	New Hampshire	0.367	28.	Ohio	0.058
4.	South Dakota	0.332	29.	Alaska	0.034
5.	Idaho	0.298	30.	Massachusetts	0.025
6.	Georgia	0.288	31.	Louisiana	0.011
7.	Indiana	0.263	32.	Connecticut	0.010
8.	Michigan	0.227	33.	Iowa	0.004
9.	Nevada	0.210	34.	Nebraska	−0.022
10.	Texas	0.200	35.	Illinois	−0.063
11.	Virginia	0.200	36.	West Virginia	−0.078
12.	Missouri	0.174	37.	Mississippi	−0.086
13.	Arizona	0.165	38.	Washington	−0.116
14.	Colorado	0.139	39.	Minnesota	−0.117
15.	Arkansas	0.137	40.	Rhode Island	−0.138
16.	Kentucky	0.137	41.	Maine	−0.158
17.	Pennsylvania	0.131	42.	Delaware	−0.195
18.	Alabama	0.125	43.	New Mexico	−0.282
19.	Wisconsin	0.110	44.	Maryland	−0.327
20.	Wyoming	0.108	45.	Vermont	−0.343
21.	Utah	0.100	46.	New Jersey	−0.424
22.	North Carolina	0.096	47.	Oregon	−0.428
23.	North Dakota	0.092	48.	California	−0.543
24.	South Carolina	0.088	49.	Hawaii	−0.601
25.	Oklahoma	0.085	50.	New York	−0.757

Note: States with the same rank are tied. States with different scores may appear identical due to rounding.

Figure 6 shows the evolution of state average economic freedom over time, excluding federalized policies. Economic freedom declined in the early 2000s, recovered briefly, took another hit in 2009, and then grew to new heights by 2017 before a modest decline since then. The upswing was consistent with what Figures 4 and 5 show: rapidly improving state fiscal policies after 2011 and a less consistent but still large average improvement in regulatory policy until 2016. We worry that the recent downward dip could be a sign of a future trend toward greater interventionism in the economy—and a greater barrier to economic recovery in the aftermath of the COVID-19 pandemic.

FIGURE 6 State Average Economic Freedom Scores over Time

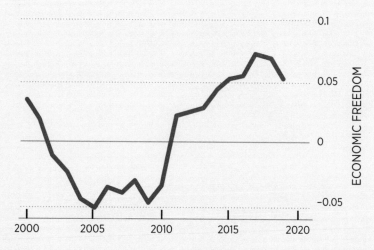

PERSONAL FREEDOM

The personal freedom versus paternalism dimension (Figure 7) consists of the following categories: (a) incarceration and arrests for victimless crimes, (b) gambling freedom, (c) gun rights, (d) marriage freedom, (e) educational freedom, (f) tobacco freedom, (g) alcohol freedom, (h) marijuana freedom, (i) asset forfeiture, (j) other mala prohibita and miscellaneous civil liberties, (k) travel freedom, and (l) campaign finance freedom. Weighting these categories is a challenge because the observable financial impacts of these policies often do not include the full harms to victims.

FIGURE 7 Personal Freedom Weights

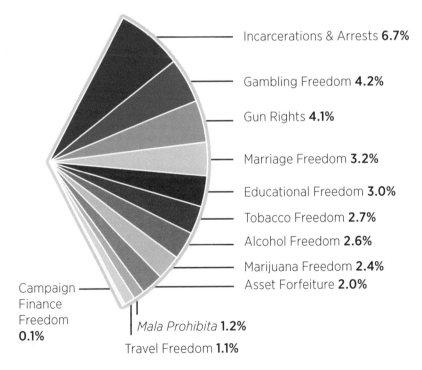

Incarcerations & Arrests **6.7%**

Gambling Freedom **4.2%**

Gun Rights **4.1%**

Marriage Freedom **3.2%**

Educational Freedom **3.0%**

Tobacco Freedom **2.7%**

Alcohol Freedom **2.6%**

Marijuana Freedom **2.4%**
Asset Forfeiture **2.0%**

Campaign
Finance
Freedom
0.1%

Mala Prohibita **1.2%**

Travel Freedom **1.1%**

With some assumptions, one can use results in the academic literature to measure, for instance, the lost consumer surplus from marijuana prohibition, or even to make a plausible guess at the disutility incurred by a year in prison. However, it is much more difficult to measure the risks prohibitionist policies pose to individuals who are not imprisoned—especially those who may not even engage in the activity prohibited, but who legitimately fear further restrictions on their freedoms.

An example may help illustrate the problem. Imagine two countries, each the size of the United States. In Country A, the average tax rate is 1 percent (of income) lower than in Country B, but unlike Country B, Country A prohibits the practice of a minor religion—say, Zoroastrianism. Assuming personal income of $12 trillion, as in the United States, the lower tax rate in Country B allows for more freedom worth $28 billion a year, by the method of calculation used in this book.

Now suppose that 10,000 Zoroastrians go to prison for their beliefs. There are few estimates of the cost of prison, including opportunity cost and psychological harms, but the estimates that exist range between $30,000 and $50,000 per year for the average prisoner.[64] Taking the higher figure, the prohibition of Zoroastrianism is found to have a victim cost of approximately $500 million per year: far, far lower than the benefit of lower taxes.

Is the country with slightly lower taxes, but with a blatant infringement of religious freedom, truly freer? Surely, the calculation above has missed some very significant costs to freedom from the infringement of religious liberty. This calculation is related to the discussion of fundamental rights in the "Regulatory Policy" section earlier. Freedom to believe (or disbelieve) in any religion and freedom to practice peacefully (or refuse to practice) any religion seem to be freedoms that every person rationally desires. They are fundamental rights. Many personal freedoms have this character, and it needs to be recognized in the freedom index.

Therefore, the index applies constitutional weights to personal freedoms—as with regulatory policies—but uses different values, because the direct, measurable costs to victims of policies that infringe on personal freedoms are generally a smaller percentage of true costs than the direct, measurable costs to victims of regulatory policies. Put another way, measuring the economic consequences that regulatory policies have on their full victim class is a relatively simple procedure, but the full costs of policies that infringe on personal freedoms are measurable only in part. Further, as mentioned in the discussion of fiscal policy, taxes and economic regulations do not necessarily infringe on the rights of all apparent victims, unlike policies

64.   John J. Donohue, "Assessing the Relative Benefits of Incarceration: The Overall Change over the Previous Decades and the Benefits on the Margin," in *Do Prisons Make Us Safer? The Benefits and Costs of the Prison Boom*, ed. Steven Raphael and Michael Stoll (New York: Russell Sage Foundation, 2008); Innocence Project, "Compensating the Wrongly Convicted," https://www.innocenceproject.org/compensating-wrongly-convicted/.

that affect personal freedoms.

Again, the index takes constitutional provisions relating to certain freedoms as prima facie evidence of a freedom's "basicness," indicating that the full victim class should be thought of as quite broad. Therefore, variables relating to fundamental, high-salience rights are multiplied by a factor of 10, on the basis of their inclusion in the federal Constitution. Variables relating to rights specified only in at least one state constitution are multiplied by a factor of 5. Variables that receive the "constitutional weights" are noted in the relevant discussion of each. There is of course nothing magical about these numbers, but they bring the personal freedom dimension into rough parity with the fiscal and regulatory policy dimensions as one-third of the overall index. In this edition, personal freedom is of slightly less weight than the regulatory dimension and 3 percent more than fiscal policy.

The following sections introduce each category within the personal freedom dimension, in order of weight.

INCARCERATION AND ARRESTS FOR VICTIMLESS CRIMES

6.7% The most heavily weighted category in the personal freedom dimension is the law enforcement statistics category, which consists of data on incarceration rates adjusted for violent and property crime rates,[65] nondrug victimless crimes arrests, the drug enforcement rate, and two variables new to the fifth edition—(a) driver's license suspensions for drug offenses and (b) prison collect phone call rates. This category is worth a bit over one-fifth of the personal freedom index. Given that the United States is frequently lambasted for having more prisoners per capita than almost every other country, and that the incarceration rate varies widely across states, it is perhaps no surprise that this category should be so important. The personal freedom dimension also includes laws that create or reduce victimless crimes in other categories, such as marijuana, gun, and prostitution laws. Our philosophy for assigning weights to these categories is to consider the forgone consumer and producer surplus due to prohibitions, while we consider within the law enforcement statistics category the costs of arrest and prison time. Given our earlier discussion of virtue libertarianism, it is important to remember that consumer and producer surplus are economic concepts rather than moral judgments that would assign any approbation to the activities themselves.

A one-standard-deviation nationwide reduction in incarceration rates adjusted for crime rates would yield about $17 billion in new value for prisoners. This figure excludes the fiscal benefits of incarcerating fewer people.

A similar reduction in drug arrests per reported drug user would benefit arrestees by $8.7 billion. Other victimless crimes arrests are calculated in two different ways, since there is no direct, state-by-state measure of the number of people who engage in these activities, as there is for drug arrests. Instead, the index takes the arrests of people over 18 for weapons, prostitution, gambling, loitering, and liquor law violations as a percentage of the population and as a percentage of total arrests. The former figure is an imperfect measure of the risk of a citizen's being arrested for one of these offenses (except that states may differ in the percentage of citizens who engage in these activities), whereas the latter is more of a measure of police priorities. Both variables are equally weighted and together amount to $5.8 billion of benefit to potential arrestees.

---

65. The adjustment involves regressing the incarceration rate on violent and property crime rates and taking the residuals. States with high scores will be those that lock up more people than would be expected given their crime rates.

The cost to drug offenders of a nationwide policy of driver's license suspensions, which typically last six months or more, would be in the neighborhood of $350 million. A standard-deviation change in the 15-minute collect phone call rate, $1.65, would roughly extract $51 million from prisoners' families if implemented nationwide.

TABLE 17

Rank	State	Incarceration and Arrests for Victimless Crimes Score	Rank	State	Incarceration and Arrests for Victimless Crimes Score
1.	Massachusetts	0.134	26.	Nebraska	0.020
2.	Rhode Island	0.116	27.	Pennsylvania	0.015
3.	Maine	0.110	28.	Montana	0.015
4.	Vermont	0.107	29.	Alabama	0.014
5.	Hawaii	0.087	30.	West Virginia	0.010
6.	Minnesota	0.086	31.	Nevada	0.010
7.	Alaska	0.085	32.	South Carolina	0.004
8.	Washington	0.078	33.	Indiana	0.003
9.	New Hampshire	0.073	34.	Ohio	0.002
10.	Connecticut	0.071	35.	Tennessee	0.001
11.	New York	0.059	36.	Wisconsin	0.000
12.	New Jersey	0.054	37.	Florida	−0.006
13.	New Mexico	0.051	38.	Missouri	−0.008
14.	Utah	0.047	39.	Virginia	−0.012
15.	Iowa	0.039	40.	Georgia	−0.016
16.	Colorado	0.036	41.	Idaho	−0.020
17.	California	0.036	42.	Kentucky	−0.021
18.	Oregon	0.034	43.	Arizona	−0.021
19.	Maryland	0.032	44.	Texas	−0.026
20.	North Carolina	0.032	45.	Oklahoma	−0.034
21.	Illinois	0.029	46.	Arkansas	−0.037
22.	Michigan	0.026	47.	South Dakota	−0.047
23.	Kansas	0.026	48.	Wyoming	−0.049
24.	North Dakota	0.023	49.	Louisiana	−0.061
25.	Delaware	0.023	50.	Mississippi	−0.062

Note: States with the same rank are tied. States with different scores may appear identical due to rounding.

GAMBLING FREEDOM

4.2%   Annual nationwide commercial casino revenues minus payouts ("win") are over $40 billion,[66] so gambling is big business. Unfortunately, no state has a free market in gaming enterprises, but an oligopolistic, state-licensed system at least permits more freedom than a total ban.

We include casino revenue data in the freedom index. We have obtained these data from the University of Nevada Las Vegas (UNLV) Center for Gaming Research and state regulatory boards' annual reports. The freedom index uses the Australian Productivity Commission's admittedly flawed[67] method (but a creditable and unique attempt) for deriving the consumer surplus, as follows:

$$S = \frac{p(1-t)q}{2e}$$

where S is the surplus, p(1 - t)q is price including tax times quantity, and e is the price elasticity of demand, assumed to be -1.3 following the academic literature and the Australian Productivity Commission's estimate for nonproblem gamblers.[68] Thus, the total gambling revenues figure is divided by 2.6 to get the consumer surplus. We also take 30 percent off for problem gamblers, whose consumer surplus might be zero (an aggressive assumption). In addition, we take two-thirds off the figure to account for interstate spillovers: gambling liberalization on the margin does not increase consumer surplus or revenue much because the national gambling market is almost saturated. For the freedom index, producer surplus is irrelevant because the producer side of the industry is heavily oligopolistic or monopolistic because of state control.

Apart from casino win, we also include dichotomous variables measuring whether states have legalized noncasino forms of gambling: pari-mutuel wagering, charitable gaming, and slot or video machines outside casinos. Some states put those revenue figures online, but we have been unable to obtain complete data, hence the dichotomous variables. Using the data we do have, however, we can roughly estimate the impact of legalization in each of those areas on consumer surplus. Slot and video machines seem to be far more popular than pari-mutuel wagering or charitable gaming. The revenues from slot machines are mind-boggling to these authors, who have little interest in this form of gambling and more than a little disapprobation. In 2016, sparsely populated Montana raked in a whopping $400 million a year in gross revenue minus

---

66.   "United States Commercial Casino Gaming: Monthly Revenues," UNLV Center for Gaming Research.

67.   Brian Dollery and John Storer, "Assessing the Impact of Electronic Gaming Machines: A Conceptual Critique of the Productivity Commission's Methodology," Gambling Research 20, no. 1 (2008): 1–12.

68.   "Estimating Consumer Surplus," Australasian Gaming Council, https://web.archive.org/web/20130426072651/www.austgamingcouncil.org.au/images/pdf/eLibrary/2330.pdf.

payouts, amounting to nearly $500 for every man, woman, and child. Clearly, quite a few Montanans are paying many thousands of dollars a year for the privilege of playing these games.

Although the aforementioned gambling variables are worth a combined 4.0 percent of the index, the remaining variables in this category have very small weights. A social gambling exception and whether "aggravated gambling" is a felony each make up 0.02 percent of the freedom index. Express prohibitions on internet gambling, which are redundant on federal prohibitions, are worth less than 0.01 percent.

TABLE 18

Rank	State	Gambling Freedom Score		Rank	State	Gambling Freedom Score
1.	Nevada	0.154		26.	Florida	−0.013
2.	Louisiana	0.048		27.	Oklahoma	−0.013
3.	West Virginia	0.035		27.	Minnesota	−0.014
4.	Pennsylvania	0.033		27.	Connecticut	−0.014
5.	Maryland	0.032		27.	California	−0.014
6.	Illinois	0.032		27.	Alabama	−0.014
7.	South Dakota	0.028		32.	Texas	−0.014
8.	Montana	0.025		32.	Nebraska	−0.014
9.	Oregon	0.025		32.	Idaho	−0.014
10.	Virginia	0.025		32.	Kentucky	−0.014
11.	Mississippi	0.018		32.	Arizona	−0.014
12.	Rhode Island	0.004		32.	Arkansas	−0.014
13.	Iowa	0.001		32.	Wyoming	−0.014
14.	Delaware	0.000		39.	Washington	−0.014
15.	Indiana	−0.003		40.	North Dakota	−0.014
16.	New Jersey	−0.004		41.	New Hampshire	−0.015
17.	Missouri	−0.006		42.	South Carolina	−0.015
18.	Ohio	−0.009		43.	Wisconsin	−0.015
19.	Michigan	−0.009		44.	Vermont	−0.015
20.	New Mexico	−0.009		44.	Alaska	−0.015
21.	Colorado	−0.010		44.	North Carolina	−0.015
22.	Kansas	−0.010		47.	Tennessee	−0.015
23.	Maine	−0.011		47.	Georgia	−0.015
24.	New York	−0.011		49.	Hawaii	−0.016
25.	Massachusetts	−0.012		50.	Utah	−0.016

Note: States with the same rank are tied. States with different scores may appear identical due to rounding.

GUN RIGHTS

4.1% Gun rights have risen across editions of the index because of new research suggesting that the price elasticity of demand for carry permits is rather low, implying high consumer surplus. Still, most of the weight of this category is because of the boost these policies receive from state and federal constitutional protection.

Only some firearms policies trigger Second Amendment scrutiny, and those are the only ones to get the full "times 10" constitutional weighting factor. We follow recent case law in our judgments on this point. On the one hand, the U.S. Supreme Court decisions in *D.C. v. Heller* [69] and *McDonald v. Chicago* [70] held that federal, state, and local governments are not allowed to ban gun ownership for self-defense purposes altogether, and state and federal appeals court decisions have also held that the Second Amendment protects a right to carry a firearm outside the home. On the other hand, the Supreme Court has opined that the U.S. Constitution permits bans on certain types of firearms and reasonable regulations on how someone may qualify to carry a weapon for self-defense. However, since the Louisiana Constitution provides that all firearms-related restrictions should be subject to strict scrutiny, we apply a "times 5" constitutional weighting factor to all those firearms policies not receiving the "times 10" boost. Variables falling into this latter category include concealed-carry permit costs, concealed-carry permit terms, restrictions on multiple purchases of handguns, licensing or regulation of gun dealers, universal background checks, registration of firearms, locking device requirements, ammunition microstamping, duty-to-retreat laws, and laws relating to National Firearms Act weapons (machine guns, sound suppressors, short-barreled rifles, short-barreled shotguns, and "any other weapon"). We eliminated non-powder-gun regulations in this edition of the index because of the lack of data.

The most significant variable in the gun rights category is the concealed-carry index, which takes into account shall-issue versus may-issue, carry in vehicles, local preemption, and the scope of places where concealed carry is allowed (1.9 percent of the freedom index). Concealed-carry permit cost (0.5 percent of the index) comes next. The existence of a local gun ban—which only Illinois had, until struck down in *McDonald v. Chicago*—is worth 0.4 percent. At about 0.3 percent of the index, we find our index of firearms owner licensing requirements and waiting periods on firearms purchases. At 0.2 percent of the index is the term of carry permits.

Other variables included in this category—and worth far less than those discussed in the previous paragraph—are our index of open-carry laws,

69. *D.C. v. Heller*, 554 U.S. 570 (2008).
70. *McDonald v. Chicago*, 561 U.S. 742 (2010).

training requirements for carry permits, stricter-than-federal minimum age to purchase firearms, assault weapons bans, duty-to-retreat laws ("castle doctrine"), restrictions on multiple purchases, locking-device requirements, dealer licensing, registration of firearms, ballistic identification or microstamping requirements, "design safety standards" (bans on cheap handguns), large-capacity magazine bans, laws regarding Class III weapons, retention of sales records, and .50-caliber rifle bans.

TABLE 19

Rank	State	Gun Rights Score	Rank	State	Gun Rights Score
1.	Kansas	0.044	26.	Indiana	0.015
2.	New Hampshire	0.044	27.	Montana	0.014
3.	Idaho	0.043	28.	Ohio	0.014
3.	Arizona	0.043	29.	Nevada	0.013
5.	Vermont	0.042	30.	South Carolina	0.013
6.	West Virginia	0.037	31.	Texas	0.013
6.	Mississippi	0.037	32.	Louisiana	0.012
6.	Kentucky	0.037	33.	New Mexico	0.012
6.	Wyoming	0.037	34.	Michigan	0.012
10.	South Dakota	0.037	35.	North Carolina	0.010
11.	North Dakota	0.036	36.	Iowa	0.009
12.	Missouri	0.036	37.	Minnesota	0.009
13.	Alaska	0.036	38.	Florida	0.006
14.	Maine	0.035	39.	Washington	0.004
15.	Arkansas	0.034	40.	Nebraska	−0.003
16.	Oklahoma	0.034	41.	Illinois	−0.009
17.	Pennsylvania	0.021	42.	Delaware	−0.027
18.	Utah	0.020	43.	New York	−0.035
19.	Wisconsin	0.019	44.	Connecticut	−0.039
20.	Colorado	0.017	45.	Maryland	−0.042
21.	Alabama	0.017	46.	Rhode Island	−0.042
22.	Oregon	0.016	47.	New Jersey	−0.047
23.	Georgia	0.016	48.	Massachusetts	−0.048
24.	Tennessee	0.016	49.	California	−0.054
25.	Virginia	0.015	50.	Hawaii	−0.077

Note: States with the same rank are tied. States with different scores may appear identical due to rounding.

MARRIAGE FREEDOM

3.2% Most of the weight of the marriage freedom category is tied to the availability of same-sex partnerships, whether civil unions or marriage. The remainder is tied to waiting periods and blood test requirements, availability of cousin marriage and covenant marriage, and sodomy laws, which were struck down by the Supreme Court in 2003. In our view, state governments should treat marriage as a contract that is "registered" or "recorded," rather than a personal status that is "licensed."

States that prohibited same-sex couples from entering private contracts that provide the benefits of marriage (whether termed "marriages" or "civil unions") clearly took away an important contract right from such couples. Some states merely refrained from providing a convenient mechanism, such as civil unions or marriage, for same-sex couples to make contracts covering inheritance, hospital visitation, medical power of attorney, and so on. Other states went further and expressly prohibited any private contracts intended to provide benefits equivalent to marriage. For instance, the Virginia Constitution states, "This Commonwealth and its political subdivisions shall not create or recognize a legal status for relationships of unmarried individuals that intends to approximate the design, qualities, significance, or effects of marriage." Such state laws are sometimes called "super-DOMAs," after the federal Defense of Marriage Act. Other states that, by statute or constitution, prohibited all marriage-like private contracts for same-sex couples are Alabama, Arkansas, Florida, Georgia, Idaho, Kansas, Kentucky, Louisiana, Michigan, Nebraska, North Carolina, North Dakota, Ohio, Oklahoma, South Carolina, South Dakota, Texas, Utah, and Wisconsin (which is a curious example of a state that has limited domestic partnerships but also a super-DOMA, banning contracts offering benefits "equal to marriage").

Now that the Supreme Court has nationalized same-sex marriage, those distinctions among states are irrelevant. The 2019 ranking on this variable is driven mostly by cousin marriage, which at 0.2 percent of the index is more important than covenant marriage and vastly more important than blood tests and waiting periods.[71]

The freedom index has long used an estimate that the freedom to marry is worth about $2,500 per year to same-sex couples, and that about 900,000 couples would take advantage of this opportunity when it became available nationwide.[72] Those estimates have proved reliable in subsequent research. Over 1 million Americans are now in same-sex marriages.[73]

---

71. Although cousin marriage is rare, bans on the practice receive the constitutional weight of 10 because they prevent certain couples from marrying altogether. Covenant marriage, waiting periods, and blood tests, by contrast, do not receive the constitutional weight.

72. M. V. Lee Badgett, "The Economic Value of Marriage for Same-Sex Couples," *Drake Law Review* 58 (2010): 1081–116.

73. Census Bureau, "U.S. Census Bureau Releases CPS Estimates of Same-Sex Households," (November 19), news release no. CB19-TPS.51, November 19, 2019. For 2016, see Richard Wolf, "Gay Marriages Up 33% in Year Since Supreme Court Ruling," *USA Today*.

TABLE 20

| | | Marriage Freedom | | | | |
Rank	State	Score		Rank	State	Score
1.	Alabama	0.028		26.	Wisconsin	0.025
1.	California	0.028		27.	Louisiana	0.025
1.	Colorado	0.028		28.	Idaho	0.022
1.	Connecticut	0.028		28.	Kentucky	0.022
1.	Georgia	0.028		28.	Minnesota	0.022
1.	Hawaii	0.028		28.	Mississippi	0.022
1.	New Mexico	0.028		28.	Missouri	0.022
1.	North Carolina	0.028		28.	Montana	0.022
1.	Rhode Island	0.028		28.	Nebraska	0.022
1.	Tennessee	0.028		28.	Nevada	0.022
1.	Vermont	0.028		28.	New Hampshire	0.022
1.	Virginia	0.028		28.	North Dakota	0.022
13.	South Carolina	0.028		28.	Ohio	0.022
14.	Maryland	0.028		28.	Oklahoma	0.022
15.	Arizona	0.028		28.	South Dakota	0.022
16.	Alaska	0.028		28.	West Virginia	0.022
16.	Florida	0.028		28.	Wyoming	0.022
16.	Massachusetts	0.028		43.	Delaware	0.022
16.	New Jersey	0.028		44.	Iowa	0.022
20.	New York	0.027		44.	Kansas	0.022
21.	Indiana	0.025		44.	Michigan	0.022
21.	Maine	0.025		44.	Oregon	0.022
21.	Utah	0.025		44.	Pennsylvania	0.022
24.	Illinois	0.025		44.	Texas	0.022
25.	Arkansas	0.025		44.	Washington	0.022

Note: States with the same rank are tied. States with different scores may appear identical due to rounding.

EDUCATIONAL FREEDOM

3.0% The single most important educational freedom variable is the index of tax credit and deduction laws for private education (1.1 percent of the whole index). We have assumed that the average "broad-eligibility" program has a per-student benefit of about $3,250. We use research on the price elasticity of demand for private schooling to estimate the number of families that would take advantage of this type of program if it were available nationwide, and we come up with an estimate of 7.5 million.[74] We also add a small bonus ($20 per student) to those students remaining in public schools, with the idea that their families also benefit slightly from the mere availability of more choice. Together, those estimates imply that moving nationwide from a situation of no tax credit scholarships to broad-eligibility programs would benefit families about $14.5 billion a year.

Other important variables for educational freedom include publicly funded voucher law size and scope, mandatory state licensure of private school teachers, mandatory state or local approval of private schools, years of compulsory schooling, and extent of private school curriculum control. Vouchers are worth less than tax credit scholarship funds because extant programs are generally more narrowly targeted and come with more strings attached. Since the closing of our data, West Virginia has enacted a broad-eligibility education savings account bill; such a policy will have a heavy weight in our index given how we calculate variable weightings (something we noted in the fifth edition of the index).

Less significant are public school choice ("open enrollment" policies), mandatory registration of private schools, existence of a homeschool law, homeschool curriculum control, homeschool teacher qualifications, homeschool standardized testing, homeschool notification index, and homeschool record-keeping index. All the homeschool variables combined make up 0.13 percent of the index. Their weight is small because few students are homeschooled (though the COVID-19 pandemic educational experience may have permanently increased the homeschool population), and the variance in state policies is not as significant in the post-2000 period as it was in the 1980s.

Educational freedom is an area in which states continue to be active in a generally positive direction. In the fifth edition, we noted that we expected several states would climb in the rankings in this edition of the index. That has now been borne out. For instance, in 2017, New Hampshire passed a law allowing all school districts to adopt a private school choice program for stu-

---

74. Andrew Coulson, "Choosing to Save: The Fiscal Impact of Education Tax Credits on the State of Nevada," Nevada Policy Research Institute, January 12, 2009, https://www.npri.org/issues/publication/choosing-to-save.

dents in grades not covered by a school district's own schools. In 2021, New Hampshire went even further, which should improve its ranking even more by the next edition.

TABLE 21

Rank	State	Educational Freedom Score	Rank	State	Educational Freedom Score
1.	Arizona	0.058	26.	Kansas	0.003
2.	Florida	0.045	27.	Idaho	0.001
3.	Indiana	0.042	28.	Tennessee	−0.001
4.	Georgia	0.036	29.	New Jersey	−0.002
5.	New Hampshire	0.033	30.	Missouri	−0.002
6.	North Carolina	0.028	31.	Delaware	−0.003
7.	Illinois	0.027	32.	Colorado	−0.003
8.	Virginia	0.026	33.	Texas	−0.004
9.	Wisconsin	0.024	34.	New Mexico	−0.004
10.	Louisiana	0.021	35.	Oregon	−0.005
11.	Oklahoma	0.018	36.	New York	−0.005
12.	Pennsylvania	0.017	37.	Kentucky	−0.005
13.	Rhode Island	0.017	38.	California	−0.005
14.	Montana	0.015	39.	Alaska	−0.006
15.	Vermont	0.013	40.	West Virginia	−0.007
16.	Mississippi	0.012	41.	Connecticut	−0.007
17.	Ohio	0.011	42.	Massachusetts	−0.010
18.	Iowa	0.010	43.	Hawaii	−0.010
19.	South Carolina	0.007	44.	Wyoming	−0.011
20.	Minnesota	0.007	45.	Maine	−0.012
21.	Nevada	0.006	46.	Maryland	−0.015
22.	Utah	0.006	47.	Nebraska	−0.015
23.	Alabama	0.005	48.	Michigan	−0.017
24.	South Dakota	0.004	49.	Washington	−0.022
25.	Arkansas	0.004	50.	North Dakota	−0.023

Note: States with the same rank are tied. States with different scores may appear identical due to rounding.

TOBACCO FREEDOM

2.7% In the tobacco freedom category, representing 2.7 percent of the index, we consider the effect of cigarette taxes, minimum legal sale age of 21, smoking and vaping bans (in privately owned workplaces, restaurants, and bars), flavored electronic cigarette bans, vending machine bans, and internet sales regulations on freedom. The vaping variables are new to this sixth edition of the index.

Cigarette taxes are the most important variable in this category. A $1-per-pack tax increase is associated with about a 16.7 percent increase in the price of a pack.[75] Nobel Prize–winning economist Gary S. Becker and his colleagues calculate that the long-run price elasticity of demand for cigarettes is about −0.75.[76] In 2010, 303 billion cigarettes were sold in the United States, typically at 20 cigarettes per pack.[77] These facts are sufficient to calculate the deadweight loss (dividing by 2 under the assumption of perfectly elastic supply) and the total cost to consumers. As with alcohol taxes, we divide the latter element by 2.5 to capture the fact that taxes have the conditional consent of some taxpayers, but not by 4 as we did for general taxes (see discussion in the "Fiscal Policy" section), because "sin taxes" disproportionately hit consumers of these products, who are more likely to be opposed to high taxes on the goods they consume.

Economics professor Michael L. Marlow examines the consequences of Ohio's comprehensive smoking ban for its losers. State and local governments issued 33,347 citations, with an average expense of about $1,250 per citation (given that each cited location averaged about five citations).[78] Extrapolating from Ohio's population supplies the national numbers for the freedom index.

The second set of costs from smoking bans has to do with lost business and the associated disutility to smokers. There is an unfortunate lack of good studies with quasi-random treatment; however, a reasonable assumption is that the costs of bans must be at least as high as (and possibly much greater than) the fines establishments are willing to risk to permit smoking. Thus, a simple approach is to multiply an estimate of this amount by 2.5, assuming that the lost revenue is slightly greater than the fines businesses are willing to incur. Because bars are affected by smoking bans much more than restaurants and workplaces are, we assign 80 percent of the weight to

75. Ann Boonn, "State Cigarette Excise Tax Rates and Rankings," Campaign for Tobacco-Free Kids, Washington, December 13, 2012, http://www.tobaccofreekids.org/research/factsheets/pdf/0097.pdf.

76. Gary S. Becker, Michael Grossmann, and Kevin M. Murphy, "Rational Addiction and the Effect of Price on Consumption," *American Economic Review* 81, no. 2 (1991): 237–41.

77. "Economic Facts about U.S. Tobacco Production and Use," Centers for Disease Control and Prevention, November 15, 2012, http://www.cdc.gov/tobacco/data_statistics/fact_sheets/economics/econ_facts/.

78. Michael L. Marlow, "The Economic Losers from Smoking Bans," *Regulation,* Summer 2010, pp. 14–19, http://www.cato.org/sites/cato.org/files/serials/files/regulation/2010/6/regv33n2-4.pdf.

smoking bans in bars and 10 percent each to the latter bans.

Banning 18- to 20-year-olds from buying tobacco products nationwide could eliminate about $5 billion of annual sales. Assuming the price elasticity of demand is –0.2, the lost consumer surplus is about 2.5 times that.

Banning flavored electronic cigarettes is worth 0.2 percent of the index. Flavored electronic cigarette bans reduce overall e-cigarette sales. Because of technological change, we apply a time-varying weight. Massachusetts's flavored vape ban appears to have reduced sales 24 percent.[79] Another economic impact study predicts a more than 58 percent drop in sales from a federal ban.[80] We average these figures to get a cross-elasticity of substitution of –0.41. We consider both the lost consumer surplus and the deadweight loss of a flavor ban. According to one source, the U.S. e-cigarette market was worth $12.8 billion in 2020.[81] The vape market was about $2.5 billion in 2014.[82] It apparently doubled each year between 2010 and 2014, and we assume it doubled back to 2008, which we use as the first year of vaping. In the preregulation era, nontobacco flavors made up to 86 percent of vape sales.[83] Recently, federal regulation has driven nonmenthol and nontobacco flavors out of the market. E-cigarette sales remain strong, suggesting that flavor bans are not nearly as severe as total bans. However, flavor bans do seem to drive youth toward cigarette smoking.[84]

Vending machine bans, vaping bans, and internet sales regulations are together worth less than 0.1 percent of the index.

79. Patrick Gleason, "One State's Flavored Tobacco & Vape Ban Is a Cautionary Tale for the Nation," *Forbes*, January 31, 2021.

80. John Dunham, "The Economic Impact of a Ban on Flavored Vapor Products," memorandum to Vapor Technology Association, November 21, 2019.

81. "United States E-Cigarette and Vape Market," Expert Market Research, December 2020.

82. "Activities of the Cigarette Companies," Chapter 4 in *E-Cigarette Use among Youth and Young Adults: A Report of the Surgeon General* (Atlanta: U.S. Department of Health and Human Services, Centers for Disease Control and Prevention, 2016), https://www.ncbi.nlm.nih.gov/books/NBK538679/.

83. Dunham, "Economic Impact of a Ban on Flavored Vapor Products."

84. Ed Cara, "San Francisco's Flavored Vape Ban Linked to More Teen Smoking, Study Finds," Gizmodo, May 25, 2021.

TABLE 22

Rank	State	Tobacco Freedom Score		Rank	State	Tobacco Freedom Score
1.	Georgia	0.019		25.	Michigan	−0.008
2.	Wyoming	0.016		27.	Kansas	−0.012
3.	South Carolina	0.015		28.	Wisconsin	−0.015
4.	Mississippi	0.015		29.	Arkansas	−0.022
5.	North Carolina	0.015		30.	Texas	−0.028
6.	Idaho	0.014		31.	Virginia	−0.031
7.	North Dakota	0.013		32.	Maryland	−0.036
8.	Tennessee	0.013		33.	Maine	−0.037
9.	Nebraska	0.012		34.	Ohio	−0.038
10.	Alabama	0.010		35.	Pennsylvania	−0.041
11.	Kentucky	0.010		36.	Delaware	−0.041
12.	Indiana	0.009		37.	Colorado	−0.047
13.	Louisiana	0.008		38.	Minnesota	−0.052
14.	Missouri	0.007		39.	Rhode Island	−0.054
15.	West Virginia	0.007		40.	Vermont	−0.055
16.	Florida	0.004		41.	Hawaii	−0.056
17.	Iowa	0.002		42.	Oregon	−0.057
18.	Nevada	0.001		43.	New Jersey	−0.064
19.	South Dakota	−0.002		44.	Alaska	−0.064
20.	Oklahoma	−0.002		45.	California	−0.067
21.	New Hampshire	−0.003		46.	Washington	−0.068
22.	Montana	−0.004		47.	Connecticut	−0.072
23.	Utah	−0.004		48.	Massachusetts	−0.086
24.	New Mexico	−0.007		49.	New York	−0.108
25.	Arizona	−0.008		50.	Illinois	−0.126

Note: States with the same rank are tied. States with different scores may appear identical due to rounding.

ALCOHOL FREEDOM

2.6% The alcohol distribution system ("control"—which means that the state has a monopoly on distribution—versus "license"—which means that the state licenses distributors) makes up almost 1.0 percent of the whole index on its own. Research shows that state distribution of alcohol imposes significant costs on consumers in time and inconvenience.[85]

The freedom index assumes a "full-price elasticity" (including formal and informal prices) of –0.2 for all alcohol types, which is similar to what has been discovered in the literature cited earlier. Reducing consumption of alcohol by 5 percent with a state monopoly, according to University of California, Los Angeles professors Stanley I. Ornstein and Dominique M. Hanssens, therefore implies a 25 percent "tax" due to transaction cost. According to the U.S. Department of Agriculture, packaged alcoholic beverage sales in 2010 amounted to $91 billion. If all such sales had to go through state monopolies, then one might expect a transaction-cost "tax" of close to $23 billion.[86]

Blue laws (bans on Sunday sales) would, if implemented nationwide, reduce consumer welfare by over $4.5 billion and are worth 0.4 percent of the index. Preventing wine, spirits, or in a few states even beer from being sold in grocery stores has a similar cost. Taxes on beer, wine, and spirits each make up 0.2–0.3 percent of the index as a whole, followed by direct wine shipment bans, keg registration and bans, and "happy hour" bans. Mandatory server training, worth less than 0.01 percent of the index, rounds out this category.

With its strong brewing industry, it is no surprise that Wisconsin finishes first in this ranking. Nor is Utah's last-place finish shocking.

---

85. Stanley I. Ornstein and Dominique M. Hanssens, "Alcohol Control Laws and the Consumption of Distilled Spirits and Beer," *Journal of Consumer Research* 12, no. 2 (1985): 200–213.

86. Björn Trolldal and William Ponicki, "Alcohol Price Elasticities in Control and License States in the United States, 1982–1999," *Addiction* 100, no. 8 (2005): 1158–65. Our comparison here is from minimum to maximum values for this variable.

TABLE 23

Rank	State	Alcohol Freedom Score		Rank	State	Alcohol Freedom Score
1.	Wisconsin	0.019		26.	South Carolina	0.004
2.	Missouri	0.019		27.	Tennessee	0.003
3.	Arizona	0.018		28.	Georgia	0.003
4.	Nevada	0.018		29.	Maine	0.002
5.	Indiana	0.018		30.	Rhode Island	0.001
6.	California	0.018		31.	Delaware	0.001
7.	Louisiana	0.016		32.	West Virginia	0.001
8.	South Dakota	0.016		33.	Minnesota	0.001
9.	Illinois	0.015		34.	Kansas	0.000
10.	Texas	0.015		35.	Iowa	0.000
11.	New Mexico	0.014		36.	Ohio	0.000
12.	Massachusetts	0.013		37.	New Hampshire	−0.001
13.	Hawaii	0.013		38.	Arkansas	−0.002
14.	Colorado	0.011		39.	Alaska	−0.004
15.	Nebraska	0.011		40.	North Carolina	−0.004
16.	Wyoming	0.011		41.	Oregon	−0.004
17.	Florida	0.010		42.	Virginia	−0.005
18.	North Dakota	0.010		43.	Kentucky	−0.006
19.	New Jersey	0.010		44.	Mississippi	−0.007
20.	New York	0.009		45.	Alabama	−0.011
21.	Connecticut	0.008		46.	Montana	−0.015
22.	Maryland	0.008		47.	Vermont	−0.015
23.	Oklahoma	0.008		48.	Idaho	−0.020
24.	Michigan	0.004		49.	Pennsylvania	−0.021
25.	Washington	0.004		50.	Utah	−0.061

Note: States with the same rank are tied. States with different scores may appear identical due to rounding.

MARIJUANA FREEDOM

2.4%   Marijuana freedom has been on the rise in the states for many years now, and states such as Vermont, Maine, and Massachusetts have risen in the rankings since the fifth edition because of policy changes in a pro-freedom direction. As mentioned earlier in the section "Incarceration and Arrests for Victimless Crimes," we consider here only the lost consumer and producer surplus due to prohibition, not the costs of arrests and incarceration.

Recent work has yielded inconsistent findings on marijuana policy and consumption. Rand Corporation economist Rosalie Liccardo Pacula and her coauthors[87] find that marijuana penalties have a small impact on marijuana use among youth (a one-standard-deviation increase in minimum jail time is associated with a 1.2 percent decline in annual risk of use), but "decriminalization" or "depenalization" as such retains a small (about 2 to 3 percent) effect even when these penalty variables are controlled for, which the authors cannot explain. In a different study, Pacula and others[88] find that reduced penalties for users increase consumption and therefore price, resulting in higher profits for sellers. They also calculate that prohibition probably doubles the price of a pound of marijuana, at least (adding $200 to $300 to the cost).

A reasonable estimate of the amount of marijuana sold in the United States in a year is 50 million pounds.[89] Unfortunately, absolutely no evidence exists on the consequences of supplier penalties. We conservatively assume total seller profits of $200 per pound (including compensation for risk). We estimate the new consumer surplus conservatively, assuming a price elasticity of demand of −0.2 (like alcohol) and unit elasticity of supply.

Looking at decriminalization of small-scale possession first, we assume this policy boosts consumption by 3 percent, which implies a transaction-cost tax of roughly 15 percent. We then calculate the deadweight loss and the forgone producer surplus, assuming a price per pound of $330. This underestimate is small because decriminalization also correlates with strength of criminal penalties, which Pacula and others[90] find affect consumption. Moving from criminalization to decriminalization nationwide should then increase consumer and producer welfare by about $2.3 billion. Our coding of this variable assumes that the benefits of full legalization of possession are

87.   Rosalie Liccardo Pacula, Jamie F. Chriqui, and Joanna King, "Marijuana Decriminalization: What Does It Mean in the United States?," NBER Working Paper no. 9690, National Bureau of Economic Research, Cambridge, MA, May 2003.

88.   Rosalie Liccardo Pacula et al., "Risks and Prices: The Role of User Sanctions in Marijuana Markets," NBER Working Paper no. 13415, National Bureau of Economic Research, Cambridge, MA, September 2007.

89.   Jon Gettman, "Lost Taxes and Other Costs of Marijuana Laws," DrugScience.org, 2007.

90.   Pacula et al., "Marijuana Decriminalization."

about five times as large.

The most important variable in the marijuana freedom category is our index of medical marijuana laws, which takes into account the scope of qualifying conditions, the maximum amount permitted, whether home cultivation is permitted, and whether dispensaries are permitted. Pacula and others find that some features of medical marijuana laws, such as home cultivation and (especially) dispensaries, may increase overall consumption, but their results are not easily interpretable in a supply-and-demand model, nor are they generally statistically significant.[91] Other research has found no effect on consumption.[92] But several studies now seem to show that legal dispensaries result in lower prices by shifting out the supply curve. Wen, Hockenberry, and Cummings find that allowing nonspecific pain as a reason for medical marijuana recommendations increases use by those over age 21 significantly.[93] The bottom line is that the total effect of medical marijuana laws on consumption is modest, probably a bit more than decriminalization, but much is unknown. We choose a weight for this variable of 1.5 times that for decriminalization.

The next most important variable is the maximum penalty for a single marijuana offense not involving a minor, which in some states is life in prison. Such penalties depress supply and raise price. We also include whether high-level possession or cultivation of cannabis is a misdemeanor or felony and any mandatory minimum sentence for "low-level" cultivation or sale. All these variables are assumed together to have a similar effect on decriminalization of possession.

The next most important variable is whether some recreational cannabis sales are legal. Recreational sales of marijuana in Colorado—the first state to implement legal recreational sales—have not decreased medical marijuana sales.[94] It is unclear what the effect has been on total sales—that is, whether legalization simply reduces the black market or also increases total consumption. Even under the former scenario, the big increase in recreational sales over time suggests that many consumers benefit by buying on the legal market rather than the black market. In the 12 months through June 2015, legal recreational sales amounted to about $450 million in Colorado. Assume 20 percent of that reflects producer costs (a common statistic is that in the absence of prohibition and any taxes, the price of marijuana would fall by

91.   Rosalie Liccardo Pacula et al., "Assessing the Effects of Medical Marijuana Laws on Marijuana and Alcohol Use: The Devil Is in the Details," NBER Working Paper no. 19302, National Bureau of Economic Research, Cambridge, MA, August 2013.

92.   Rosalie Liccardo Pacula and Eric L. Sevigny, "Marijuana Legalization Policies: Why We Can't Learn Much from Policy Still in Motion," *Journal of Policy Analysis and Management* 33, no. 1 (2014): 212–21.

93.   Hefei Wen, Jason M. Hockenberry, and Janet R. Cummings, "The Effect of Medical Marijuana Laws on Adolescent and Adult Use of Marijuana, Alcohol, and Other Substances," *Journal of Health Economics* 42, issue C (2015): 64–80.

94.   Ricardo Baca, "Colorado Pot Sales Spike in June, Top $50 Million for First Time," *Cannabist*, August 13, 2015, http://www.thecannabist.co/2015/08/13/colorado-marijuana-taxes-recreational-sales-june-2015-50-million/39384/.

80 percent). The remainder reflects producer and consumer surplus. We assume one-quarter of that surplus is due to the legalization of sales specifically, rather than possession and cultivation. After adjusting to national population, we estimate then that legalizing some marijuana sales would create $5.4 billion of benefit nationally.

Finally, we consider the effect of *Salvia divinorum* bans within this category. A 2006 study found that 750,000 people used salvia that year, compared with 26 million marijuana users per year.[95] Therefore, we add together all the marijuana weights and multiply by 0.75/26. An objection to this strategy is that the variance among states is greater on salvia policy, so this weight understates the importance of the policy (in no state is marijuana completely unregulated). On the other hand, the per-user quantity of salvia consumed is surely much lower than that for marijuana, so this weight may overstate the importance of the policy. Because we cannot assess the relative magnitudes of these biases, we simply assume that they cancel out. Salvia bans are therefore worth less than 0.1 percent of the index.

---

95.   National Survey on Drug Use and Health, "Use of Specific Hallucinogens: 2006," *NSDUH Report,* February 14, 2008, https://roar.nevadaprc.org/public/resources/1127.

TABLE 24

Rank	State	Marijuana Freedom Score		Rank	State	Marijuana Freedom Score
1.	California	0.076		26.	Arkansas	0.005
2.	Maine	0.066		27.	Connecticut	0.005
3.	Alaska	0.061		28.	New York	0.003
4.	Massachusetts	0.059		29.	West Virginia	0.003
5.	Oregon	0.058		30.	Pennsylvania	0.002
6.	Michigan	0.058		31.	New Jersey	0.002
7.	Colorado	0.054		32.	Florida	0.001
8.	Nevada	0.052		33.	North Carolina	−0.006
9.	Washington	0.051		34.	Idaho	−0.007
10.	Illinois	0.047		35.	Indiana	−0.007
11.	Vermont	0.042		36.	Kansas	−0.008
12.	Maryland	0.021		37.	Louisiana	−0.008
13.	Hawaii	0.016		38.	Wisconsin	−0.009
14.	New Hampshire	0.015		39.	Kentucky	−0.009
15.	New Mexico	0.013		40.	Wyoming	−0.010
16.	Oklahoma	0.013		41.	Nebraska	−0.010
17.	Delaware	0.012		42.	Mississippi	−0.010
18.	Missouri	0.012		43.	South Dakota	−0.011
19.	Utah	0.011		44.	South Carolina	−0.011
20.	Rhode Island	0.010		45.	Iowa	−0.012
21.	Ohio	0.009		46.	Tennessee	−0.014
22.	North Dakota	0.009		47.	Georgia	−0.014
23.	Arizona	0.008		48.	Texas	−0.015
24.	Montana	0.007		49.	Alabama	−0.017
25.	Minnesota	0.006		50.	Virginia	−0.017

Note: States with the same rank are tied. States with different scores may appear identical due to rounding.

ASSET FORFEITURE

2.0%   Civil asset forfeiture is the government's ability to take a
person's property by accusing him or her of a crime. Often
the seized cash or proceeds of auctioning the property accrue to the seizing
agency, providing incentives for "policing for profit." Typically, the person
whose property is seized must file suit and prove innocence to get the property back. Both federal and state and local law enforcement engage in asset
forfeiture.

We measure not only state laws, including the extent to which a few
states limit federal "adoption" of state-initiated forfeiture cases, but also
the amount of "equitable-sharing" revenue state and local law enforcement
receives from the Department of Justice in each state. A standard-deviation
change in equitable-sharing forfeitures nationwide amounts to $4.6 billion.
We give state forfeiture laws the same weight even though we have no consistent data on state-level forfeitures.

TABLE 25

Rank	State	Asset Forfeiture Score		Rank	State	Asset Forfeiture Score
1.	New Mexico	0.056		26.	Arkansas	0.011
2.	South Dakota	0.051		27.	Mississippi	0.010
3.	Wisconsin	0.038		28.	Indiana	0.010
4.	New Hampshire	0.036		29.	Michigan	0.010
5.	Nebraska	0.035		30.	Nevada	0.009
6.	North Dakota	0.032		31.	Illinois	0.007
7.	Colorado	0.030		32.	Oklahoma	0.004
8.	Missouri	0.026		33.	Alabama	0.003
9.	California	0.025		34.	Louisiana	0.002
10.	Connecticut	0.024		35.	New York	0.002
11.	Iowa	0.023		36.	West Virginia	0.002
12.	Pennsylvania	0.022		37.	Delaware	0.002
13.	Oregon	0.021		38.	Virginia	0.001
14.	Arizona	0.021		39.	Texas	−0.001
15.	Utah	0.020		40.	South Carolina	−0.002
16.	Florida	0.018		41.	Idaho	−0.002
17.	Ohio	0.018		42.	Massachusetts	−0.003
18.	Wyoming	0.018		43.	Tennessee	−0.003
19.	North Carolina	0.015		44.	Washington	−0.003
20.	Maryland	0.014		45.	New Jersey	−0.004
21.	Vermont	0.014		46.	Kentucky	−0.008
22.	Montana	0.014		47.	Georgia	−0.009
23.	Minnesota	0.014		48.	Alaska	−0.009
24.	Hawaii	0.013		49.	Kansas	−0.009
25.	Maine	0.012		50.	Rhode Island	−0.029

Note: States with the same rank are tied. States with different scores may appear identical due to rounding.

MALA PROHIBITA

1.2% The term *mala prohibita* refers to acts defined as criminal in statute, even though they are not harms in common law (*mala in se*). This category is a grab bag of mostly unrelated policies, including raw milk laws, fireworks laws, prostitution laws, physician-assisted suicide laws, religious freedom restoration acts, rules on taking DNA samples from criminal suspects without a probable cause hearing, trans-fat bans, state equal rights amendments, mixed martial arts legalization, and, new to this edition, bans on racial preferences in the public sector.[96]

Of these, the policies with the greatest potential cost to victims are racial preferences in the public sector (more than half of this category), prostitution prohibition, and trans-fat bans.

The biggest effect of state affirmative action bans appears to be in public university admissions.[97] White and Asian enrollment appears to grow about 5 percent when affirmative action is banned. The annual benefit to these students of attending a preferred college is probably on the order of, say, $5,000—that is, a fraction of typical public tuition.

If Nevada-style policies legalizing but regulating brothels were in effect nationwide, the industry would garner an estimated $5 billion in revenue, a comparatively small sum compared with other vice industries, such as alcohol, gambling, tobacco, and even marijuana.[98]

After racial preferences in the public sector and prostitution prohibition, the next most important is California's restaurant trans-fat ban, which, if implemented nationwide, would cost consumers—at a reasonable estimate—more than $3.5 billion worth of pleasure a year.[99] Next is the legalization of raw milk, then legalization of mixed martial arts, followed closely by fireworks laws. Then comes physician-assisted suicide, which receives the "times five" constitutional weighting factor, since the Montana Constitution has been held to protect a right thereto. Rounding out this category, in order, are state equal rights amendments, state DNA database laws, and religious freedom restoration acts.

---

96. To be clear, we do not necessarily condone prostitution, but we defend the rights of willing adults to engage in consensual exchange of sex. We completely condemn all nonconsensual sex trafficking as unjust and deserving of legal prohibition.

97. Hayley Munguia, "Here's What Happens When You Ban Affirmative Action in College Admissions," FiveThirtyEight.com, December 9, 2015.

98. Daria Snadowsky, "The Best Little Whorehouse Is Not in Texas: How Nevada's Prostitution Laws Serve Public Policy, and How Those Laws May Be Improved," *Nevada Law Journal* 6, no. 1 (2005): 217–19.

99. Gary Becker, "Comment on the New York Ban on Trans Fats," Becker-Posner Blog, December 21, 2006, https://www.becker-posner-blog.com/2006/12/comment-on-the-new-york-ban-on-trans-fats--becker.html.

TABLE 26

Rank	State	*Mala Prohibita* Score	Rank	State	*Mala Prohibita* Score
1.	Nebraska	0.026	26.	Arkansas	−0.002
2.	Arizona	0.026	26.	Mississippi	−0.002
3.	Oklahoma	0.026	28.	Kentucky	−0.002
4.	Michigan	0.026	28.	Tennessee	−0.002
5.	California	0.019	30.	Minnesota	−0.002
6.	Washington	0.014	30.	New York	−0.002
7.	New Hampshire	0.013	32.	Idaho	−0.002
8.	Florida	0.011	33.	Virginia	−0.002
9.	Nevada	0.008	34.	Wisconsin	−0.002
10.	Oregon	−0.001	35.	Iowa	−0.002
11.	Pennsylvania	−0.001	36.	Massachusetts	−0.002
12.	New Mexico	−0.001	37.	Kansas	−0.002
13.	Maine	−0.001	38.	New Jersey	−0.002
14.	Wyoming	−0.001	39.	Maryland	−0.003
15.	Colorado	−0.001	40.	Alabama	−0.003
16.	Connecticut	−0.001	41.	Louisiana	−0.003
17.	Vermont	−0.001	42.	North Carolina	−0.003
18.	Utah	−0.002	42.	West Virginia	−0.003
19.	Hawaii	−0.002	44.	South Dakota	−0.003
19.	Montana	−0.002	45.	Georgia	−0.003
21.	Illinois	−0.002	46.	Delaware	−0.003
22.	South Carolina	−0.002	47.	North Dakota	−0.003
23.	Missouri	−0.002	48.	Rhode Island	−0.003
24.	Alaska	−0.002	49.	Indiana	−0.003
25.	Texas	−0.002	50.	Ohio	−0.004

Note: States with the same rank are tied. States with different scores may appear identical due to rounding.

TRAVEL FREEDOM

1.1% Two variables—the use and retention of automated license plate reader data and the availability of driver's licenses to those without Social Security numbers (such as undocumented workers)—together make up about half of the travel freedom category's total weight in the index.

There are about 11.1 million undocumented immigrants in the United States, and we assume that 60 percent of them would be willing to get driver's licenses, slightly lower than the rate of licensed drivers in the general population. We then assume the mean value of a license per driver per year is $750. For automated license plate readers, we assume that the average driver—of whom there are 210 million in the United States—would be willing to pay $15 a year to avoid being subject to their unlimited use.

Seat belt laws are weighted on the basis of estimated costs of tickets. A fingerprint or thumbprint requirement for a driver's license is worth slightly less.

Suspicionless sobriety checkpoints invade privacy and create anxiety among those stopped and searched. Extrapolating from two different sources, we estimate about 9 million drivers a year are searched at sobriety checkpoints nationwide, or would be if checkpoints were legal nationwide. We assume a cost of $20 per driver searched in lost time, privacy, and anxiety. We multiply the variable by 5 because some state constitutions prohibit these checkpoints.

After that come uninsured/underinsured motorist insurance coverage requirements, motorcycle helmet laws, open-container laws, and bans on driving while using a cell phone, in that order.

These variables were included in previous editions of *Freedom in the 50 States,* and some of them generated a fair number of comments by readers and audience members at public presentations. In particular, it was argued that some of these variables seem to be justified on the grounds of enhancing public safety. But not every measure that enhances public safety is morally justifiable—consider random searches of pedestrians. A preferable approach would use penalties for "distracted driving" of whatever cause, rather than a blanket ban on using a handheld phone while driving, which does not always pose a risk to others. Likewise, it would be better to focus on penalties for drunk driving rather than punishing people for having opened beverage containers in their vehicles, another behavior that does not necessarily pose a direct risk to others. In states with a federally conforming open-container law, having an unsealed but closed wine bottle on the floor of the passenger side of a car is sufficient to trigger a misdemeanor violation and possible jail time.

No state does extremely well on travel freedom. Utah scores at the top despite having sobriety checkpoints, an open-container law, and a primary-enforcement seat belt law, because it is one of the few states allowing someone to obtain a driver's license without a Social Security number and places some limits on automated license plate reader data retention and, unlike number two Vermont, does not mandate underinsured motorist coverage.

TABLE 27

Rank	State	Travel Freedom Score		Rank	State	Travel Freedom Score
1.	Utah	0.010		26.	Tennessee	−0.002
2.	Vermont	0.009		27.	Arizona	−0.002
3.	Colorado	0.008		28.	Virginia	−0.002
4.	Nevada	0.007		29.	Georgia	−0.002
5.	California	0.007		30.	Alaska	−0.003
6.	Maryland	0.007		30.	Iowa	−0.003
7.	Washington	0.007		30.	Michigan	−0.003
8.	New Hampshire	0.007		33.	Rhode Island	−0.003
9.	Delaware	0.006		34.	Wisconsin	−0.003
10.	New Mexico	0.006		35.	North Dakota	−0.003
11.	Oregon	0.005		35.	South Dakota	−0.003
12.	Connecticut	0.005		37.	Missouri	−0.003
13.	Montana	0.004		38.	North Carolina	−0.004
14.	Illinois	0.003		39.	Massachusetts	−0.004
15.	New York	0.002		40.	Indiana	−0.004
16.	Hawaii	0.000		40.	Kentucky	−0.004
17.	Arkansas	0.000		42.	Nebraska	−0.004
18.	Maine	−0.001		43.	South Carolina	−0.005
19.	Idaho	−0.001		44.	Mississippi	−0.005
19.	Wyoming	−0.001		45.	New Jersey	−0.006
21.	Minnesota	−0.002		46.	Alabama	−0.006
22.	Florida	−0.002		46.	Louisiana	−0.006
22.	Oklahoma	−0.002		48.	Kansas	−0.006
24.	Ohio	−0.002		49.	West Virginia	−0.007
24.	Pennsylvania	−0.002		50.	Texas	−0.007

Note: States with the same rank are tied. States with different scores may appear identical due to rounding.

CAMPAIGN FINANCE

0.1% Citizens should have the right to express and promote their political opinions in a democracy, including their support for or opposition to candidates for office. By regulating contributions to parties and candidates, governments effectively limit citizens' ability to spread their ideas.

The campaign finance policy category covers public financing of campaigns and contribution limits (individuals to candidates, individuals to parties, an index of individuals to political action committees [PACs] and PACs to candidates, and an index of individuals to PACs and PACs to parties). Although these policies receive "constitutional weights" boosting them by a factor of 10 because of their First Amendment implications, they receive low weights even so because little evidence exists that current contribution limits significantly reduce private actors' involvement in politics, unless the limits are extremely low (and Vermont's extremely low limits were struck down by the U.S. Supreme Court in 2006).[100]

Also, there just is not much money in state elections, even in states without contribution limits. According to the National Institute on Money in State Politics, in the past three election cycles nationwide individual contributions to state legislative candidates amounted to about $850 million per two-year cycle, or less than $3 per person in the country.[101] Finally, even being prevented from making, say, a $1,000 donation to a candidate does not result in a $1,000 loss to the frustrated donor because the donor can put those funds to a different use. The freedom index assumes a utility loss equivalent to 10 percent of the planned contribution when calculating victim cost. In sum, the nationwide victim losses from state campaign finance restrictions come to a figure in the tens of millions of dollars a year, at most.

100.   *Randall v. Sorrell*, 548 U.S. 230 (2006).
101.   National Institute on Money in State Politics website, http://www.followthemoney.org.

TABLE 28

Rank	State	Campaign Finance Freedom Score		Rank	State	Campaign Finance Freedom Score
1.	Indiana	0.001		26.	Missouri	0.000
1.	Mississippi	0.001		27.	Maine	0.000
1.	Nebraska	0.001		28.	Arkansas	0.000
1.	North Dakota	0.001		29.	Delaware	0.000
1.	Oregon	0.001		30.	Arizona	0.000
1.	Pennsylvania	0.001		31.	Vermont	0.000
1.	Texas	0.001		32.	North Carolina	0.000
8.	Alabama	0.001		33.	Wisconsin	0.000
8.	Virginia	0.001		34.	Illinois	0.000
10.	Iowa	0.001		35.	South Carolina	0.000
10.	Utah	0.001		36.	Rhode Island	0.000
12.	Wyoming	0.000		37.	Maryland	0.000
13.	South Dakota	0.000		38.	California	0.000
14.	Nevada	0.000		39.	West Virginia	0.000
15.	Tennessee	0.000		40.	Hawaii	0.000
16.	Georgia	0.000		41.	Kansas	0.000
17.	Michigan	0.000		42.	Louisiana	0.000
18.	New Mexico	0.000		43.	New Jersey	0.000
19.	New York	0.000		44.	Alaska	0.000
20.	Idaho	0.000		45.	New Hampshire	−0.001
21.	Montana	0.000		46.	Oklahoma	−0.001
22.	Washington	0.000		47.	Kentucky	−0.001
23.	Florida	0.000		48.	Massachusetts	−0.001
24.	Ohio	0.000		49.	Connecticut	−0.001
25.	Minnesota	0.000		50.	Colorado	−0.001

Note: States with the same rank are tied. States with different scores may appear identical due to rounding.

OVERALL PERSONAL FREEDOM RANKING

33.2% The top states in the personal freedom dimension tend to be more western and northeastern, while the bottom states are either socially conservative and southern or mid-Atlantic and liberal. As in past editions, we find a strong rural–urban division. One reason for the rural–urban relationship is likely voters' fears of crime, which leads them to support harsh policing and prosecutorial tactics, stricter drug and gun laws, and more limits on civil liberties. However, no statistical relationship exists between personal freedom and actual violent crime rates (however, it is weakly negatively correlated with property crime rates). It is well known that public perceptions of crime can diverge widely from the truth.[102] An alternative explanation is that there are more negative externalities of personal behavior in urban settings. But if that were the case, one would also expect urbanized states to have more economic regulation and higher taxation, and they do not. Socially conservative states tend to restrict alcohol, gambling, marijuana, and marriage freedoms but permit greater freedom in education and have more respect for gun rights and for private property on smoking policy.

---

102. Lydia Saad, "Perceptions of Crime Problem Remain Curiously Negative," Gallup, October 22, 2007; Mark Warr, "Public Perception of Crime Remains Out of Sync with Reality, Criminologist Contends," University of Texas, November 10, 2008.

TABLE 29

Rank	State	Overall Personal Freedom Score		Rank	State	Overall Personal Freedom Score
1.	Nevada	0.302		26.	California	0.069
2.	New Hampshire	0.225		27.	Pennsylvania	0.068
3.	Maine	0.190		28.	Utah	0.056
4.	Vermont	0.167		29.	Louisiana	0.055
5.	New Mexico	0.159		30.	Illinois	0.049
6.	Arizona	0.157		31.	Kansas	0.047
7.	Colorado	0.123		32.	Maryland	0.045
8.	Michigan	0.122		33.	Rhode Island	0.045
9.	Oregon	0.118		34.	Georgia	0.043
10.	Alaska	0.108		35.	South Carolina	0.037
11.	Indiana	0.105		36.	Mississippi	0.029
12.	Florida	0.104		37.	Alabama	0.028
13.	North Dakota	0.103		38.	Virginia	0.026
14.	West Virginia	0.100		39.	Tennessee	0.024
15.	Missouri	0.100		40.	Ohio	0.022
16.	North Carolina	0.097		41.	Wyoming	0.020
17.	Montana	0.096		42.	Idaho	0.016
18.	South Dakota	0.093		43.	Connecticut	0.007
19.	Iowa	0.090		44.	Arkansas	0.005
20.	Nebraska	0.081		45.	Kentucky	−0.001
21.	Wisconsin	0.081		46.	Hawaii	−0.002
22.	Minnesota	0.076		47.	Delaware	−0.008
23.	Oklahoma	0.075		48.	New Jersey	−0.036
24.	Washington	0.073		49.	Texas	−0.046
25.	Massachusetts	0.069		50.	New York	−0.056

Note: States with the same rank are tied. States with different scores may appear identical due to rounding.

Figure 8 shows state average personal freedom scores over time. This chain-linked index excludes such federalized policies as same-sex marriage, sodomy laws, and removal of local gun bans. After personal freedom dropped nationwide between 2000 and 2008, partially due to a wave of new tobacco restrictions, it has grown even more substantially since 2010, due in large part to ballot initiatives loosening marijuana regulations, to the spread of legal gambling, and to legislative criminal justice and asset forfeiture reforms. If we were to plot the average personal freedom scores, including federalized scores, the improvement in personal freedom would be even more dramatic, as judicial engagement on personal freedoms has generally enhanced rather than reduced them. We hope that the small dip in 2019 is merely noise in a larger trend. However, a growing paternalistic mindset, exacerbated by the COVID-19 pandemic and often characterized by excessive deference to "experts," could spell trouble ahead in those policy areas where the secular progressive consensus of those who dominate the commanding heights does not already favor liberalization (such as prostitution and marijuana).

FIGURE 8 State Average Personal Freedom Scores Over Time

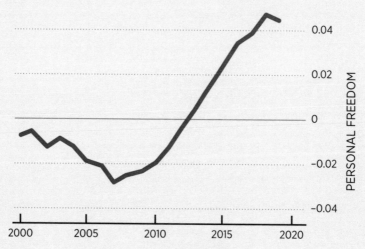

OVERALL FREEDOM RANKING

TABLE 30

Rank	State	Overall Freedom Score	Rank	State	Overall Freedom Score
1.	New Hampshire	0.592	26.	Wyoming	0.128
2.	Florida	0.552	27.	Kansas	0.127
3.	Nevada	0.511	28.	South Carolina	0.125
4.	Tennessee	0.441	29.	Iowa	0.094
5.	South Dakota	0.425	30.	Massachusetts	0.094
6.	Indiana	0.368	31.	Ohio	0.080
7.	Michigan	0.349	32.	Louisiana	0.066
8.	Georgia	0.330	33.	Nebraska	0.059
9.	Arizona	0.322	34.	Maine	0.032
10.	Idaho	0.313	35.	West Virginia	0.022
11.	Missouri	0.274	36.	Connecticut	0.017
12.	Colorado	0.262	37.	Illinois	−0.013
13.	Virginia	0.226	38.	Minnesota	−0.041
14.	Pennsylvania	0.200	39.	Washington	−0.043
15.	North Dakota	0.195	40.	Mississippi	−0.057
16.	North Carolina	0.192	41.	Rhode Island	−0.093
17.	Wisconsin	0.190	42.	New Mexico	−0.123
18.	Montana	0.177	43.	Vermont	−0.176
19.	Oklahoma	0.160	44.	Delaware	−0.203
20.	Utah	0.156	45.	Maryland	−0.282
21.	Texas	0.155	46.	Oregon	−0.311
22.	Alabama	0.153	47.	New Jersey	−0.460
23.	Arkansas	0.143	48.	California	−0.474
24.	Alaska	0.141	49.	Hawaii	−0.603
25.	Kentucky	0.136	50.	New York	−0.813

Note: States with the same rank are tied. States with different scores may appear identical due to rounding.

OVERALL FREEDOM RANKING

The weighted sum of all the variables is used to produce the overall freedom ranking of the states. The overall freedom scores rate states on how free they are relative to other states. A score of 1 would correspond to a state's being one standard deviation above average in every single variable, although in reality, every state scores better on some variables and worse on others. A score of 0 would be equivalent to a state's being absolutely average on every variable, and a score of –1 to a state's being one standard deviation below average on every variable. Table 30 presents the overall freedom rankings as of year-end 2019.

New Hampshire, Florida, and Nevada are the freest states in the country and now significantly outpace their peers. States that have always done well in our index—such as Tennessee, South Dakota, Indiana, and Arizona—also find themselves in the top 10. New York is the least free state again, as it has been in every version of the index and every year covered by this index since 2000. Hawaii has fallen enough to put itself well below California now. New Jersey and Oregon round out the bottom five. Because states' freedom scores represent their situation at the beginning of the year 2020, they include changes made by legislatures that in most states were elected in November 2018. Figure 9 shows the evolution of the top and bottom states over time using the chain-linked index, so that it focuses specifically on decisions made by state governments and voters.

New Hampshire is once again the freest state in the Union. In 2000, on the full index, Nevada was number one, just ahead of New Hampshire. Florida was the freest in the fifth edition, published in 2018. But the Granite State, which first claimed the top spot in 2011, regained the crown in this edition. However, it did so not because of Florida's becoming less free but because of greater gains by New Hampshire. Historically, freedom in New Hampshire declined substantially with the legislatures elected in 2006 and 2008, then recovered all the ground it lost in those years in the legislature elected in 2010. The legislature elected in 2012 diminished freedom slightly, but the 2014-elected legislature then increased it again even more, as we expect will be the case with the 2020-elected legislature given its wide-ranging freedom-enhancing policy changes. Today, absolute freedom in the

Granite State stands above the level it did in 2000.

Florida's rise since 2009 has been nothing short of stunning. Most states have improved on freedom in that time if federalized policies are excluded; however, Florida's post-2010 improvement has been the third greatest in the United States (after Wisconsin and Michigan). Florida's improvement has lain almost entirely in fiscal policy, where the numbers tell a consistent story: government consumption, local taxes, state taxes, debt, and government employment have all fallen as a share of the private economy. The only area of deterioration in fiscal policy has been liquid assets, which have fallen slightly. Clearly, Florida's state leadership deserves great credit for making freedom a priority over the past decade, and it shows.

Nevada comes in just behind Florida at number three. It has been a consistent top-five state, though others have leapfrogged it in relative terms since 2000. Freedom in Nevada declined with the legislatures elected in 2006, but it has bounced back strongly since then. Overall freedom there today is nearly as high as it was in 2000. Most notably, Nevada is the number-one state on personal freedom, which fits the stereotype. In fact, it has always been the number-one state on that dimension. Twenty-nineteen was the first year in which Nevada has been in the top 10 on economic freedom since 2006. So Nevada's ranking isn't just due to its less personally paternalistic ways.

Tennessee is the fourth-freest state, just ahead of South Dakota. Their rankings are largely due to high scores on economic freedom. Tennessee, for example, is number two on economic freedom, due mainly to its tax policies. But it ranks 39th on personal freedom. Thus, it is the stereotypical "red state," though the general stereotype is oftentimes false. South Dakota is similar, coming in at number four on economic freedom and number 18 on personal freedom. It bottomed out on the latter in 2010 and has been rising notably since in relative and absolute terms.

Residents of these top five states have much to be proud of, and the rest of us should be more willing to look to states like New Hampshire, Florida, Nevada, Tennessee, and South Dakota as models to emulate. One interesting thing about this top five is that they have similar levels of freedom despite substantial differences on other margins.

When it comes to the bottom states, we see that the Empire State has consistently placed last by a wide margin. The difference between the scores for New York, New Hampshire, and Florida corresponds to one and one-third standard deviations on every single variable. New York also performs poorly across the board, ranking at or near the bottom in all three dimensions of freedom. Thus, New Yorkers feel the heavy hand of government in every area of their lives. Is it any wonder that people are fleeing the state in droves? According to the U.S. Census Bureau's components of population

FIGURE 9 Freedom Evolution of Selected States

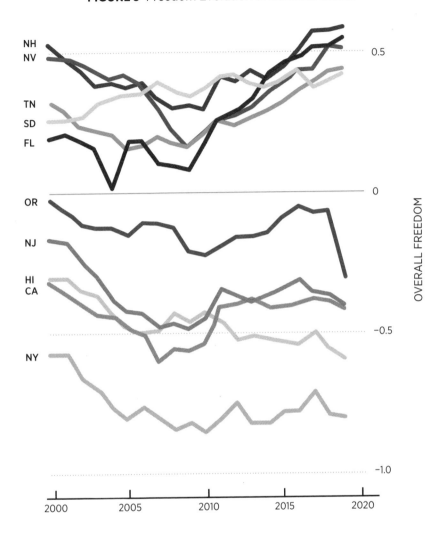

change data, about 1.4 million people, on net, fled New York for other states between 2010 and 2019, a whopping 7.1 percent of the state's 2010 population.[103] In calendar year 2019 alone, 185,000 more people moved from New York to another state than moved in.[104] That occurred pre-COVID-19. We expect that 2020 will be even worse, especially given the policy responses

103. "State Population Totals and Components of Change: 2010–2019," U.S. Census Bureau, 2021.
104. "State-to-State Migration Flows," U.S. Census Bureau, 2021.

from state and local leaders that alienated many, failed to contain the crisis, and harmed key parts of the economy. The only reason that New Yorkers haven't noticed the great emptying out of the state is its still positive international in-migration. Foreign immigration represents a source of population growth for New York, but overall population growth remains well below the national average. Indeed, its international migration also lags California, Florida, and Texas.

Hawaii is no paradise when it comes to freedom. The Aloha State has declined gradually since the Great Recession, and that decline is even more precipitous once we take into account the effects of its native son's PPACA, because Hawaii formerly had one of the most free-market health insurance systems in the country. Fiscal policy accounts for most of Hawaii's decline, due to big increases in tax burden in 2011 and 2012, as well as additional increases in fiscal policy burdens in 2018 and 2019 (tax increases in 2021 will continue its woes into the next edition). Land-use, labor, and property and casualty insurance regulations have also gotten tougher since 2013. Since 2011, real income and income per capita growth have fallen behind the rest of the country, and Hawaii's real per capita income is below the level of West Virginia's.

California lives up to its big government reputation, coming in as the third-worst state for freedom. Its overall freedom (even controlling for federalization of some policies in an anti-freedom direction) has declined substantially since 2000, owing to declines in regulatory policy that have swamped improvements in personal freedom. State taxation rose substantially from 2011 to 2014, then leveled off. Local taxes, debt, government consumption, and government employment have all fallen since the Great Recession. That has helped improve fiscal policy, especially in the years 2009 to 2011. From 2000 to 2012, California had the worst real personal income growth performance of any state other than Michigan. Since then, the economy has recovered somewhat. California's personal freedom grew from 2008 to 2016, but other states have improved even faster in that dimension. Given some policy and cultural trends, we expect Sacramento to further burden state-level freedom ahead and undermine its natural economic advantages.

New Jersey is just above California and substantially worse than Oregon at number 46. It has actually fallen faster than California in the period from 2000 to 2019. It appears to want to join New York rather than outcompete it on the freedom margin. New Jersey is 49th on regulatory policy and 48th on personal freedom. Although it is in the middle on fiscal policy, taxes have risen since 2016 but are not yet as high as New York's. We would expect some further convergence unless a different mindset emerges across the state.

Figure 10 plots each state's personal freedom score against its economic freedom score. There appears to be a small positive correlation between personal and economic freedom, but it is not statistically significant. Most of the top states on overall freedom do well on both economic and personal freedoms. However, a few states in the top 10 still do relatively poorly on personal freedom but outstandingly well on economic freedom, such as Tennessee, South Dakota, and Georgia.

The outlier states are instructive. In the bottom part of the lower-right quadrant, we see economically freer, personally less-free states, such as Idaho, South Dakota, Georgia, Texas, Alabama, Kentucky, Arkansas, Virginia, and Tennessee. Texas is a paradigmatic case, finishing second to last in personal freedom despite a top-10 economic freedom score. Texans may be unhappy with their weak personal freedom showing, but it reflects poor criminal justice policies and the fact that the Lone Star State is increasingly behind the curve on cannabis, education, and gambling freedoms.

Oklahoma is an especially interesting case. It was a classic, stereotypical red state, performing well on economic freedom but poorly on personal freedom. However, since 2017, it has gained substantially on personal freedom (gun rights, marijuana and alcohol freedom, and criminal justice reform), whereas economic freedom has stagnated relatively. Given its openness to policy innovation, Oklahoma could stand to turn its attention to economic matters and outcompete neighbors like Texas and Kansas (which is great on regulatory policy but quite poor on fiscal policy).

FIGURE 10 Economic and Personal Freedom in 2019

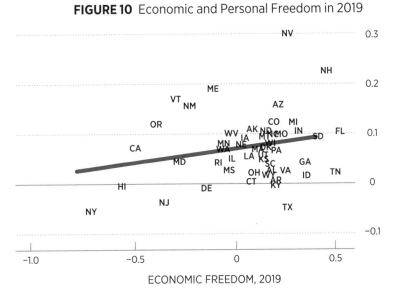

In the upper-right quadrant are economically and personally free states, such as New Hampshire, Nevada, Arizona, Indiana, Michigan, and Florida. Far out on the bottom left is New York, which scores quite poorly on both economic and personal freedoms. New Jersey and Hawaii are not as extreme as New York on economic freedom but still score quite badly on economic freedom as well as personal freedom. Finally, in the upper-left quadrant are Vermont, Maine, New Mexico, California, and Oregon, which are performing poorly on economic freedom but doing a bit better on personal freedom (or, in the case of New Mexico, Vermont, and Maine, a lot better). These are the stereotypical left-liberal states that do well on personal freedom but are economically collectivist. Generally, then, conservative states do better than left-liberal states on economic freedom, and rural/western/New England states do better than urban/southern/mid-Atlantic states on personal freedom.

Figure 11 shows the evolution of nonfederalized overall freedom scores over time. There is a pronounced J-shape since 2000, with the upward trend beginning in 2011. When we include federalized policies, the average state score in 2019 is almost identical to the score in 2000. Thus, federal subversion of state autonomy has on balance been detrimental to the freedom that citizens experience since 2000. Indeed, in general, economic freedom has declined in the United States since 2000, but the blame for this trend essentially belongs on the federal government, not state and local governments.[105]

FIGURE 11 State Average Overall Freedom Over Time

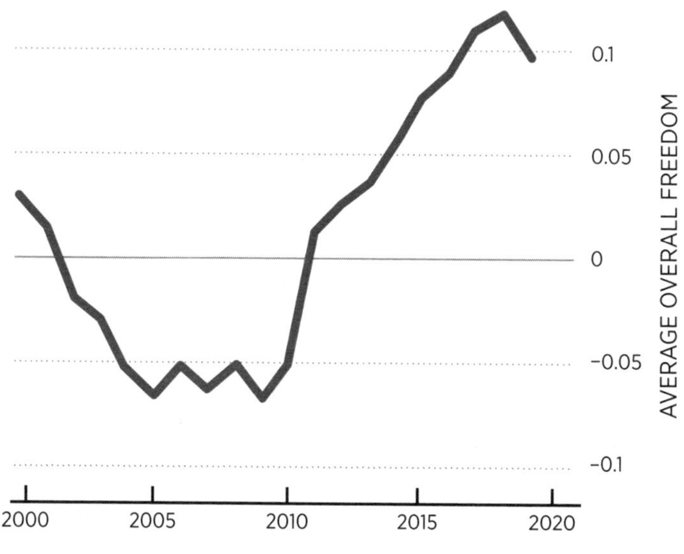

105. James Gwartney, Robert Lawson, and Joshua Hall, "Economic Freedom of the World: Lessons for the U.S.," *Huffington Post,* September 25, 2011, http://www.huffingtonpost.com/james-gwartney/economic-freedom-of-the-w_b_980441.html.

CHANGE OVER TIME

The following list pulls out the most improved and worsened states from year-end 2018 to year-end 2019 (Table 31). It is important to recognize that short-term changes will be caused by a great deal of noise in the fiscal data that may or may not be due to significant policy changes, especially since our FY 2020 tax data are estimates that exclude minor categories of taxation (and changes in local taxation since FY 2019). Nonetheless, it is worth noting which states saw the most change in individual freedom in the period covered by our newest data.

South Dakota is our most improved state in that short window, driven by both economic and personal freedom policy changes. Like most states after the decentralization of the individual health insurance mandate, South Dakota allowed the mandate to lapse. It also passed constitutional carry while benefiting from gradual fiscal policy and incarceration and arrest rate improvements. Florida, Missouri, and Michigan are all right behind South Dakota; in fact, all four states cluster at the top.

The last list showing changes over time (Table 32) highlights the big picture since our first comprehensive set of data in 2000, and is limited to non-federalized policies. Thus, this list covers policies from year-end 2000 until year-end 2019. We have data for every year between those dates.

Over this long period, Florida is the biggest gainer, followed closely by Michigan. As previously discussed, Florida's rise has been remarkable. It has gained primarily in the fiscal policy category, where the numbers tell a consistent story: government consumption, local taxes, state taxes, debt, and government employment have all fallen as a share of the private economy. It has also improved on personal freedom and gained relatively on regulatory policy (even as it has declined absolutely).

Michigan is also a fascinating story. A Rust Belt state with declining fortunes in the American consciousness, it has actually liberalized its economy in ways similar to Wisconsin and Indiana. The vast majority of its rise has come since 2012. Regulatory reforms such as passing a right-to-work law in that year have helped. It has also improved on fiscal policy, going from 34th in 2009 to 13th today. Its overall economic score was 18th in 2000 and today stands at 8th. Personal freedom has seen an even larger relative uptick. It is now 8th overall, moving up remarkably since 2000 when it was 31st in the country. It improved on guns and alcohol policy, legalized marijuana, banned racial preferences in public services, and improved on incarceration and arrest rates.

TABLE 31

Rank	State	Freedom Growth, 2018-2019
1.	South Dakota	0.086
2.	Florida	0.085
3.	Missouri	0.081
4.	Michigan	0.080
5.	Connecticut	0.077
6.	Kentucky	0.070
7.	Idaho	0.067
8.	New Hampshire	0.065
9.	Oklahoma	0.063
10.	Louisiana	0.062
11.	Tennessee	0.061
12.	Iowa	0.059
13.	North Carolina	0.057
14.	South Carolina	0.055
15.	Kansas	0.055
16.	Indiana	0.052
17.	Georgia	0.050
18.	Alabama	0.050
19.	Pennsylvania	0.049
20.	Mississippi	0.047
21.	Maine	0.044
22.	Nevada	0.044
23.	Wisconsin	0.041
24.	New York	0.040
25.	Nebraska	0.035
26.	Arkansas	0.034
27.	Wyoming	0.032
28.	Texas	0.030
29.	Alaska	0.030
30.	North Dakota	0.030
31.	Arizona	0.029
32.	Minnesota	0.027
33.	Colorado	0.024
34.	Montana	0.017
35.	Ohio	0.017
36.	Hawaii	0.017
37.	Vermont	0.017
38.	West Virginia	0.014
39.	Maryland	0.011
40.	Washington	0.002
41.	Illinois	0.002
42.	Delaware	−0.005
43.	Virginia	−0.012
44.	Utah	−0.023
45.	California	−0.025
46.	New Jersey	−0.034
47.	Rhode Island	−0.035
48.	Massachusetts	−0.037
49.	New Mexico	−0.061
50.	Oregon	−0.192

Note: States with the same rank are tied. States with different scores may appear identical due to rounding.

TABLE 32

Rank	State	Freedom Growth, 2000–2019		Rank	State	Freedom Growth, 2000–2019
1.	Florida	0.364		26.	Pennsylvania	0.081
2.	Michigan	0.350		27.	North Dakota	0.076
3.	Wisconsin	0.322		28.	Nebraska	0.068
4.	Oklahoma	0.321		29.	New Hampshire	0.067
5.	Georgia	0.291		30.	Kansas	0.058
6.	Idaho	0.258		31.	Maine	0.051
7.	Arizona	0.248		32.	Colorado	0.043
8.	New Mexico	0.210		33.	Virginia	0.041
9.	Ohio	0.204		34.	Nevada	0.013
10.	South Carolina	0.203		35.	Minnesota	0.011
11.	Missouri	0.188		36.	Mississippi	0.010
12.	Utah	0.181		37.	Illinois	0.007
13.	South Dakota	0.172		38.	Rhode Island	−0.014
14.	Alaska	0.164		39.	Washington	−0.023
15.	Montana	0.159		40.	Maryland	−0.029
16.	Texas	0.134		41.	Massachusetts	−0.029
17.	Louisiana	0.131		42.	Iowa	−0.031
18.	Alabama	0.129		43.	Connecticut	−0.047
19.	Kentucky	0.127		44.	California	−0.098
20.	West Virginia	0.122		45.	Delaware	−0.189
21.	Tennessee	0.120		46.	New York	−0.229
22.	Wyoming	0.118		47.	New Jersey	−0.234
23.	North Carolina	0.112		48.	Vermont	−0.253
24.	Arkansas	0.100		49.	Oregon	−0.280
25.	Indiana	0.093		50.	Hawaii	−0.290

Note: States with the same rank are tied. States with different scores may appear identical due to rounding.

Hawaii is our biggest loser over the two-decade period. As noted earlier, its tax burden increased and its fiscal freedom has declined. Land-use, labor, and property and casualty insurance regulations have gotten tougher since 2013, while its real income and income per capita growth have fallen behind the rest of the country.

Oregon and Vermont are the next states that have declined the most. Vermont provides a dramatic contrast with the freest state, its neighbor to the east, New Hampshire. Although many people outside of the Northeast confuse the two, Vermont is "Bizarro New Hampshire" or "Upside-Down New Hampshire" when it comes to freedom. Beginning in 1997, Vermont's school funding system was dramatically altered in such a way as to cause a big increase in fiscal centralization. Property taxes are now considered a state tax rather than a local tax, although towns still have some control over the rate. More importantly, taxes have continued to go up despite the "fix." State taxes have risen from 8.0 percent to 9.8 percent of the tax base (excluding motor fuel and alcohol and tobacco taxes), while local taxes have fallen only from 2.4 percent to 2.1 percent since 2000. Government employment and consumption have risen slightly as a percentage of the economy. Regulatory policy has also gotten much worse, with the vast majority of the losses concentrated in land-use and environmental regulation. As near as we can tell using our admittedly imperfect data, residential building restrictions have tightened enormously. One reflection of that is the frequency of the term "land use" in appellate court decisions; that frequency is now much higher, when divided by population, in Vermont than anywhere else. Vermont has enacted one of the country's most costly renewable portfolio standards. Personal freedom has also not grown much over this period despite marijuana freedom increasing substantially. Most of the country has gained more in this area. Gun rights have declined slightly, while a large tobacco freedom decline has effectively cancelled out its freedom-enhancing change on cannabis. This latter point we find particularly rich given its hypocrisy from the public health standard that drove tobacco restrictionism.

Last, it is worth pointing out policy areas that have received significant attention throughout the 2000–2019 period. Tobacco policy is the most notable area in which state policies have become more restrictive of personal freedom, with significant increases in taxes, as well as greater and greater restrictions on where one can smoke. Laws dealing with domestic partnerships, civil unions, and gay marriage also changed dramatically, especially in the years 2010–2015. Criminal justice reforms have swept the country at both the federal and state levels. In fact, they became pretty much a transpartisan consensus issue where little opposition existed before the summer of 2020 created some turbulence in the air (especially on policing).

Civil asset forfeiture reform stands out here, as well as criminal penalties affected by criminal justice reform efforts. Marijuana laws are undergoing rapid liberalization, first in states with citizen ballot initiatives. Gun laws and educational policies have been gradually liberalized across the country, and state bans on direct-to-consumer wine shipments have been removed in many places.

On the regulatory side, eminent domain reform occurred in some fashion in most states following the infamous *Kelo v. City of New London* decision by the U.S. Supreme Court in 2005. Several states have recently enacted right-to-work laws, and there is still some space for further change across the country (including New Hampshire). Policies dealing with new technologies—such as DNA databases, electronic cigarettes, and automated license plate readers—have also seen change. Twenty-nineteen, in particular, saw some changes in a few states on concealed carry, which bucked what we might have thought in light of prominent mass shootings. A quite significant arena for policy change occurred in the sports and online gambling area since the fifth edition, with many states jumping on the betting freedom bandwagon. Several states also repealed Sunday sales blue laws since our fifth edition to go along with more legalized marijuana, including some in 2020 and 2021 that wouldn't be captured here but would in the seventh edition. One might speculate that this is part of a trend of greater "lifestyle libertinism" over time—which has certainly benefited our political economy but it could be viewed with a jaundiced eye from the perspective of other values, such as overall human flourishing (especially if the arm of the state increases in other ways simultaneously, perhaps even related to that cultural trend). Of course, it could be that more Americans have simply come to appreciate that toleration is a better tool than legal punishment for promoting personal responsibility or at least a healthier relationship between the state and society.

One ongoing feature of policy change is the displacement of state discretion with federal mandates, for both good and ill with regard to pure individual liberty (leaving aside the damage done to federalism, a long-term institutional bulwark of freedom). Federal courts have forced states to liberalize gun laws, sodomy laws, and marriage laws, though in all those areas state governments were reforming long before the federal courts chose to intervene conclusively. In health insurance regulation, all three branches of the federal government have acted in concert to dramatically raise the regulatory threshold, mostly via the PPACA. States may still choose to regulate health insurance even more tightly than the federal government, but they may not choose more market-oriented models of regulation. There has been one important exception to this trend: the individual health insurance mandate of Obamacare was stripped by Congress.

Leaving aside the cases where there has been liberalization at the federal level, centralization is a dangerous trend. For one thing, it reduces the ability of federalism as an institutional system to check government overreach. For another, it makes it harder for citizens to find freedom by voting with their feet, as they cannot go anywhere for different and better policies unless they emigrate.

CONSTRUCT VALIDITY AND ROBUSTNESS

In this edition of the index, we test the construct validity and robustness of our overall freedom measure by examining correlations in overall freedom measures across editions (for the year 2006, which appears in all editions). Between the second and third editions, we switched from an impressionistic to a quantified, "victim cost" method for weighting variables. Nevertheless, the correlation between the sixth-edition and first-edition scores for 2006 overall freedom is a hefty 0.82. The correlation between third- and fifth-edition scores is 0.88. These extremely high correlation coefficients suggest that the overall freedom ranking is robust to within-reason perturbations of weights on the variables and addition and subtraction of variables.

INDEX OF CRONYISM

As in the fourth edition, we present a "freedom from cronyism" state ranking that takes into account blatantly anti-competitive regulations: (a) general sales below cost/minimum markup law, (b) sales below cost/minimum markup law for gasoline, (c) certificate of public convenience and necessity for household goods movers, (d) direct auto sales bans, (e) certificate of need for hospital construction, (f) all occupational licensing variables, (g) eminent domain laws, (h) bans on direct shipment of wine, and (i) alcohol sales blue laws.

Table 33 shows how the states come out on cronyism in 2019 (higher values/lower rankings indicate less cronyism). The numbers in the table represent the weights of each variable multiplied by the standardized value (number of standard deviations greater than the mean). As noted in the previous section, a state that is one standard deviation better—freer—than the average on every single policy will score 1 on overall freedom. Because the index of cronyism draws on a subset of the freedom index, the values in this table fall within a much smaller range. Idaho's score of 0.046, therefore, means that, taking cronyist policies into account, Idaho's positions on those issues contribute 0.046 to its overall freedom score. Idaho is the least cronyist state. The freedom from cronyism index can be found in the "Regulatory" tab of the spreadsheet at http://freedominthe50states.org.

TABLE 33

Rank	State	Freedom from Cronyism Score		Rank	State	Freedom from Cronyism Score
1.	Idaho	0.046		26.	Nevada	−0.005
2.	New Hampshire	0.036		27.	Indiana	−0.006
3.	Wyoming	0.035		28.	Michigan	−0.006
4.	Colorado	0.033		29.	Massachusetts	−0.006
5.	Arizona	0.027		30.	Oregon	−0.007
6.	Kansas	0.026		31.	Washington	−0.007
7.	New Mexico	0.023		32.	West Virginia	−0.010
8.	Minnesota	0.019		33.	Georgia	−0.010
9.	Vermont	0.019		34.	Kentucky	−0.013
10.	South Dakota	0.018		35.	Oklahoma	−0.013
11.	Alaska	0.015		36.	Florida	−0.014
12.	Hawaii	0.013		37.	Tennessee	−0.016
13.	Rhode Island	0.011		38.	Virginia	−0.018
14.	Utah	0.011		39.	New York	−0.018
15.	North Dakota	0.010		40.	North Carolina	−0.018
16.	Missouri	0.009		41.	South Carolina	−0.018
17.	Nebraska	0.008		42.	New Jersey	−0.019
18.	Wisconsin	0.007		43.	Alabama	−0.020
19.	Connecticut	0.005		44.	Louisiana	−0.021
20.	Iowa	0.004		45.	Ohio	−0.022
21.	Delaware	0.002		46.	Illinois	−0.022
22.	Pennsylvania	0.001		47.	Maryland	−0.025
23.	Maine	0.001		48.	Arkansas	−0.028
24.	Montana	0.000		49.	California	−0.028
25.	Mississippi	0.000		50.	Texas	−0.030

Note: States with the same rank are tied. States with different scores may appear identical due to rounding.

We compare our cronyism scores with state corruption scores based on a survey of statehouse journalists.[106] The correlation between 2019 cronyism and 2007 corruption is –0.35, indicating that states scoring higher on freedom from cronyism score lower on corruption. In other words, cronyist states are more corrupt. The correlation weakens when cronyism is measured around the same time as corruption, perhaps implying a causal path from corruption to cronyism rather than vice versa.

FIGURE 12 Relationship Between Lobbyist Ratio and Cronyism

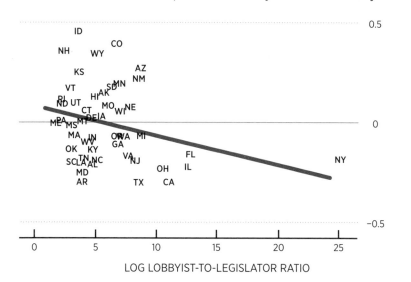

We also compare our cronyism scores with state lobbyist-to-legislator ratios from the mid-2000s.[107] The correlation between the two is –0.32, indicating that states with more lobbyists relative to legislators a decade ago are more cronyist today. (Again, the correlations weaken when they are measured closer together in time.) Figure 12 shows how the freedom from cronyism index relates to the logged number of lobbyists per legislator for all 49 states for which lobbyist data are available (Nevada is excluded).

When freedom from cronyism is regressed on both corruption and lobbyist ratio, each independent variable enters the equation with a negative sign and is statistically significant. We do not know whether corruption and lobbying cause cronyism, or vice versa, but the statistical relationship suggests

106.   Bill Marsh, "Illinois Is Trying. It Really Is. But the Most Corrupt State Is Actually . . .," *New York Times*, December 14, 2008.

107.   Center for Public Integrity, "Ratio of Lobbyists to Legislators 2006," December 21, 2007; updated May 19, 2014.

a connection, the plausibility of which in turn increases our confidence in the validity of the cronyism index.

In Part 2, we will take a closer look at the causes and consequences of freedom, as well as important changes in state policies during the pandemic years 2020 and 2021.

PART 2
POLITICS OF FREEDOM

I n this part, we consider the causes and consequences of freedom in the states. We also provide an up-to-date qualitative assessment of freedom across the 50 states that takes into account policy changes since our data cutoff for the quantitative analysis.

More specifically, we first examine the relationship between public opinion and freedom. Next, we consider the consequences of freedom for economic growth and migration. We follow with some observations about the political economy of freedom at the state level. Finally, we discuss policy changes made across the states in 2020 and the first half of 2021, as well as how responses to COVID-19 at the state and local levels affected freedom.

PUBLIC OPINION AND FREEDOM

We now move to analyzing in a more systematic fashion the relation-ship between public opinion ideology—as measured by presidential election results by state—and economic, personal, and overall freedom.

Figure 13 is a scatterplot of economic freedom in 2000 against presiden-tial voting in 1996. (We chose presidential elections before the year that the policy is measured, because we think a lag exists between changes in public opinion and changes in law.) The x-axis measures the number of percentage points to the left of each state's popular vote, summing up Democratic and Green vote shares for the state minus the same for the country as a whole. We see a strong negative relationship between leftward lean in the elector-ate and economic freedom. However, strongly conservative states are no more economically free on average than mildly conservative or centrist states, such as Tennessee, New Hampshire, Missouri, and Florida.

FIGURE 13 Partisanship and Economic Freedom in 2000

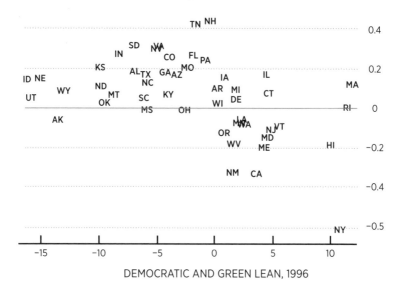

Figure 14 shows the same scatterplot for 2019, allowing us to see how the relationship between ideology and economic freedom has changed over the entire range of our time series. The relationship between ideology and freedom looks curvilinear again. We noted in the fourth edition that West Virginia looked like a big outlier, having moved substantially to the right since 2000. If right-wing ideology leads to more economic freedom, economic freedom should rise in West Virginia in future years. However, other low-income, southern states tend not to do well on economic freedom (e.g., Mississippi, Arkansas, and Kentucky), suggesting that West Virginia's room for improvement may be limited.

In fact, West Virginia did improve on economic freedom, and it is now a much smaller outlier.

FIGURE 14 Partisanship and Economic Freedom in 2019

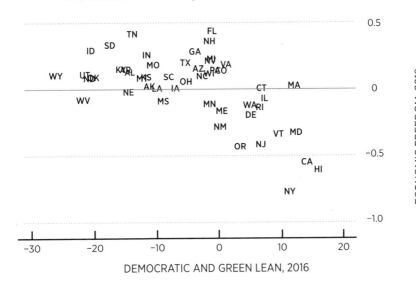

Figure 15 plots personal freedom in 2000 against partisan lean in 1996. The relationship between partisanship and personal freedom in that year was extremely noisy. Slightly right-of-center Nevada topped the charts, followed by slightly left-of-center Maine and Vermont. Centrist West Virginia, New Hampshire, and Oregon followed. Left-leaning Maryland and Illinois did poorly, but they were joined by deeply conservative Nebraska, Oklahoma, and Alabama. The only southern state that was much above average was North Carolina.

FIGURE 15 Partisanship and Personal Freedom in 2000

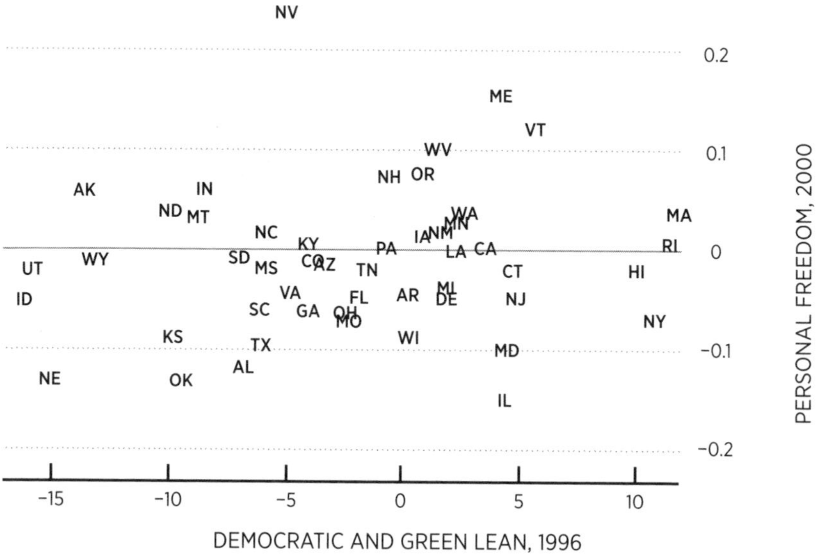

Figure 16 shows the relationship between partisanship and personal freedom at the end of our time series. Now, centrist states enjoy an apparent advantage on personal freedom, and the relationship is much noisier than the one between partisanship and economic freedom. Southern states no longer perform as relatively poorly as they have in the past, and because personal freedom has improved over time, few states remain below the post-2000 average.

FIGURE 16 Partisanship and Personal Freedom in 2019

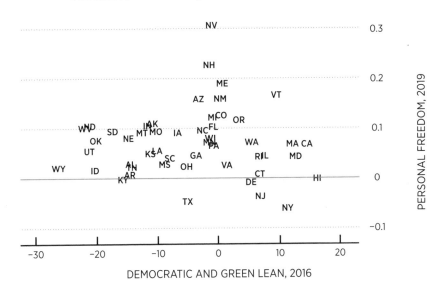

Figure 17 puts economic and personal freedom together to show how partisanship relates to overall freedom. Again, we see a curvilinear relationship in which conservative and moderate states do much better than strongly left ones. New York sits in a class of its own at the bottom of the scale. It is actually quite remarkable how different it is from other states with regard to freedom, which we chalk up to policy ideology more than anything special about New York in relation to its urbanism or other factors. (Political scientists understand policy ideology as the relative orientation of a state's policies on the left–right spectrum, observed as a correlation across policy domains[108].) In other words, New York is a strongly left-of-center state, and most strongly left-of-center states do quite poorly on freedom. If we imagine a regression line among just the observations to the right of zero on the x-axis, it would slope sharply downward, and New York would sit comfortably on or near that line. The more surprising performances come from Rhode Island and Massachusetts in this period, whose freedom scores are not as low as their ideology would predict. The presence of New York City alone cannot account for New York's outlier position because other urban states or states with megacities perform significantly better.

108. Robert Erikson, Gerald Wright, and John McIver, *Statehouse Democracy: Public Opinion and Policy in the American States* (New York: Cambridge University Press, 1993).

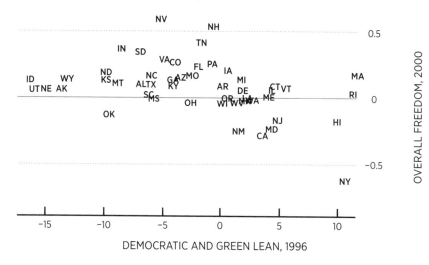

FIGURE 17 Partisanship and Overall Freedom in 2000

Figure 18 shows the overall freedom and partisanship relationship at the end of our time series. A distinct and tighter negative relationship exists between leftward tilt and overall freedom. However, the outliers are still noteworthy. New York is still abysmal even for a strongly left-wing state. Wyoming, West Virginia, Mississippi, Louisiana, and Nebraska all underperform other conservative states. California and Hawaii aptly represent the stereotype of progressive states. Florida, New Hampshire, and Nevada significantly outperform the rest of the center, while Massachusetts does better than one would expect for such a progressive state.

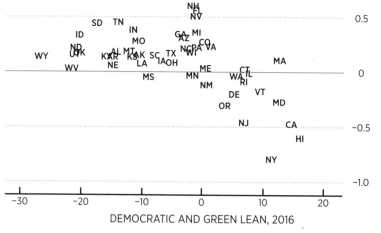

FIGURE 18 Partisanship and Overall Freedom in 2019

To study the dynamics of public opinion and freedom over time, we regressed, for each state, its overall freedom score on partisanship (Democratic and Green lean) from four years ago. (For years between presidential elections, we linearly interpolate partisanship.) The regression includes year dummies and assumes state fixed effects, and it covers the years from 2000 to 2019. The fixed-effects specification forces the regression to focus on over-time change within each state.[109] The results are shown in Table 34.

TABLE 34

Partisanship and Overall Freedom: Difference-in-Differences Estimates

Variable	Coefficient	Std. Error
$Partisanship_{t-4}$	−0.0056	0.029
R^2 (within)	34.0%	
N	1,000	

Note: Assumes clustered standard errors. R^2 = proportion of the total variance explained by the model.

The statistically significant results suggest that when public opinion in a state moves left, freedom falls somewhat. For instance, if a state begins 2 percentage points to the left of the national median voter in presidential elections, then moves 6 percentage points to the left, the predicted change in freedom four years in the future is 4 × −0.0056 = −0.022. That is a fairly modest but not unimportant change, about the difference between Illinois and Connecticut in 2019.

FREEDOM, MIGRATION, AND GROWTH

America is a land of immigrants. Indeed, immigrants throughout America's history have boarded ships (and eventually planes) in droves to escape tyranny and to breathe the cleaner air of a nation founded on the idea of individual freedom. Sometimes that story is dramatic, as when the Puritans hurriedly left Europe to realize greater religious liberty or when Vietnamese boat people escaped murderous communist oppression to start anew in the New World. Other times it is less stark, as in the case of a German family fed up with the modern paternalist state and looking for a place to build a business and to raise a family or in the case of Mexican migrants looking for the better economic opportunities afforded by a freer economy.

109.   Despite Nickell bias, we also tried including a lagged dependent variable, but it was not statistically significant.

Unsurprisingly, given our foreign ancestors, it is also the case that we are a land of internal migrants. According to a Gallup poll, approximately one in four Americans "have moved from one city or area within their country to another in the past five years."[110] That factor puts the United States (with countries like New Zealand and Finland) in the top ranks globally for internal mobility (the worldwide average is 8 percent).

But why do those Americans move? They certainly aren't moving one step ahead of oppressive regimes and violence like those fleeing recently from Syria, Venezuela, or Zimbabwe. More likely they move for reasons like economic opportunity and locational amenities, such as better weather or beaches. But freedom might matter too when it comes to internal migration, given the differences across the 50 states we identify in the first part of this study. Those differences aren't as severe as those between the United States and the least free countries of the world. But they are meaningful, especially considering that New York is far less free than the average state, while other states also score substantially worse or better than others.

But do Americans value freedom as we define it? One way to try to answer that question is to analyze the relationship between freedom and net interstate migration—that is, the movement of people between states. If, all else being equal, Americans prefer to move to freer states, that would be evidence in favor of the hypothesis that Americans value freedom. In other words, it looks at preferences revealed by behavior rather than mere expressed views. That does not mean that people are responding directly to changes in policy, packing up moving vans, and heading from New York to New Hampshire or the Dakotas. But it could be that they are moving within their region to freer places like Pennsylvania and New Jersey.

We try to answer the question posed in the previous paragraph by examining the statistical correlations between freedom at particular moments and net interstate migration over several subsequent years. Figures 19–24 plot states' net migration rates from July 1, 2000, to July 1, 2010, and from July 1, 2010, to July 1, 2019, against their overall, economic, and personal freedom scores in 2000 and 2010, respectively. This division essentially splits our sample in half and roughly separates pre– and post–Great Recession periods. The net migration rate is defined as the number of people moving *to* a state *from* other states minus the number of people moving from that state to other states, divided by the initial resident population of the state. The migration data are from the Census Bureau's "components of population change" tables. These figures represent a simple "first cut" at the question. They do not control for any other factors that might drive migration.

110. Neli Esipova, Anita Pugliese, and Julie Ray, "381 Million Adults Worldwide Migrate within Countries," Gallup, May 15, 2013.

Figure 19 shows the relationship between overall freedom and net migration over the earlier period from 2000 to 2010. It shows a strong relationship between the starting level of freedom and subsequent net migration, suggesting that people are moving to freer states. We can see that from the example of New York, which suffered the worst net outmigration of any state—8.8 percent of its 2000 population—and is also the least free state. Louisiana is obviously anomalous because Hurricane Katrina drove away hundreds of thousands of people, resulting in large net outmigration despite an average level of freedom. At the top end, Nevada and Arizona are big outliers in net in-migration, as Americans during this period were flocking to the so-called sand states because of their supposedly desirable climates.[111] Those anomalies illustrate the importance of controlling for potential confounders.

FIGURE 19 Overall Freedom and Net Domestic Migration, 2000–2010

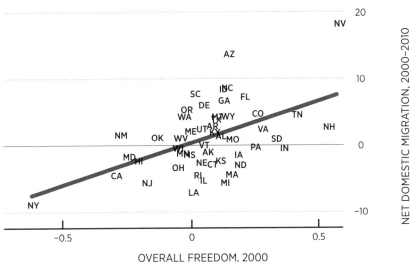

Figure 20 shows the relationship between year-end 2010 freedom and migration over the next nine years. We see less evidence of amenity-driven migration over this period, which includes the aftermath of the Great Recession. However, warm states like the Carolinas, Arizona, Nevada, and Texas lie mostly above the line of best fit, whereas cold states like Alaska, New Hampshire, Illinois, and South Dakota lie mostly below that line. The relationship between freedom and net migration appears equally strong in both the earlier and later periods.

---

111.   Thomas Davidoff, "Supply Elasticity and the Housing Cycle of the 2000s," *Real Estate Economics* 41, no. 4 (2013): 793–813.

FIGURE 20 Overall Freedom and Net Domestic Migration, 2010–2019

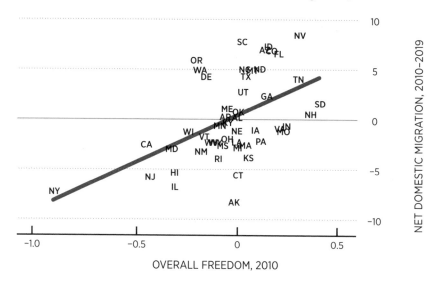

Figure 21 shows the relationship between economic freedom and net migration in the first half of our period of analysis. Again, a strong relationship exists between economic freedom and in-migration.

FIGURE 21 Economic Freedom and Net Domestic Migration, 2000–2010

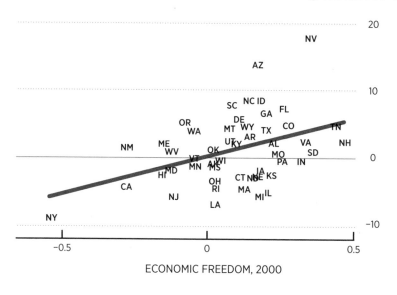

Figure 22 shows how economic freedom in 2010 relates to subsequent migration. The line of best fit expresses a strong, positive relationship between a state's economic freedom at the beginning of the period and subsequent in-migration. North Dakota lies significantly above the regression line in part because of its discovery of shale oil and gas. Michigan lies significantly below the regression line mostly because of the travails of its automobile-manufacturing industry in international markets.

FIGURE 22 Economic Freedom and Net Domestic Migration, 2010–2019

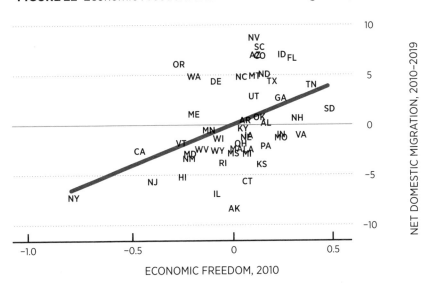

Figure 23 moves to personal freedom. Here, we do not find as strong a relationship between freedom and migration as we found for overall freedom and economic freedom. The line of best fit is nearly flat, implying a weak relationship between personal freedom and net migration. Recall that personal freedom correlates slightly negatively with economic freedom. If economic freedom is a more important driver of net in-migration than personal freedom, the bivariate relationship between personal freedom and migration expressed here will probably be biased downward.

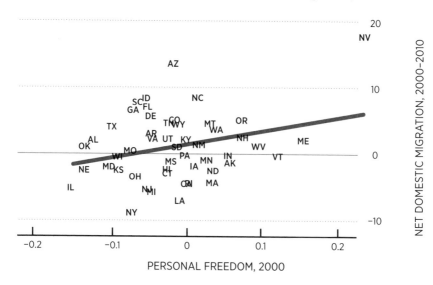

FIGURE 23 Personal Freedom and Net Domestic Migration, 2000–2010

Figure 24 shows the relationship between personal freedom at the end of 2010 and subsequent net migration. The line of best fit is again nearly flat, indicating a weak relationship. However, economic freedom is an important confounder.

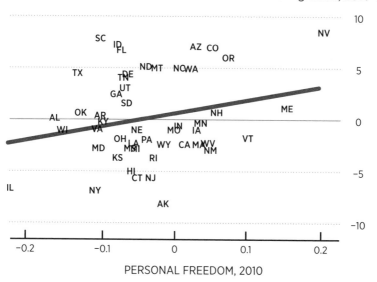

FIGURE 24 Personal Freedom and Net Domestic Migration, 2010–2019

To deal with confounding variables that affect migration, we turn to multiple regression analysis, which allows us to control for factors such as climate. Doing so permits us to meet the most obvious challenge to our conclusions about the relationship between freedom and migration patterns among the states. In previous editions, we have found a positive relationship between each dimension of freedom and migration, although regulatory policy has been related to net migration solely through the channels of cost of living and economic growth. In other words, a lighter regulatory touch may improve the productivity of the economy, but low taxes and personal freedom seem to be amenities that the marginal migrant values for their own sake.

In this edition, we are again able to look at how freedom associates with net migration in two different time periods. By looking at how later-period freedom relates to migration and growth, we are making a kind of "out of sample" prediction from our prior results. Previous results of preregistered models showed that personal freedom dropped in significance as a driver of migration after the Great Recession, but all three dimensions of freedom positively correlated with the subsequent net in-migration during the first eight years of the 21st century. This time, we compare results for the 2000–2010 period with those for the 2010–2019 period.

We present results from two types of estimations: monadic and matched neighbors. The monadic regressions simply compare all 50 states with each other. The matched-neighbors regressions subtract the weighted average of neighboring states' values (on migration, freedom, and controls) from each state's value. The weights are the distances between the "centroids" (geographic centers) of each state. The purpose of these regressions is to examine whether freedom has a stronger effect on in-migration when neighboring states are more different on freedom. We expect that a freer state surrounded by less free states will attract more migrants than a freer state surrounded by equally free states, all else being equal.

Table 35 presents seven regression equations of net migration over the 2000–2010 period.[112] The tables display coefficients and standard errors. A rough rule of thumb for statistical significance is that when the ratio of the coefficient to the standard error is greater than two, the coefficient is statistically significant at the 95 percent confidence level; however, statistical significance is best thought of as a continuum rather than a switch.

The first equation simply regresses the net migration rate on the three dimensions of freedom, which are measured as averages for the years 2000 to 2004. Fiscal, regulatory, and personal freedom are all independently, positively, statistically significantly correlated with net in-migration. Model (2) adds cost of living in 2000, as measured by William Berry, Richard Fording, and Russell Hanson.[113] Cost of living is potentially a bad control, because regulatory policy, especially land-use freedom, can influence migration through the channel of cost of living. Model (3) adds accommodation GDP per capita, which proxies the size of the tourist industry. States with bigger hospitality sectors appear to attract more migrants, presumably because they have more locational amenities. Model (4) controls for capital stock per worker from Gasper Garofalo and Steven Yamarik.[114] Model (5) adds the percentage of state population age 65 and older. Model (6) adds the violent crime rate. Finally, model (7) adds population-weighted annual heating degree days—a measure of how cold a climate is—and area-weighted statewide average annual precipitation.

Except for cost of living, adding each of those controls does not substantially affect the statistical estimates of the correlation between fiscal, regulatory, and personal freedom, on the one hand, and net migration, on the other hand. The coefficient on regulatory freedom does fall when cost of living is added, a post-treatment collider: states lower on regulatory freedom suffer from higher cost of living, which is the more immediate cause of lower in-migration.

Table 36 performs the same set of analyses on the 2010–2019 data, with freedom variables measured as the average of 2010 through 2013 values. Again, fiscal and regulatory freedom look like important drivers of interstate migration over this period, whereas personal freedom loses much of its importance, as we expected. The last, personal freedom, also looks less important for migration in 2010–2019 than in 2000–2010. The relationship between fiscal and regulatory freedom, on the one hand, and migration, on the other hand, looks robust to the addition of controls.

112.   As in the fourth edition, we tried dropping the outlier case of Louisiana, with only trivial differences in results.

113.   William D. Berry, Richard C. Fording, and Russell L. Hanson, "An Annual Cost of Living Index for the American States, 1960–1995," *Journal of Politics* 62, no. 2 (2000): 550–67.

114.   Gasper A. Garofalo and Steven Yamarik, "Regional Growth: Evidence from a New State-by-State Capital Stock Series," *Review of Economics and Statistics* 84, no. 2 (2002): 316–23.

TABLE 35

Monadic Estimates of Freedom and Migration, 2000–2010

Variable	(1) Coef. (SE)	(2) Coef. (SE)	(3) Coef. (SE)	(4) Coef. (SE)	(5) Coef. (SE)	(6) Coef. (SE)	(7) Coef. (SE)
Fiscal freedom	0.94 (0.50)	1.39 (0.40)	0.90 (0.45)	0.82 (0.51)	1.03 (0.50)	0.90 (0.45)	1.42 (0.53)
Regulatory freedom	2.77 (0.58)	1.29 (0.56)	2.65 (0.55)	3.01 (0.76)	2.70 (0.56)	3.06 (0.54)	2.44 (0.59)
Personal freedom	2.09 (0.74)	2.41 (0.66)	1.41 (0.61)	2.33 (0.86)	2.08 (0.71)	2.68 (0.65)	1.91 (0.57)
Cost of living		−4.03 (0.97)					
Accommodations			1.35 (0.58)				
Capital per worker				0.55 (0.72)			
Retirees					−0.55 (0.67)		
Violent crime						1.40 (0.52)	
Heating degree days							−1.50 (0.97)
Precipitation							−1.37 (0.76)
Constant	0.75 (0.61)	−1.84 (0.66)	0.64 (0.56)	0.69 (0.60)	0.78 (0.60)	0.48 (0.50)	0.94 (0.58)
R^2	36.3%	50.8%	40.6%	37.1%	37.6%	45.2%	44.4%

Note: All independent variables are standardized to mean zero and variance one. Robust standard errors. Coef. = coefficient; R^2 = proportion of the total variance explained by the model; SE = standard error.

TABLE 36

Monadic Estimates of Freedom and Migration, 2010–2019

Variable	(8) Coef. (SE)	(9) Coef. (SE)	(10) Coef. (SE)	(11) Coef. (SE)	(12) Coef. (SE)	(13) Coef. (SE)	(14) Coef. (SE)
Fiscal freedom	1.17 (0.53)	1.18 (0.53)	1.20 (0.53)	1.05 (0.50)	1.16 (0.53)	1.12 (0.51)	1.46 (0.53)
Regulatory freedom	1.81 (0.51)	1.60 (1.00)	1.79 (0.51)	2.07 (0.57)	1.82 (0.51)	1.83 (0.49)	1.54 (0.50)
Personal freedom	1.46 (0.53)	1.47 (0.54)	1.26 (0.59)	1.66 (0.58)	1.46 (0.55)	0.66 (0.64)	1.26
Cost of living		−0.24 (0.84)					
Accom-modations			0.37 (0.37)				(0.47)
Capital per worker				0.57 (0.60)			
Retirees					0.14 (0.82)		
Violent crime						0.66 (0.64)	
Heating degree days							−1.05 (0.76)
Precipitation							−1.09 (0.53)
Constant	0.91 (0.58)	0.91 (0.60)	0.84 (0.59)	0.92 (0.57)	0.91 (0.60)	0.95 (0.58)	0.37 (0.49)
R^2	30.3%	30.4%	31.0%	31.6%	30.4%	32.4%	36.2%

Note: All independent variables are standardized to mean zero and variance one. Robust standard errors. Coef. = coefficient; R^2 = proportion of the total variance explained by the model; SE = standard error.

Table 37 presents the results for the 2000–2010 period when we match each state to its neighbors, on the (true) assumption that migration flows between neighboring states are greater than they are between distant states. These matched-neighbor results are somewhat sharper than the monadic results. They suggest that fiscal and regulatory freedom drive migration even when cost of living is controlled. As expected, more costly states repel migrants, whereas states with locational amenities attract them. Model (17)—which controls for cost of living and accommodations GDP per capita—and model (18)—which controls for the previous two plus capital per worker—explain more than two-thirds of all the variance in relative-to-neighbors net migration across all 50 states as measured by R-squared.

TABLE 37

Matched-Neighbors Estimates of Freedom and Migration, 2000–2010

Variable	(15) Coef. (SE)	(16) Coef. (SE)	(17) Coef. (SE)	(18) Coef. (SE)
Fiscal freedom	0.90 (0.44)	1.53 (0.47)	1.60 (0.40)	1.46 (0.40)
Regulatory freedom	2.97 (0.89)	2.36 (0.76)	1.85 (0.62)	2.20 (0.78)
Personal freedom	1.95 (0.56)	1.56 (0.56)	0.81 (0.45)	0.85 (0.45)
Cost of living		−6.4 (2.0)	−7.5 (1.6)	−7.7 (1.7)
Accommodations			1.7 (0.3)	1.8 (0.4)
Capital per worker				0.48 (0.51)
Constant	−0.34 (0.54)	−0.4 (0.47)	−0.46 (0.42)	−0.29 (0.46)
R^2	54.2%	64.7%	70.8%	71.3%

Note: All independent variables are standardized to mean zero and variance one. Robust standard errors. Coef. = coefficient; R^2 = proportion of the total variance explained by the model; SE = standard error.

Table 38 presents the matched-neighbors results for the 2010–2019 period. All variables have smaller coefficients, due in part to the fact that absolute rates of net migration were lower during this period compared with the previous period. R-squareds are also lower, showing that net migration was simply less predictable during this period, presumably because of idiosyncratic shocks that state economies suffered during the Great Recession. Fiscal freedom is again robustly related to net in-migration, and personal freedom is nearly statistically significant in all models. Regulatory freedom appears less important to migration in this period, but the standard errors are apparently inflated, possibly owing to multicollinearity.

TABLE 38

Matched-Neighbors Estimates of Freedom and Migration, 2010–2019

Variable	(19) Coef. (SE)	(20) Coef. (SE)	(21) Coef. (SE)	(22) Coef. (SE)
Fiscal freedom	1.07 (0.47)	1.19 (0.52)	1.26 (0.56)	0.96 (0.49)
Regulatory freedom	1.26 (0.75)	0.73 (1.07)	0.48 (1.22)	1.11 (1.15)
Personal freedom	1.34 (0.56)	1.12 (0.52)	0.93 (0.56)	0.90 (0.51)
Cost of living		−0.93 (0.95)	−1.12 (1.03)	−1.8 (1.2)
Accommodations			0.3 (0.37)	0.63 (0.41)
Capital per worker				1.19 (0.77)
Constant	−0.25 (0.51)	−0.30 (0.54)	−0.32 (0.55)	0.12 (0.52)
R^2	31.5%	33.0%	33.7%	38.0%

Note: All independent variables are standardized to mean zero and variance one. Robust standard errors. Coef. = coefficient; R^2 = proportion of the total variance explained by the model; SE = standard error.

Our migration models do not control for state economic growth, which is endogenous (more migration of workers will induce higher economic growth). It is plausible that regulatory freedom, in particular, influences migration almost entirely by affecting the economic climate (cost of living and growth), rather than as a direct amenity. Few workers are likely to study different states' labor laws or tort liability systems before deciding where to live, but it is quite plausible that businesses do so when deciding where to invest.

Therefore, we now turn to analyzing the statistical relationship between economic growth in each state and its economic freedom. The dependent variable in these regression equations is annual real personal income growth. The Bureau of Economic Analysis has produced real personal income estimates for the 2008–2019 period at the state level, using state-specific price indexes. We present four models, all with region dummies and two with year dummies in addition. Two of the models include economic freedom, and the other two separate out the fiscal and regulatory indexes (Table 39).

TABLE 39

Economic Freedom and Real Personal Income Growth Estimates, 2008–2019

Variable	(23) Coef. (SE)	(24) Coef. (SE)	(25) Coef. (SE)	(26) Coef. (SE)
Economic freedom	0.012 (0.004)		0.0074 (0.0032	
Fiscal freedom		0.009 (0.011)		0.010 (0.006)
Regulatory freedom		0.015 (0.018)		0.003 (0.007)
Region dummies?	Yes	Yes	Yes	Yes
Year dummies?	No	No	Yes	Yes
R^2	62.1%	62.0%	76.6%	76.7%

Note: Coef. = coefficient; R^2 = proportion of the total variance explained by the model; SE = standard error.

The results show that economic freedom is positively associated with subsequent income growth. A one-point increase in economic freedom is associated with a percentage point increase of between 0.7 and 1.2 in the growth rate of personal income the following year. Since the average personal income growth rate in the data set is 2.1 percent, and the standard deviation of growth rates is 2.6 percent (i.e., 0.026), this effect is substantial. Although fiscal and regulatory freedom are not individually significant in their models, a test that results in the linear combination of their coefficients being zero rejects the null in each case.

In conclusion, there is robust evidence that economic freedom is associated with subsequent income growth, even when we control for the previous year's rate of growth and region and year fixed effects. Part of the reason fiscal and regulatory policy scores correlate with greater in-migration may be that a good economic policy regime promotes economic growth, which in turn attracts investment and workers.

POLICY CHANGES SINCE JANUARY 2020, INCLUDING THOSE RELATED TO COVID-19

GENERAL POLICY CHANGES

Finally, we discuss policy changes made across the states in 2020 and the first half of 2021, as well as how responses to COVID-19 at the state and local levels affected freedom. Given that the ongoing COVID-19 pandemic has affected freedom across the country since our data cutoff—even if only temporarily in some cases—we find it valuable to describe policy changes that have occurred at the state and local levels since that time. In the past, we have tried to capture major policy changes that occurred after our data cutoff in the state profiles, and readers can also find them here in this edition.

As always, we do not try to shoehorn up-to-date data from some variables into the index, given that some other variables have a lag in availability, such as fiscal and criminal justice data. Our goal is to capture the state of freedom at a particular slice in time. However, we think it is worth capturing these changes in a qualitative way in this section so that readers will have as up-to-date an understanding of the state of freedom in the states as possible. So what follows is not only a COVID-19-specific discussion, but also a broader discussion of the policy changes of 2020 and 2021.

We turn first to relating policy changes more broadly, with a focus on those policies that fall within the purview of the index, and then we deal with policies dealing specifically with COVID-19. We can observe simultaneous pro-freedom and anti-freedom trends around the country in different policy domains. Some of these trends predated the pandemic, whereas others seem more likely to have been a reaction either to the pandemic itself or to the changing economic and social conditions it has brought about.

Pro-freedom trends can be observed in domains such as school choice, criminal justice and policing, drug reform, alcohol laws, gambling laws, and tax policy. This last trend has been facilitated in part by federal profligacy, so that it is hard to say whether Americans in general have enjoyed a true tax cut—taking into account the growth in the future tax burden due to federal spending increases—from the pandemic years.

Anti-freedom trends are visible in labor laws and tobacco and e-cigarette policies. Land-use freedom has become a hot topic as housing costs have escalated, and some positive state-level reforms have occurred. However, it is unclear at best whether these initial efforts to break the housing logjam clear much of the ever-deepening thicket of local zoning regulations.

Turning first to fiscal policy, we see several states that have cut income tax rates. In 2021, 10 states reduced individual income taxes, and 5 states reduced corporate income taxes.[115] Most states cutting income taxes also simplified their tax structures. The most significant overall cuts in tax burden occurred in Idaho, Nebraska, New Hampshire, Ohio, Oklahoma, and Wisconsin. By eliminating the interest and dividends tax, New Hampshire will become the ninth state without an individual income tax. The pandemic also reduced tax collections initially because of the decline in economic activity.[116] A number of states tapped their rainy-day funds, allowing them to avoid raising taxes.[117] However, fiscal 2021 revenues mostly came in above projections, allowing a few states to cut taxes in 2021.[118] The most significant tax increases came from states that took advantage of the *Wayfair* decision to enact sales taxes on out-of-state internet retailers: as of June 2021, all states that have a general sales tax have made this change. Washington also enacted a new capital gains tax, even though it lacks a general income tax.[119] New York raised its top marginal income tax rate significantly, though the change applies only to those earning more than $25 million in a year.[120] Many states also increased government spending, particularly because the CARES Act and American Rescue Plan together shoveled more than $600 billion into states and localities.[121] Readers will rightly worry that states—and those

115. Tax Foundation, "States Respond to Strong Fiscal Health with Income Tax Reforms," July 15, 2021, https://taxfoundation.org/2021-state-income-tax-cuts/.

116. National Association of State Budget Officers, *The Fiscal Survey of States: Fall 2020* (Washington: NASBO, 2020), p. 54.

117. Barb Rosewicz, Justin Theal, and Joe Fleming, "States' Total Rainy Day Funds Fall for First Time Since Great Recession," The Pew Charitable Trusts, May 21, 2021.

118. National Association of State Budget Officers, *The Fiscal Survey of States: Spring 2021* (Washington: NASBO, 2021), p. 52.

119. Melissa Santos, "Eight Big Things the Washington State Legislature Passed in 2021," Crosscut.com, April 26, 2021.

120. "New York State: Tax Measures in 2021 Budget Agreement," KPMG, April 7, 2021.

121. Richard McGahey, "Why Didn't Covid-19 Wreck State and City Budgets? Federal Spending," *Forbes*, September 1, 2021.

groups and individuals who benefit from the spending (at the cost of the forgotten man, the federal taxpayer now and in the future)—will get hooked on this federal "drug" and try to maintain at least some of this spending.

In the area of regulatory policy, we have seen significant changes to health insurance regulation and labor regulation in several states, as well as some efforts at opening up housing production. Licensing regulations were sometimes suspended temporarily to permit telehealth across state lines, but most of those changes were not permanent. New technologies like virtual currencies continue to attract legislative attention.

In the field of labor regulation, 25 states have increased their minimum wages since the closing date on our study: Alaska, Arizona, Arkansas, California, Colorado, Connecticut, Florida, Illinois, Maine, Maryland, Massachusetts, Minnesota, Missouri, Montana, Nevada, New Jersey, New Mexico, New York, Ohio, Oregon, Rhode Island, South Dakota, Vermont, Virginia, and Washington. Several Democrat-controlled states also enacted or expanded mandatory paid sick leave, paid family leave, and restrictions on independent contractor status.[122] Colorado enacted paid sick leave and equal pay regulation. Connecticut created a paid family leave program. California expanded its existing family leave program and mandated racial and sexual diversity on corporate boards. Maine created a general paid leave mandate. Massachusetts enacted paid family leave.[123] New York enacted paid sick leave. Virginia tightened restrictions on independent contractors and non-compete agreements. Washington also expanded exemptions from noncompetes. New Jersey "banned the box" for private employers, and New York City and St. Louis have done so at the local level.[124]

In the area of health insurance regulation, Washington pioneered a state-level public option plan that was passed in 2019 and went into effect in 2021, with Colorado and Nevada following suit in 2021. In all three states, the "public option" is really a government-controlled, public–private partnership rather than a fully government-run insurer.[125] As Pew noted earlier this year: "The early results from Washington state's experiment are disappointing. In many parts of the state, premiums for the public option plans cost more than premiums for comparable commercial plans. Many of the state's hospitals have refused to take part in the public option, prompting lawmakers to introduce more legislation this year to force participation if there

122. Susan Gross Sholinsky et al., "Roadmap to Compliance: Major Employment Laws Effective as of January 2021 and Beyond," *Act Now Advisory*, Epstein Becker Green, January 26, 2021.

123. Heather St. Clair and Bruce Sarchet, "New State Employment Laws Set to Take Effect on January 1, 2021," Littler Mendelson, November 9, 2020.

124. New York City Council, Law 2021/004, prohibiting discrimination based on one's arrest record, pending criminal accusations of criminal convictions, enacted January 10, 2021, File #: Int 1314-2018; City of St. Louis, Ordinance 71074, effective January 1, 2021.

125. Dylan Scott, "The Public Option Is Now a Reality in 3 States," Vox, June 17, 2021.

aren't sufficient health insurance options in a geographic area. And consumer buy-in is also meager."[126] We will need to include this policy choice in any subsequent edition of this index.

State-level housing legislation does not figure directly in the index, but the goal of most state legislation on this topic is to loosen up local restrictions, which should eventually make an observable difference in our data. Important legislation includes California's accessory dwelling unit laws of 2020 and 2021, which are expected to ease the construction of thousands of new units.[127] New Hampshire enacted a similar law in 2017. Oregon essentially banned single-family zoning in cities in 2019, requiring residential districts in cities of at least 10,000 people to allow duplexes.[128]

Cryptocurrency is an emerging area of regulation at both state and federal levels. Wyoming has gone furthest to define new legal regimes for crypto firms, and in 2021 it recognized decentralized autonomous organizations as legal entities.[129] In 2017, New Hampshire expressly exempted cryptocurrency from state regulation.[130] At the other extreme, New York requires a state license for crypto firms.

Occupational licensing was also an area of at least temporary liberalization during the pandemic. Many states moved to allow audio-only telemedicine and to relax licensure requirements for out-of-state providers.[131] Florida, North Carolina, and Wyoming were the only states not to legalize audio-only telehealth.[132] Maryland had one of the broadest reforms for health care practitioners, allowing all health care professionals the authority to work beyond their current scope of practice in health care facilities. New York enacted a more limited reform for select professionals. Eight states—Idaho, Maine, Michigan, Missouri, New Hampshire, New York, Pennsylvania, and Texas—waived or modified licensing requirements for all professionals. Nurse practitioners specifically received expanded scope of practice in Kentucky, Louisiana, New Jersey, New York, Wisconsin, and other states that did not previously grant it.[133] Fifteen states enacted reforms

126. Michael Ollove, "3 States Pursue Public Option for Health Coverage as Feds Balk," The Pew Charitable Trusts, July 22, 2021.

127. Californians for Homeownership website, www.caforhomes.org.

128. Laurel Wamsley, "Oregon Legislature Votes to Essentially Ban Single-Family Zoning," NPR, July 1, 2019.

129. Heather Morton, "Cryptocurrency 2021 Legislation," National Conference of State Legislatures, May 14, 2021.

130. Jennifer L. Moffitt, "The Fifty U.S. States and Cryptocurrency Regulations," CoinATMRadar, July 27, 2018.

131. Iris Hentze, "COVID19: Occupational Licensing during Public Emergencies," National Conference of State Legislatures, October 30, 2020, www.ncsl.org/research/labor-and-employment/covid-19-occupational-licensing-in-public-emergencies.aspx; Ethan Bayne, Conor Norris, and Edward J. Timmons, "A Primer on Emergency Occupational Licensing Reforms for Combating COVID-19," policy brief, Mercatus Center at George Mason University, Arlington, VA, March 26, 2020.

132. Julia Raifman et al., "COVID-19 US State Policy Database," www.openicpsr.org/openicpsr/project/119446/version/V129/view.

133. Sara Heath, "Mass. Law Expands Nurse Scope of Practice, Patient Access to Care," PatientEngagementHIT, January 5, 2021; "Scope of Practice—Nurse Practitioners," American Academy of Family Physicians, March 2021, www.aafp.org/dam/AAFP/documents/advocacy/workforce/scope/BKG-Scope-NursePractitioners.pdf.

allowing out-of-state licensed medical professionals to get a temporary license to practice in-state. Several states that had previously not allowed pharmacists to administer vaccines changed their laws to permit it.[134]

In the area of personal freedom, we see major legislative action in education, drugs (including alcohol), tobacco, guns, criminal justice, and gambling over the past two years. Most of that action, but not all, has been in a pro-freedom direction.

Turning first to drugs, the trend toward liberalization has continued. Arizona, Connecticut, Montana, New Jersey, New Mexico, New York, South Dakota, and Virginia have legalized recreational marijuana in 2020 or 2021.[135] Alabama legalized medical marijuana, and Louisiana decriminalized possession of up to 14 grams. Texas now allows low-THC medical marijuana.[136] Oregon was the first state in the country to decriminalize small-scale possession of all drugs. Oregon was also the first state to legalize medical psilocybin.[137] A growing number of states are authorizing medical research into psychedelics.[138]

In the wake of George Floyd's death, states moved to enact policing reforms that had been brewing for years as part of the larger criminal justice reform effort. Many states banned the use of chokeholds, including California, Colorado, Delaware, Indiana, Iowa, Louisiana, Massachusetts, Minnesota, Nevada, New Hampshire, New York, Oregon, Texas, Utah, Vermont, Virginia, and Wisconsin.[139] Tennessee and Illinois were previously the only states to ban the practice.[140] More significantly, New Mexico has banned the defense of qualified immunity for public employees, and Colorado has ended it for police officers (in 2020).[141] Another common reform has been to limit the circumstances under which police officers may use deadly force and to require officers to intervene when they observe excessive use of force.

In other criminal justice news, Maine became the fourth state to abolish civil asset forfeiture,[142] and Arizona moved to require a criminal conviction before civil forfeiture proceedings.[143] The Maine law also prohibits

134. Kelsie George, "Pharmacists Boosting Access to COVID Vaccine," *State Legislatures Magazine*, May 18, 2021.

135. "2021 Marijuana Policy Reform Legislation," Marijuana Policy Project, June 22, 2021.

136. "Texas Medical Marijuana," State of Texas, 2021, Texas.gov.

137. "The Complete Guide to Psychedelic Legalization," Psychedelic Invest, 2021.

138. Joyce E. Cutler, "Texas the Latest State to Legalize Psychedelic Medical Research," Bloomberg Law, June 23, 2021.

139. National Conference of State Legislatures, "Legislative Responses for Policing—State Bill Tracking Database," NCSL, June 16, 2021.

140. Farnoush Amiri, Colleen Slevin, and Camille Fassett, "Floyd Killing Prompts Some States to Limit or Ban Chokeholds," AP News, May 23, 2021.

141. Brooke Seipel, "Colorado Governor Signs Sweeping Police Reform Bill Ending Qualified Immunity, Banning Chokeholds," *The Hill*, June 19, 2020.

142. C. J. Ciaramella, "Maine Becomes 4th State to Repeal Civil Asset Forfeiture," Reason.com, July 14, 2021.

143. C. J. Ciaramella, "Arizona Legislature Passes Bill Requiring Convictions for Asset Forfeiture," Reason.com, April 29, 2021.

equitable sharing participation, giving it the best forfeiture laws in the nation. Minnesota made more modest changes.[144]

Red states continue to adjust their gun laws in a pro-freedom direction. In 2021, five states enacted constitutional carry: Iowa, Montana, Tennessee, Texas, and Utah. Arkansas adopted Stand Your Ground,[145] whereas Ohio adopted a more limited version preventing civil liability.[146] Colorado's supreme court specified no duty to retreat in a recent decision. Meanwhile, blue states went in the other direction. Virginia adopted a package of significant changes, including universal gun registration, safe storage regulation, a one-gun-a-month limit, and red flag seizures.[147] Cities are now allowed to ban guns on their property. Colorado also enacted a safe storage law.

Alcohol laws were at least temporarily liberalized during the pandemic in many states and localities as drinking establishments and breweries suffered from the restrictions and reduced demand for public socializing that occurred from March 2020 through the summer of 2021. Michigan, Nevada, New Mexico, North Dakota, South Dakota, and Utah were the only states *not* to allow restaurants to serve takeout alcohol. Thirty-two states further allowed restaurants to deliver alcohol. Normally, liquor licensees must get permission to expand outdoor dining from state agencies, but states passed legislation allowing them to expand outdoor dining with only local zoning approval (e.g., Arkansas 2021 Act 705). New Jersey expanded the period during which seasonal retail consumption license holders could sell alcohol (A.B. 4589). The success of these policies for consumers suggests the policies should stick, and perhaps many states will make their temporary legislation permanent, especially since the fears promoted for decades by the "Bootlegger and Baptist" coalition did not play out.

The year 2021 became the "year of school choice" in the wake of widespread parent dissatisfaction with public school remote learning. The most significant changes included the enactment of a new tax-credit scholarship in Arkansas and the establishment of educational savings accounts in Florida, Indiana, Kentucky, Missouri, New Hampshire, and West Virginia.[148] Numerous states expanded existing tax-credit scholarship programs. Many states are also, through legislation or court decisions, expanding existing school choice programs to religious schools.

144. Stephen Montemayor, "Changes to Minnesota's Civil Asset Forfeiture Laws Pass Legislature," *Star Tribune*, July 3, 2021.

145. Monisha Smith, "Gun Laws—Good and Bad—Are Changing in States across the Country: Here's What's Going into Effect in July 2021," Everytown for Gun Safety, July 1, 2021.

146. Senate Bill 175, Ohio Legislature, signed into law January 4, 2021.

147. Jackie DeFusto, "Five New Gun Control Laws Take Effect July 1 in Virginia," WRIC.com, June 28, 2021.

148. "The Year of School Choice," American Federation for Children, May 16, 2021.

Online sports betting took off in a big way in the last few years because of the innovations of DraftKings and related apps and websites. As of mid-2021, 27 states had legalized online sports betting, a complete turnaround from 2018 when only Nevada had done so.[149]

As we have seen throughout the pandemic, when government gets out of the way, businesses and professionals rush to provide goods and services that consumers demand, such as sidewalk and parking space dining (parking spaces are oversupplied because of government parking minimums), alcohol to go, in-person private schooling, and telehealth. Will state and local governments take notice and keep these consumer-friendly policies, or will they go back to satisfying entrenched interests with regulatory barriers unresponsive to consumer needs?

COVID-19-RELATED POLICIES

Fellow classical liberals have diverse views on the appropriate policy responses to infectious diseases. In principle, it is clear that intentionally or negligently exposing others to a serious infectious disease is a violation of their freedom. Even unknowingly exposing others is a regrettable act that should be prevented if possible. Behaviors that pose serious risks to others in this way constitute a significant, direct, negative externality. Therefore, there is room for coercive public policies to prevent or punish such acts.

But what kind of policy response is appropriate? Classical liberals can understandably disagree on the thresholds of risk at which coercion becomes justifiable. Activities that create a risk of transmitting a deadly and highly contagious disease presumably merit more sanction than activities that create a risk of transmitting a usually harmless and only mildly contagious disease. Thus, extreme action such as bans on travel and quarantines may well have been justified in early modern cities to prevent the spread of plague, given its contagion and fatal consequences during the era. COVID-19 lies more at the other end of the spectrum from early modern plague, fatal only to a small minority (under 2 percent of those infected by every estimate) and moderately contagious (R_0 below measles but above influenza).[150]

Moreover, risk isn't always obvious when a new threat emerges, and a varied range of responses can help society learn the true level of risk and how to mitigate it. In those situations of uncertainty, decentralized and deliberative processes, rather than top-down and bureaucratic ones, are most needed. For these reasons, we are skeptical of open-ended gubernatorial emergency powers, such as those exercised in some states during the pandemic.

149. "State by State Legal Sports Betting Guide," SportsBetting.Legal.

150. "COVID-19 Pandemic Planning Scenarios," Centers for Disease Control and Prevention, March 19, 2021.

Thus, the most extreme COVID-19 policies, such as mandatory stay-at-home orders, do not appear in hindsight to have been justified given what we now know about its deadliness and contagion. Had policymakers known the full characteristics and consequences of COVID-19, they would have realized that mandatory stay-at-home orders were excessive. Defenders of the policy might admit that while it turned out not to have been desirable, the lack of knowledge early in the pandemic meant that lockdown was the safer choice and, thus, the caution was warranted. However, the knowledge problem cuts both ways. States clearly did not know what the negative consequences of lockdowns would be for the economy, education, mental health, and crime, to name a few apparent downstream effects. Even if the early lockdowns could be justified, state legislators could still be faulted for the extent to which they delegated emergency powers to executives. Moreover, the governments that enacted second-wave lockdowns in late 2020 and early 2021 should have known better. There is a legitimate debate to be had, however, about policies such as mask mandates and vaccine incentives.

Turning to state policies, a small number of states, to their credit, avoided mandatory lockdowns in 2020: Arkansas, Iowa, Nebraska, North Dakota, South Dakota, Utah, and Wyoming.[151] Some states maintained lockdowns long after it was apparent that they were not needed to "flatten the curve," most notably California and New Mexico. Most lockdowns were short-lived, however: "By mid-May, all 50 states had begun the process of easing restrictions, seeking a balance between reopening economies and protecting public health."[152] Mandatory stay-at-home orders may have reduced infection rates in 2020,[153] but few studies examine the tradeoffs of the policy, such as the long-run effects on death rates relative to other, more focused protection policies.[154]

Moreover, stay-at-home orders may have gotten more attention than they deserve, compared with other policies. For example, every state but South Dakota closed restaurants, bars, movie theaters, gyms, and hair salons for several weeks or months in 2020.[155] (Casinos and liquor stores got special treatment: only 22 states closed casinos, and only one state—Nevada—closed liquor stores.) Some states required quarantine for individuals entering the state. Thirty-one states suspended elective medical procedures. Iowa,

151.   "States That Issued Lockdown and Stay-at-Home Orders in Response to the Coronavirus (COVID-19) Pandemic, 2020," Ballotpedia.

152.   Rachel Treisman, "How Is Each State Responding to COVID-19?," NPR, December 4, 2020.

153.   Renan C. Castillo, Elena D. Staguhn, and Elias Weston-Farber, "The Effect of State-Level Stay-at-Home Orders on Covid-19 Infection Rates," *American Journal of Infection Control* 48, no. 8 (2020): 958–60; M. Keith Chen et al., "Causal Estimation of Stay-at-Home Orders on SARS-CoV-2 Transmission," working paper, arXiv.org, May 11, 2020.

154.   Shaowen Luo, Kwok Ping Tsang, and Zichao Yang, "The Impact of Stay-at-Home Orders on US Output: A Network Perspective," April 20, 2020.

155.   Raifman et al., "State Policy Database."

Mississippi, and New Mexico suspended elective medical procedures a second time, during the winter of 2020/21. Some states shut down in-person private schooling in addition to public schooling.[156] Some states limited the size of outdoor gatherings, including but not limited to California, Colorado, Connecticut, Delaware, Hawaii, Maine, Massachusetts, Michigan, New Jersey, New York, North Carolina, Pennsylvania, and Vermont. Given what we now know about how COVID-19 is spread, these restrictions seem pointless at best.

In 2021, mask mandates have been the pandemic policy of choice, not business closures. (As noted earlier, this kind of restriction on freedom may be justifiable—at least, it seems there is scope for reasonable debate on the question.) As of September 2021, seven states had mask mandates for indoor places that applied even to vaccinated individuals: Hawaii, Illinois, Louisiana, Nevada, New Mexico, Oregon, and Washington.[157] Many localities in the other 43 states also had mask mandates. The only states never to have had a mask mandate are Arizona, Florida, Georgia, Idaho, Missouri, Nebraska, Oklahoma, South Carolina, South Dakota, and Tennessee.[158]

Another policy to have emerged recently, with a very clear anti-freedom orientation, is prohibitions on vaccination requirements by private institutions. According to Ballotpedia, "20 states—Alabama, Alaska, Arizona, Arkansas, Florida, Georgia, Idaho, Indiana, Iowa, Missouri, Montana, North Dakota, Ohio, Oklahoma, South Carolina, South Dakota, Tennessee, Texas, Utah, and Wyoming"—ban vaccination requirements in the private sector.[159]

In the wake of lengthy, pandemic-related public emergencies, sometimes granting governors unilateral powers to implement widespread shutdowns of the private economy, legislatures have taken a second look at gubernatorial emergency powers.[160] The most significant changes occurred where strongly Republican legislatures faced off against Democratic governors, as in Kentucky and Pennsylvania. Kentucky's legislature limited the governor's emergency orders to 30 days unless extended by the legislature and required the governor to seek approval from the attorney general when issuing orders that suspend statutes during an emergency. Pennsylvania adopted constitutional amendments limiting emergency declarations to 21 days unless extended by the legislature and allowed the Pennsylvania General Assembly to pass resolutions terminating emergencies (i.e., without legislation that would require a governor's signature).

156. "US Appeals Court Sides with KY Governor in Closing Schools," *Lexington Herald Leader,* November 29, 2020.
157. Andy Markowitz, "State-by-State Guide to Face Mask Requirements," AARP, September 16, 2021.
158. Raifman et al., "State Policy Database."
159. "State Government Policies about Vaccine Requirements (Vaccine Passports)," Ballotpedia.
160. "Changes to State Emergency Power Laws in Response to the Coronavirus (COVID-19) Pandemic, 2020–2021," Ballotpedia.

As noted in the prior section, many pro-freedom trends were prompted by the pandemic, particularly in the areas of education, health care licensing, and alcohol takeout and delivery. The lockdowns were mostly short-lived, and it seems unlikely that states will return to them. Thus, despite the initial overreaction of most states to the pandemic, the American states can generally be credited with reasonable, freedom-respectful responses to the pandemic in the long run, especially compared with international governments. To be sure, not a single state distinguished itself with a consistently pro-freedom orientation throughout the pandemic, but many states have now an essentially free-market approach to pandemic policies, letting private institutions lead the way and discover how best to manage what is rapidly becoming an endemic part of our life as a species.

CONCLUSIONS

In the first section of the book, we built and justified our index of freedom across the 50 states in the period 2000–2019. Our index of freedom can be broken down into three dimensions: fiscal freedom, regulatory freedom, and personal freedom. Fiscal and regulatory freedoms together we dub "economic freedom."

It turns out that economic freedom is more often found in more conservative states that tend to vote Republican in presidential elections, although exceptions exist, and the relationship was weaker in 2000 than it is now. Personal freedom is all over the map. It doesn't seem to have any relationship with more or less conservative or progressive states. The relationship is just noisier and more uncertain than that between ideology and economic freedom.

Another reason that freedom tends to prosper in some places and falter in others is institutional design. Much research has been conducted on the effects of institutions on government spending across countries,[161] as well as on institutions and the dynamics of policy change in the American states.[162] Variables of interest include size of the legislature, gubernatorial power, professionalization of the legislature, fiscal decentralization, term limits, and initiative and referendum. In theory, institutions could have consistent effects on individual liberty in one direction or the other, but it is more likely that most institutions affect freedom positively in some areas and negatively in others. For instance, popular initiatives have helped pass strict tax limitation rules, such as Colorado's Taxpayer Bill of Rights, but have also allowed

---

161. See, for instance, Torsten Persson and Guido Tabellini, *The Economic Effects of Constitutions* (Cambridge, MA: MIT Press, 2003).

162. See, for instance, Charles R. Shipan and Craig Volden, "Bottom-Up Federalism: The Diffusion of Antismoking Policies from U.S. Cities to States," *American Journal of Political Science* 50, no. 4 (2006): 825–43.

massive spending increases to become law, such as Florida's 2002 initiative requiring that universal prekindergarten be offered throughout the state and a 2000 initiative requiring construction of a high-speed rail system to connect Florida's five major cities.

Although macro phenomena like partisan lean and corruption have a big impact on freedom, we must not discount the role of political entrepreneurs and individual activists at the state and local levels. The late Jerry Kopel, a Colorado legislator and activist, authored the original "sunrise" and "sunset" legislation for occupational licensing agencies and maintained a website where he kept a close watch on licensing regulation.[163] Quite probably because of Kopel's indefatigable efforts, Colorado remains among the highest-rated states in the nation for occupational freedom.

Next, we examine the consequences of freedom for migration and economic growth. We find strong evidence that states with more freedom attract more residents. We can be especially confident of the relationships between economic freedom (both a lighter fiscal impact and the regulatory impact of government policy) and net in-migration; both were statistically significant in every model we ran. Personal freedom was significant in 21 of 22 models, and the only model in which it was not significant controlled for violent crime and found a positive relationship between violent crime and in-migration, which seems likely to be spurious. More important than statistical significance, the estimates suggested that the effects of each dimension of freedom on in-migration are economically significant as well.[164]

One channel by which economic freedom affects in-migration is by increasing economic growth. We found a robust relationship between economic freedom in one year and income growth in the next. It was impossible, however, to disentangle the relative contributions of fiscal and regulatory policy from this result, as the two are positively correlated with each other.

Freedom is not the only determinant of personal satisfaction and fulfillment, but as our analysis of migration patterns shows, it makes a tangible difference for people's decisions about where to live. Moreover, we fully expect people in the freer states to develop and benefit from the kinds of institutions (such as symphonies and museums) and amenities (such as better restaurants and cultural attractions) seen in some of the older cities on the coast, and in less free states such as California and New York, as they grow and prosper. Indeed, urban development expert and journalist Joel Kotkin recently made a similar point about the not-so-sexy urban areas that

163. See Jerry Kopel's website, jerrykopel.com.

164. On the distinction between economic and statistical significance, see Stephen T. Ziliak and Deirdre N. McCloskey, *The Cult of Statistical Significance: How the Standard Error Costs Us Jobs, Justice, and Lives* (Ann Arbor: University of Michigan Press, 2008).

were best situated to recover from the 2008–2009 economic downturn:

> Of course, none of the cities in our list competes right now with New York, Chicago, or L.A. in terms of art, culture, and urban amenities, which tend to get noticed by journalists and casual travelers. But once upon a time, all those great cities were also seen as cultural backwaters. And in the coming decades, as more people move in and open restaurants, museums, and sports arenas, who's to say Oklahoma City can't be Oz?[165]

These things take time, but the same kind of dynamic freedom enjoyed in Chicago or New York in the 19th century—that led to their rise—might propel places in the middle of the country to be a bit hipper to those with urbane tastes.

Lastly, we would stress that the variance in liberty at the state level in the United States is quite small in the global context. Even New York provides a much freer environment for the individual than most countries. There are no Burmas or North Koreas among the American states. Still, our federal system allows states to pursue different policies in a range of important areas. The policy laboratory of federalism has been compromised by centralization, most recently in health insurance, but it is still functioning. We saw the capacity of states to innovate in the direction of freedom nearly a decade ago when Colorado and Washington legalized recreational marijuana. More recently, Arizona's experiments in occupational licensing universality, New Hampshire's Housing Appeals Board, and the expansion of new forms of online gambling in many states show that this capacity is still very much alive.

Regardless of one's views about freedom as we define it, the information this study provides should prove useful to those looking for a better life. As Americans—especially those who are currently less fortunate—grow richer in future years, quality of life will matter more to residence decisions, whereas the imperative of higher-paying employment will decline by comparison. For many Americans, living under laws of which they approve is a constituent element of the good life. As a result, we should expect more ideological "sorting" of the kind economist and geographer Charles Tiebout foresaw. High-quality information on state legal and policy environments will matter a great deal to those seeking an environment friendlier to individual liberty.

---

165.   Joel Kotkin, "Welcome to Recoveryland: The Top 10 Places in America Poised for Recovery," November 9, 2010, joelkotkin.com.

PART 3
FREEDOM STATE BY STATE

The following state profiles contain (a) a chart of each state's personal, economic, and overall freedom rankings over time (because these are ranks, *lower* numbers are better); (b) key facts on each state; (c) a descriptive analysis of each state's freedom situation; and (d) three specific policy recommendations that would increase freedom in each state. We have chosen policy recommendations that would have the greatest effects on the state's freedom score, consistent with its political environment. For instance, urging New York to pass a right-to-work law would be futile, but eliminating rent control through state legislation might be more feasible. The discussions for each state represent the policy environment as of our data cutoff date, although we have attempted to note some of the most significant policy changes that occurred after that date.

KEY TO THE PROFILES

The following profiles contain some basic information about each state, including the state's freedom rankings over time and various institutional, political, demographic, and economic indicators of interest. The next page provides a brief description of each element contained in the profiles, keyed to the sample profile below. It also supplies more information about the variables we have chosen to include.

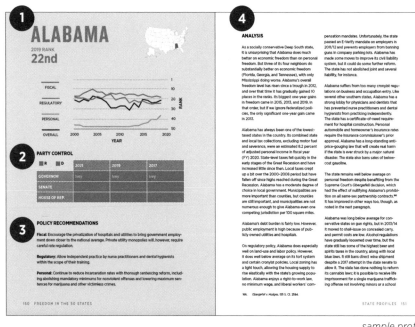

sample profile

1. STATE ID

State Name

State profiles appear in alphabetical order. The District of Columbia and unincorporated organized territories are not included in this index.

State Rankings

Each state's overall rank for 2019 is displayed prominently at the top of the spread, next to the state name. A chart below the state name presents the state's segmented, historical rankings for each year from 2000 to 2019.

2. PARTY CONTROL

This section provides information on party control of the legislature and governorship between 2017 and 2021. Red indicates Republican control; blue indicates Democratic control. The table also gives the name of the governor. Unified party control of the legislature and governor's office allows observers to ascribe responsibility for policy actions to the party in control. One topic for political science research is how unified Republican, unified Democratic, and divided state governments affect the policy environment on fiscal, regulatory, and personal freedom issues.

3. POLICY RECOMMENDATIONS

There are three policy recommendations for each state, corresponding to the three dimensions of freedom: fiscal policy, regulatory policy, and personal freedom, in that order. We considered three criteria as we decided which policy recommendations to include in this book:

1. **Importance.** The recommended policy change would result in a significant boost to the state's freedom score.

2. **Anomalousness.** The policy change would correct a significant deviation of the state's policies from national norms.

3. **Feasibility.** The policy change would likely prove popular, taking into account the state's ideological orientation and the political visibility of the issue.

4. ANALYSIS

The analysis section of each state profile begins with an introduction and then discusses fiscal, regulatory, and personal freedom issues in the state, in that order.

ALABAMA

2019 RANK
22nd

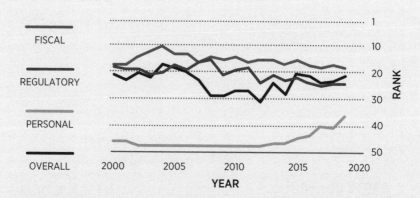

	FISCAL
	REGULATORY
	PERSONAL
	OVERALL

RANK axis: 1, 10, 20, 30, 40, 50
YEAR axis: 2000, 2005, 2010, 2015, 2020

PARTY CONTROL

■ R ■ D

	2021	2019	2017
GOVERNOR	Ivey	Ivey	Ivey
SENATE			
HOUSE OF REP.			

POLICY RECOMMENDATIONS

Fiscal: Encourage the privatization of hospitals and utilities to bring government employment down closer to the national average. Private utility monopolies will, however, require careful rate regulation.

Regulatory: Allow independent practice by nurse practitioners and dental hygienists within the scope of their training.

Personal: Continue to reduce incarceration rates with thorough sentencing reform, including abolishing mandatory minimums for nonviolent offenses and lowering maximum sentences for marijuana and other victimless crimes.

ANALYSIS

As a socially conservative Deep South state, it is unsurprising that Alabama does much better on economic freedom than on personal freedom. But three of its four neighbors do substantially better on economic freedom (Florida, Georgia, and Tennessee), with only Mississippi doing worse. Alabama's overall freedom level has risen since a trough in 2012, and over that time it has gradually gained 10 places in the ranks. Its biggest one-year gains in freedom came in 2015, 2013, and 2019, in that order, but if we ignore federalized policies, the only significant one-year gain came in 2013.

Alabama has always been one of the lowest-taxed states in the country. Its combined state and local tax collections, excluding motor fuel and severance, were an estimated 8.2 percent of adjusted personal income in fiscal year (FY) 2020. State-level taxes fell quickly in the early stages of the Great Recession and have increased little since then. Local taxes crept up a bit over the 2000–2008 period but have fallen off since highs reached during the Great Recession. Alabama has a moderate degree of choice in local government. Municipalities are more important than counties, but counties are still important, and municipalities are not numerous enough to give Alabama even one competing jurisdiction per 100 square miles.

Alabama's debt burden is fairly low. However, public employment is high because of publicly owned utilities and hospitals.

On regulatory policy, Alabama does especially well on land-use and labor policy. However, it does well below average on its tort system and certain cronyist policies. Local zoning has a light touch, allowing the housing supply to rise elastically with the state's growing population. Alabama enjoys a right-to-work law, no minimum wage, and liberal workers' com-

pensation mandates. Unfortunately, the state passed an E-Verify mandate on employers in 2011/12 and prevents employers from banning guns in company parking lots. Alabama has made some moves to improve its civil liability system, but it could do some further reform. The state has not abolished joint and several liability, for instance.

Alabama suffers from too many cronyist regulations on business and occupation entry. Like several other southern states, Alabama has a strong lobby for physicians and dentists that has prevented nurse practitioners and dental hygienists from practicing independently. The state has a certificate-of-need requirement for hospital construction. Personal automobile and homeowner's insurance rates require the insurance commissioner's prior approval. Alabama has a long-standing anti-price-gouging law that will create real harm if the state is ever struck by a major natural disaster. The state also bans sales of below-cost gasoline.

The state remains well below average on personal freedom despite benefiting from the Supreme Court's *Obergefell* decision, which had the effect of nullifying Alabama's prohibition on all same-sex partnership contracts.[166] It has improved in other ways too, though, as noted in the next paragraph.

Alabama was long below average for conservative states on gun rights, but in 2013/14 it moved to shall-issue on concealed carry, and permit costs are low. Alcohol regulations have gradually loosened over time, but the state still has some of the highest beer and spirits taxes in the country, along with local blue laws. It still bans direct wine shipment despite a 2017 attempt in the state senate to allow it. The state has done nothing to reform its cannabis laws; it is possible to receive life imprisonment for a single marijuana trafficking offense not involving minors or a school

---

166.   *Obergefell v. Hodges*, 135 S. Ct. 2584.

zone. Alabama long had a much higher incarceration rate than the national average, even adjusting for its violent and property crime rates. But since 2014, that rate has come down substantially. Alabama's police do not actually pursue arrests for victimless crimes very vigorously. The state continues to suspend driver's licenses for drug offenses unrelated to driving. Despite substantially reducing its prison collect call rate in 2015, the state still has one of the highest rates in the country. Alabama does much better than average on tobacco freedom because of low taxes and relatively lenient smoking bans on private property. The state is mediocre on educational freedom but did enact a modest private scholarship tax-credit law in 2013/14.

ALASKA

24th

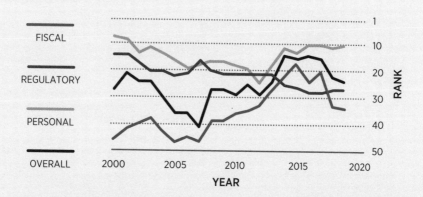

- FISCAL
- REGULATORY
- PERSONAL
- OVERALL

RANK — 1, 10, 20, 30, 40, 50

YEAR — 2000, 2005, 2010, 2015, 2020

PARTY CONTROL

■ R   ■ D

	2021	2019	2017
GOVERNOR	Dunleavy	Dunleavy	Walker, Ind.
SENATE			
HOUSE OF REP.			

POLICY RECOMMENDATIONS

Fiscal: Cut spending in the areas of grossest overspending relative to national averages: education, corrections, administration (especially financial administration and public buildings), housing and community development spending, and "miscellaneous commercial activities." Use the proceeds to reduce the corporate income tax permanently, helping the economy diversify away from energy.

Regulatory: Enact a right-to-work law to attract manufacturing investment.

Personal: Reform asset forfeiture to require a criminal conviction before forfeiture and to require Department of Justice equitable sharing proceeds to follow the same procedure.

ANALYSIS

Alaska is an unusual state because of its enormous oil and gas reserves and revenues. Its fiscal policy scores fluctuate wildly depending on the global price of oil. With the end of the commodity boom in the 2000s, corporate income tax collections plummeted in Alaska, and the state buffered the decline with large withdrawals from its enormous rainy-day fund. Alaska has by far the highest cash-to-liability ratio of any state.[167] Since 2017, state-level revenues have rebounded, making it look like a deteriorating fiscal policy position. In reality, the true long-term stance of Alaskan fiscal policy is likely about average, and it has improved since the 2000s when the size of government was clearly bigger.

Alaska's enviable net asset position has also made for something of a "resource curse" in the state's expenditures. Of the employed population in Alaska, 15 percent work in state or local government, nearly 2 standard deviations above average—but it was nearly 17 percent back in 2002. Government consumption is similarly high. Although local taxes outstrip state taxes (which are quite low)—lately by a wide margin—local jurisdictions are so consolidated that virtually no choice exists among local government options.

Despite its attractive overall fiscal situation, or perhaps because of it, Alaska does poorly on several important regulatory policy indicators and does middling overall. The labor market is far more regulated than one would expect for such a conservative state. There is no right-to-work law; the state has strict workers' compensation mandates and a high minimum wage ($10.34 per hour in 2020). Many occupations are licensed in Anchorage and Fairbanks, where about half of the state's population lives. On the one hand, insurance is pretty heavily regulated. On the other hand, Alaska gives a good bit of practice freedom to nurses and dental hygienists, does not zone out low-cost housing, and has one of the nation's best civil liability systems (an area in which the state has improved a great deal during the past 25 years).

As one of the country's most libertarian states, Alaska has always done well on personal freedom and reached the top 10 in 2016 for the first time since 2001. Drug arrests are quite low (1.5 standard deviations below average); crime-adjusted incarceration is below the national average and, like most places, dropping; marijuana is legal; homeschooling is unregulated; and gun rights are secure (for instance, concealed carry of handguns does not require a license). However, the state used to have one of the most anti-gay-marriage laws in the nation, forbidding even private partnership contracts for same-sex couples. (Of course, *Obergefell* federalized the issue and overturned such laws.) The state's civil asset forfeiture law is among the worst in the country, which probably accounts for why local police do not bother to ask the Department of Justice to "adopt" many cases. The burden of proof is on the owner of the property to prove innocence, property is subject to forfeiture from mere probable cause, and the proceeds largely go to law enforcement. Sales of all alcohol, even beer, are prohibited in grocery stores. Alcohol taxes, especially for beer, are also among the highest in the country. Gambling freedom is low, and the cigarette tax is high at $2 per pack in 2019 ($5 a pack in Juneau). There is no helmet law for motorcyclists.

---

167.   Eileen Norcross, "Ranking the States by Fiscal Condition," Mercatus Research, Mercatus Center at George Mason University, Arlington, VA, July 2015.

ARIZONA

2019 RANK
9th

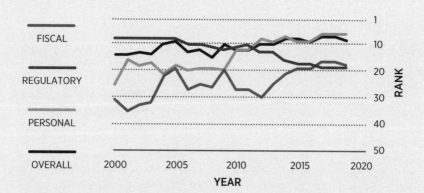

FISCAL

REGULATORY

PERSONAL

OVERALL

RANK

YEAR

PARTY CONTROL

■ R   ■ D

	2021	2019	2017
GOVERNOR	Ducey	Ducey	Ducey
SENATE			
HOUSE OF REP.			

POLICY RECOMMENDATIONS

Fiscal: Provide an easy procedure for small groups of neighborhoods to incorporate new municipalities, either out of unincorporated areas or out of existing cities. Keep state aid to localities at a low level to allow local jurisdictions to provide different levels and mixes of public goods according to the desires of their residents.

Regulatory: Provide for full competition in telecommunications and cable, allowing different wireline and wireless companies to attract customers without service mandates, price controls, or local franchising exactions.

Personal: Legalize for-profit casinos and card games.

ANALYSIS

Arizona has moved up in the overall rankings during the past two decades, improving considerably on personal freedom while maintaining above-average performance on economic freedom. It has lost ground consistently on regulatory policy but is still ranked in the top 20.

Fiscal policy has typically been more of a problem than regulatory policy, but the two have converged over the years. State and local taxes are 8.9 percent of adjusted personal income, well below average. Although local taxes are around the national average, state-level taxes are reasonably low. The state depends heavily on sales taxes, permitting generally low individual and business income taxes. Arizona has very little scope for choice among local jurisdictions. Although municipalities are more important than counties, there are only 91 municipalities in the whole state. Debt and government consumption are below average, and government employment is a lot better than average, at only 10.5 percent of the private sector.

On regulatory policy, Arizona is one of the best in the country with regard to anti-cronyism. In most industries, business entry and prices are quite liberalized. However, occupational licensing has ratcheted up substantially over time. The state has no certificate-of-need laws for hospital construction or movers. The right-to-work law probably attracts manufacturing businesses, and the state passed statewide cable franchising in 2018. It has a higher-than-federal minimum wage that has risen significantly because of Proposition 206, which was passed by popular vote in 2016. That law meant a rise from $8.05 per hour to $10 per hour, with subsequent increases to $10.50 per hour in 2018, $11 per hour in 2019, and $12 per hour in 2020. It also has an E-Verify mandate. Although land-use regulation tightened in the 1990s and early 2000s, a regulatory takings initiative may have curbed its growth a little since 2006.

Arizona's personal freedom improvements are due to growing gun rights ("constitutional carry" passed in 2009/10); a medical marijuana law; school vouchers (passed in 2011/12); declining victimless crime arrests; the abolition of its sodomy law because of the Supreme Court decision in *Lawrence v. Texas*;[168] the judicial legalization of same-sex marriage; liberalization of its wine shipment laws; and a significant asset forfeiture reform in 2017. On the other side of the ledger, incarceration rates are still quite high, climbing relatively consistently until reaching their peak in 2014 and then moving down slightly after that. Arizona's cigarette taxes are higher than average, and smoking bans have become comprehensive and airtight. (The latter, like the state's minimum wage, is explained in part by the ballot initiative, which really does result in some observable "tyranny of the majority.") There are local vaping bans. The state banned driving while talking or texting on a handheld cell phone in 2019. Not much change has been observed in alcohol freedom, where the state is better than average, or gambling freedom, where the state is worse than average.

---

168.   *Lawrence v. Texas*, 539 U.S. 558 (2003).

ARKANSAS

2019 RANK

23rd

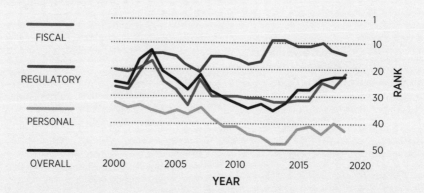

FISCAL

REGULATORY

PERSONAL

OVERALL

RANK

YEAR

PARTY CONTROL

		2021	2019	2017
■ R ■ D				
GOVERNOR		Hutchinson	Hutchinson	Hutchinson
SENATE				
HOUSE OF REP.				

POLICY RECOMMENDATIONS

Fiscal: Cut the state sales and use tax, which is high. Let local governments vary property taxes to meet local needs and desires, reducing state aid for education and other purposes.

Regulatory: Roll back occupational licensing. Some occupations that could be deregulated include sanitarians, title abstractors, interpreters, dietitians and nutritionists, pharmacy technicians, veterinary technologists, opticians, athletic trainers, occupational therapist assistants, massage therapists, private detectives, security guards, landscaping contractors, tree trimmers (locally), funeral apprentices, collection agents, 911 dispatchers, tree injectors, construction contractors, security alarm installers, well drillers, mobile home installers, and boiler operators.

Personal: Enact a generous tax credit for contributions to private scholarships for K–12 education.

ANALYSIS

Arkansas has been mediocre on economic freedom for most of the past two decades, but it improved on regulatory policy in the early 2010s and on fiscal policy in the past four years, restoring the state nearly to heights not seen since George W. Bush's first term. Arkansas has ranked consistently worse than most states on personal freedom, declining substantially relative to others since 2007 and receiving very little bump from the Supreme Court's legalization of same-sex marriage in 2015.

Arkansas's tax burden is about average, but the state is highly fiscally centralized. State taxes are way above the national average, and local taxes are way below. The overall tax burden has drifted downward since FY 2014. Debt is low, but government employment at 13.1 percent of private employment is high (though declining consistently since 2010). Government gross domestic product (GDP) has fallen from 11.3 percent of income in 2013 to 9.9 percent in 2019.

Arkansas does well on land use despite its unreformed eminent domain laws. Still, our proxies for zoning stringency show a growth in such restrictions over time. The state has above-average labor-market freedom, although it began regular minimum-wage increases in 2014 because of a popular initiative; minimum wage stands at $11 as of 2021. The state has a problem with cronyism, especially on entry and price controls. The

extent of occupational licensing is more than a standard deviation worse than the national average. Hospital construction requires a certificate of need, the state has an anti-price-gouging law, and also a general law against "unfair pricing" or sales below cost. However, Arkansas does better than most other southern states, and indeed better than the national average, on its civil liability regime. Like most other states, it did not replace the federal government's health insurance individual mandate and, therefore, saw a bump up on health insurance freedom in 2019.

Arkansas is one of the worst states in the country on criminal justice policies. Its crime-adjusted incarceration rate is more than a standard deviation worse than the national average and has not come down much recently, while its drug enforcement rate has moved in the wrong direction. It also suspends driver's licenses for those with drug offenses unrelated to driving. In contrast, it has improved significantly on gun rights with the adoption of constitutional carry for both concealed and open carry in 2018. Marijuana laws are largely unreformed, although voters did pass a medical marijuana initiative in 2016. Arkansas deviates little from the average on many personal freedom policies. School choice remains an opportunity for improvement, given the state's fiscal centralization (education funding comes substantially from the state), its generally conservative ideological orientation, and its minority student populations. A voucher program for students with disabilities was adopted in 2017.

CALIFORNIA

2019 RANK

48th

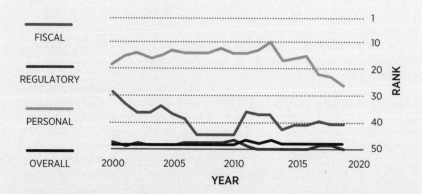

FISCAL

REGULATORY

PERSONAL

OVERALL

RANK

YEAR

PARTY CONTROL

		2021	2019	2017
GOVERNOR		Newsom	Newsom	Brown
SENATE				
ASSEMBLY				

■ R ■ D

POLICY RECOMMENDATIONS

Fiscal: Cut spending in the areas of health and hospitals, public welfare operations, and employee retirement. Use the proceeds to reduce indebtedness.

Regulatory: Liberalize the housing market with targeted preemption, incentives, and institutional changes.

Personal: Expand legal gambling. California's political culture is unlikely to have many qualms about gaming, but legalizing nontribal casinos would require a constitutional amendment.

ANALYSIS

California is one of the least free states in the country, largely because of its long-standing poor performance on economic freedom. However, California's economic freedom has improved since the late 2000s and, perhaps as a result, so has its economic performance. California has long suffered from a wide disparity between its economic freedom and personal freedom ranking, but it is not as if the state is a top performer in the latter dimension. Indeed, it is quite mediocre on personal freedom, although its recent decline in rank has more to do with other states catching up and passing it than any backsliding in the state itself.

Despite Proposition 13, California is one of the highest-taxed states in the country. California's combined state and local tax collections were 10.9 percent of adjusted personal income. Moreover, because of the infamous *Serrano*[169] decision on school funding, California is a fiscally centralized state. Local taxes are about average nationally, whereas state taxes are well above average. But the fiscal situation in California is much better now than in the 2000s, and the state's government employment is now much lower than the national average, at 11.0 percent of private employment. Government GDP has fallen from 12.3 percent of income in 2009 to 10.3 percent in 2019.

Regulatory policy is more of a problem for the state than fiscal policy. California is one of the worst states on land-use freedom. Some cities have rent control, new housing supply is tightly restricted in the coastal areas despite high demand, and eminent domain reform has been nugatory. The state even mandates speech protections in privately owned shopping malls. Labor law is anti-employment, with no right-to-work law, high minimum wages, strict workers' compensation mandates, mandated short-term disability insurance, stricter-than-federal anti-discrimination law, and prohibitions on consensual non-compete agreements. Occupational licensing is extensive and strict, especially in construction trades. The state is tied for worst in nursing practice freedom. The state's mandatory cancer labeling law (Proposition 65) has significant economic costs.[170] California is one of the worst states for consumers' freedom of choice in homeowner's and automobile insurance. On the plus side, the state has no certificate-of-need law for new hospitals and has made some moves to deregulate cable and telecommunications, and the civil liability regime has improved gradually during the past 14 years.

California is a classic left-wing state on social issues. Gun rights are among the weakest in the country and have been weakened consistently over time. It was one of the first states to adopt a smoking ban on private property, which was further tightened in 2016. Cigarette taxes were hiked substantially in 2017. It has adopted strict, anti-scientific vaping bans and bans on flavored e-cigarettes (locally and under 21 statewide). California was an early leader on cannabis liberalization and retains that position today with full legalization. Alcohol is not as strictly regulated as in most other states, and booze taxes are relatively low. Physician-assisted suicide was legalized in 2015. Private school choice programs are nonexistent, but private schools and homeschools are mostly lightly regulated. Incarceration and drug arrest rates used to be higher than average but have fallen over time, especially since 2010. The state was a leader in marriage freedom, adopting same-sex partnerships and then civil unions fairly early.

---

169.   *Serrano v. Priest*, 5 Cal.3d 584 (1971).

170.   David R. Henderson, "Proposition 65: When Government Cries Wolf," *Econlog*, April 14, 2013.

COLORADO

2019 RANK
12th

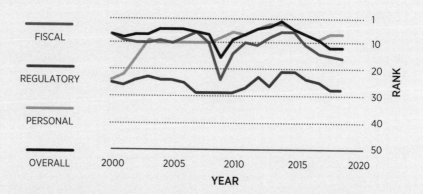

FISCAL

REGULATORY

PERSONAL

OVERALL

RANK

1
10
20
30
40
50

2000   2005   2010   2015   2020

YEAR

PARTY CONTROL

■ R   ■ D

	2021	2019	2017
GOVERNOR	Polis	Polis	Hickenlooper
SENATE			
HOUSE OF REP.			

POLICY RECOMMENDATIONS

Fiscal: Trim spending on airports, general administration, and parks and recreation (a category that excludes conservation lands), where spending is above the national average. Build up the rainy-day fund and cut taxes.

Regulatory: Remove remaining barriers to entry and competitive pricing, such as property and casualty rate classification restrictions, the drug price-gouging law, household goods mover licensing, and the sales-below-cost law.

Personal: Require all equitable sharing revenues from the Department of Justice to follow state-level procedures for civil asset forfeiture.

ANALYSIS

Colorado has long been one of America's freer states, but it falls out of the top 10 in this edition. It does best on personal and fiscal freedom. Since 2006, we note an increasing divergence: falling economic freedom and rising personal freedom, both of which roughly cancel each other out.

Colorado's overall state and local tax burden is an estimated 8.9 percent of adjusted personal income, lower than the national average. State-level taxes have remained more or less constant during the past 20 years, with some gyrations due more to economic fluctuations than policy changes. Local tax revenues have also remained roughly steady and seem to be less sensitive to economic downturns than state revenues. Although fiscal decentralization is high when measured as the ratio of local to state taxes, there isn't much choice of local government, given the importance of counties and the paucity of incorporated cities. Debt has fallen below average after peaking in FY 2010. State and local employment is lower than average and has dipped to 11.7 percent of private employment from a high of 12.8 percent less than a decade ago. But it is still higher than it was in 2000.

Colorado ranks fifth on freedom from cronyism, although it is below average on regulatory policy as a whole. It earns its good ranking in our cronyism index because of its relatively open occupational licensing system, including broad scope of practice for health care professionals and lack of a certificate-of-need law for hospitals. However, occupational freedom declined noticeably in 2019 (pharmacy technicians and athletic trainers were licensed, and restrictive statutory language increased). Colorado also requires household goods movers to get certificates of public convenience and necessity, prohibits price increases for pharmaceuticals during emergencies, and proscribes all "unfair" pricing in gasoline specifically and in other industries. Its legal regime for torts is much better than average. In 2013/14, the state deregulated telecommunications somewhat, though it still lacks statewide video franchising. It is a little below average on labor-market freedom, with no right-to-work law and a high minimum wage (because of a 2016 voter-approved amendment, the state saw regular increases through 2020 until it reached $12 per hour and is now adjusted for cost of living). Colorado's land-use freedom has declined modestly, and its renewable portfolio standard for electricity is much stricter than the national average and probably results in higher rates.

Colorado started out personally freer than the average state in 2000 and is now among the personally freest states. It has led the way with the legalization of the cultivation and sale of recreational marijuana, which occurred in stages from 2012 to 2014. Legal gambling and gun rights are above average, although the qualifications for carry licensure are fairly strict, and large-capacity firearm magazines are banned. Its beer, wine, and spirits taxes are much better than average. In 2018, beer was allowed into grocery stores. State asset forfeiture law is good, and equitable sharing participation has fallen in recent years. Crime-adjusted incarceration rates are about the national average, but drug arrests are low. The state enacted civil unions in 2013 and then was judicially granted same-sex marriage in 2014. Voters approved physician-assisted suicide in 2016. Educational freedom is somewhat below average, as the state has no private school choice programs. But the state has long enjoyed public school choice. As noted in the post-2020 update in Part 2, Colorado has become the first state to end qualified immunity across the board.

CONNECTICUT

2019 RANK
36th

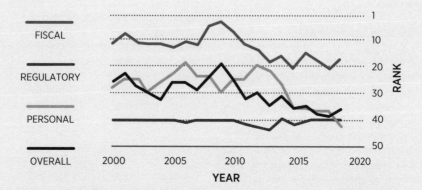

FISCAL

REGULATORY

PERSONAL

OVERALL

RANK

YEAR

PARTY CONTROL

■ R   ■ D

	2021	2019	2017
GOVERNOR	Lamont	Lamont	Malloy
SENATE			
HOUSE OF REP.			

POLICY RECOMMENDATIONS

Fiscal: Build up sinking and rainy-day funds and pay down debt to reduce the interest burden.

Regulatory: Enact statewide restrictions on eminent domain.

Personal: Legalize recreational marijuana.

ANALYSIS

Connecticut has been on a long, slow decline in freedom. As recently as 2009 it was in the top 20, but it is now flirting with the bottom 10. It suffers most from having consistently stifling regulatory policy that drags down its economic freedom ranking while—perhaps surprisingly for a New England "blue" state— also performing relatively poorly on personal freedom as other states have leapfrogged it.

After getting hit hard by the Great Recession, state revenues have bounced back strongly, and the state's fiscal policy score has suffered somewhat. Most of the decline in the state's fiscal policy rank is exaggerated by this phenomenon and by the fact that other states have passed it by, rather than Connecticut actually falling in an absolute sense. Although Connecticut residents enjoy broad scope of choice among local governments, state government tax collections are about 40 percent greater than local tax collections, making the choice of local government less valuable. Government GDP and employment have fallen over the long run, relative to private-sector equivalents, and are well below national averages. Meanwhile, debt has risen to 20.0 percent of income and is now about average, whereas cash and security assets are below average at 9.6 percent of income.

Connecticut does poorly in most areas of regulatory policy. Exclusionary zoning is common. Renewable portfolio standards are tight, keeping electric rates high. The state has a minimum wage; the legislature has repeatedly raised it, resulting in a rate of $12 per hour as of 2021. The state also lacks a right-to-work law. Like most states, Connecticut has declined over time on occupational freedom. However, in 2013/14, the state legalized independent nurse practitioner practice with prescription authority, a significant achievement. Price regulation in the property and casualty market became more interventionist from 2011 to 2016 but has now eased again. The civil liability system is mediocre. Cable franchising moved to the state level in 2007, but telecommunications has not been deregulated significantly yet.

On personal freedom, Connecticut has improved over the years in absolute terms, although it dipped slightly in 2019. However, it has not kept up with other states and has slipped in the rankings. Despite Connecticut's gun manufacturing tradition, firearms are strictly regulated. The state decriminalized low-level possession of cannabis and enacted a medical marijuana law in 2011/12. Alcohol taxes are relatively low, and alcohol blue laws were finally repealed in 2012. The state has no private school choice programs. Cigarette taxes are sky-high ($4.35 a pack in 2021), and smoking bans, except for private workplaces, are tight. Vaping was added to that ban in 2015. Crime-adjusted incarceration rates have fallen consistently since 2007 but are still higher than those of other New England states. Victimless crime arrests are much lower than the national average. Asset forfeiture was reformed in 2017. The state legalized same-sex marriage in 2007/8. Travel freedom has declined since the fourth edition because of new requirements for uninsured and underinsured coverage, but driver's licenses have been available since 2013 to residents without Social Security numbers.

DELAWARE

2019 RANK
44th

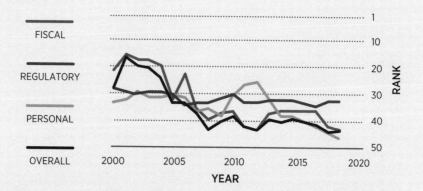

FISCAL

REGULATORY

PERSONAL

OVERALL

RANK

YEAR

PARTY CONTROL

■ R ■ D	2021	2019	2017
GOVERNOR	Carney	Carney	Carney
SENATE			
HOUSE OF REP.			

POLICY RECOMMENDATIONS

Fiscal: Reduce state-level taxes and education spending. Delaware is one of the freest-spending states in the country on education. Allow local governments to pick up more of the school spending out of their own fiscal resources.

Regulatory: Liberalize land-use regulation with targeted preemption, incentives, and institutional reforms.

Personal: Eliminate or significantly limit civil asset forfeiture, consistent with reform trends across the country aimed at protecting the individual property rights of innocent people before conviction.

ANALYSIS

How the mighty have fallen! Once a stalwart near the top of economic freedom indexes, Delaware has lost tremendous ground during the past 20 years. It now ranks in or near the bottom third on all three dimensions of freedom, earning its 44th place by all-around poor performance. Part of the reason for this low ranking is that the state had one of the most free-market health insurance systems before the enactment of the Patient Protection and Affordable Care Act (PPACA), and so it suffered disproportionately because of the federal law. Moreover, its much-touted advantage on corporate law is now significantly overstated.

On fiscal policy, Delaware has floundered ever since the mid-2000s. The overall tax burden, at about 10.9 percent of personal income, is worse than average, and the state is highly fiscally centralized with most of the tax burden at the state level. With 1.6 competing jurisdictions per 100 square miles, Delawareans would stand to benefit were the state to allow more tax space for local governments. Debt and public employment are better than average and have improved of late, but government GDP share and cash and security assets have gone the other way.

Delaware has been getting worse on regulatory policy and is below average in most regulatory policy categories. Labor law is fairly anti-employment, with a minimum wage (though not too high compared with other blue states) and no right to work. Occupational freedom is mediocre, with dental hygienists and nurse practitioners lacking sufficient practice freedom. The state has certificate-of-need laws for hospitals. Land-use regulation ratcheted up significantly in

the 2000–2010 period, as have renewable portfolio standards for utilities. For a long time, the state's insurance commissioners treated property and casualty insurance rates under "prior approval" contrary to statute, according to the Insurance Information Institute, but they have recently been following the law, which is "file and use."[171] The state remains one of a handful that have not joined the Interstate Insurance Product Regulation Compact. Even the state's vaunted liability system has actually deteriorated since 2000 to merely average, we find. The state has enacted no tort reforms, and the size of the legal sector has grown, whether measured in number of lawyers or share of GDP. In 2019, the state enacted a plastic bag ban despite the policy's known health and environmental costs.[172]

Delaware is below the national average in personal freedom. It is below average on gun rights; the biggest problem area is the "may-issue" regime for concealed-carry licensing. Gambling freedom is higher than the national average, and the state was at the forefront of legal online gambling for its own residents. There are no private school choice programs, but homeschooling is easy. Smoking bans are comprehensive, and cigarette taxes were about average until 2017, when the rate was increased 60 cents to $2.10 per pack. The state's medical cannabis law was expanded in 2011/12, and low-level possession was decriminalized in 2015. Alcohol taxes, already a bit lower than average, have eroded over time because of inflation. However, the state bans direct wine shipments. Delaware is roughly average on the overall incarceration and arrests category, but the state's civil asset forfeiture law is tied for worst in the country, with few protections for innocent owners.

---

171.   See the "Metadata" tab of the n_reg_15.xls spreadsheet.

172.   "Sustainable Shopping: Which Bag Is Best?," National Geographic Society, July 10, 2020; Bag the Ban, "Plastic Bags Are the Healthier Option—for Families and the Environment," American Recyclable Plastic Bag Alliance, 2019.

FLORIDA

2019 RANK
2nd

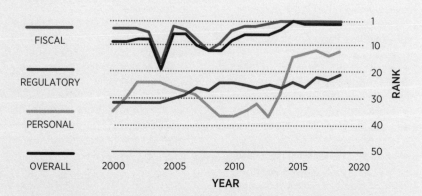

FISCAL

REGULATORY

PERSONAL

OVERALL

RANK

YEAR

PARTY CONTROL

		2021	2019	2017
■ R	■ D			
GOVERNOR		DeSantis	DeSantis	Scott
SENATE				
HOUSE OF REP.				

POLICY RECOMMENDATIONS

Fiscal: Decentralize taxing and spending powers from counties to municipalities and make it easy for municipalities to control their own school districts. More choice of local government should make Floridians freer.

Regulatory: Reform the occupational licensing system to free residents who are currently stymied by those barriers to entry and opportunity. Candidates for deregulation include farm labor contractors, interior designers, medical and clinical laboratory technologists, pharmacy technicians, dispensing opticians, funeral attendants, and bill and account collectors.

Personal: Enact the following criminal justice reforms: (a) close the loophole allowing seizure of cash and monetary instruments without an arrest and close the equitable sharing end run around state forfeiture law; and (b) end driver's license suspensions for drug convictions unrelated to driving, as most of the country has done, and provide "safety valves" from mandatory minimum sentences.

ANALYSIS

Lacking an individual income tax and featuring a hot climate, Florida has long enjoyed substantial in-migration of well-off retirees. But as we've noted in the past, the state attracts more than seniors, as others vote with their feet for good weather and the increased opportunity afforded by Florida's freer society. Florida does especially well on economic freedom, and even more so on fiscal policy. Indeed, it is our top state on both. Regulatory policy is improved but mediocre compared with the fiscal side. Florida's personal freedom has lagged in the past; however, it has improved a lot since 2014.

Florida's state-level tax collections are more than 1.5 standard deviations below the national average, whereas its local tax collections are a little lower than average. Florida's fiscal decentralization does not offer a great deal of choice to homeowners, however, because the state has only about half an effective competing jurisdiction per 100 square miles. Government consumption and debt are lower than average. Government employment is much below average, falling from 11.2 percent of private employment in 2010 to 8.3 percent in 2019.

Florida's regulatory policy is middling relative to other states but has improved in absolute terms, leaving aside federalized policies. Despite the temptations posed by high housing demand, homeowners have been unable to enact exclusionary zoning on anything like the levels of California or New Hampshire. Our two measures of local zoning give a split judgment on just how restrictive Florida is. Land-use regulation appears to be a major political issue, but the courts have tools to restrain local governments, as the state has a particularly strong regulatory takings law. Florida has gone further than just about any other state to tighten criteria for eminent domain. It does have a law restricting employers from banning guns on certain company property, such as parking lots, which violates employers' property rights. Labor law is also above average because of a right-to-work law, but the state has a minimum wage ($10 per hour in 2021). Regulations on managed health care plans are among the worst in the country, with standing referrals, direct access to specialists, and a ban on financial incentives to providers. Cable and telecommunications are partially deregulated. The civil liability system is better than average and has improved significantly since the 2000s. As we long recommended, the state finally reformed its homeowner's insurance sector along competitive lines in 2017, and it also opened up auto insurance rate setting slightly in 2018. On the other side of the ledger, the state is far below average on occupational freedom and has a certificate-of-need law for hospitals. Physician assistants are now free to prescribe, but nurse practitioners and dental hygienists are not yet free from independent practice limitations.

After falling relative to other states for a decade, Florida has improved its personal freedom score with big jumps in 2014 and 2015. It is now well above average. Part of this bump was because of the Supreme Court's nationalization of same-sex marriage. Before that decision, Florida did not recognize any kind of same-sex partnership, and it banned private contracts similar to marriage with a super-DOMA (Defense of Marriage Act). Florida also reformed its civil asset forfeiture regime in 2016, including requiring proof "beyond a reasonable doubt" for forfeitures. On the downside, the state's crime-adjusted incarceration rate has fallen a bit from its high but is still a lot worse than average (although criminal justice reform efforts promise help on that front). Arrests for victimless crimes have fallen significantly. Florida is one of the top states for educational freedom, although homeschool regulations remain substantial. The cannabis regime is largely unreformed despite recent liberalization of medical marijuana policy (which we recommended in the fourth edition), whereas alcohol is lightly regulated despite beer and wine taxes being a bit high. Gun rights are mediocre and became more restrictive in 2018, as the state has waiting periods for handguns, local dealer licensing, and virtually no open carry. It does have a "Stand Your Ground" law and protects the right to use sound suppressors. Tobacco freedom is middling. Automated license plate reader data use and retention have been partially reformed. The state takes DNA from arrestees without a probable cause hearing.

GEORGIA

2019 RANK
8th

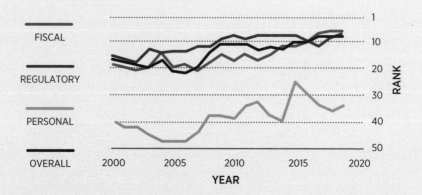

FISCAL

REGULATORY

PERSONAL

OVERALL

RANK

1
10
20
30
40
50

2000   2005   2010   2015   2020

YEAR

PARTY CONTROL

		2021	2019	2017
■ R ■ D				
GOVERNOR		Kemp	Kemp	Deal
SENATE				
HOUSE OF REP.				

POLICY RECOMMENDATIONS

Fiscal: Phase out state-level business subsidies and prohibit them at the local level.

Regulatory: Liberalize health care professions even more: (a) permit independent nurse practitioner practice with prescription authority, (b) allow dental hygienists to clean teeth wholly independently of dentist supervision, and (c) allow physician assistants to prescribe on all schedules.

Personal: Reform civil asset forfeiture by putting the burden of proof on the government, requiring evidence beyond a reasonable doubt that the property was the product of criminal activity, sending forfeiture proceeds to the general fund, and requiring all equitable sharing revenues to meet state standards.

ANALYSIS

Georgia has been one of the fastest-growing southern states, likely because of its strong performance on economic freedom. Economic freedom also drove the state's high overall freedom ranking. However, the state performs poorly on personal freedom despite some consistent absolute improvements since 2006 (even without considering the post-*Obergefell* bump because of the federalization of marriage policy).

State and local taxes were 8.3 percent of adjusted personal income, well below the national average. At 4.6 percent of personal income, state tax collections are significantly below the national average, whereas local taxes—3.7 percent of income—are average. Like most southern states, Georgia has fewer than one effective competing local government per 100 square miles, which reduces the benefit from its fiscal decentralization. Government consumption and debt are substantially lower than average. Government employment used to be around the national average, but Georgia has brought it down from 13.2 percent of private employment in 2010 to 10.4 percent in 2019, more than a standard deviation better than average.

Like other conservative southern states, Georgia does well on labor and land-use policy. It has a right-to-work law, no minimum wage, relaxed workers' compensation regulations, and moderate zoning. It has deregulated telecommunications and enacted statewide video franchising. Unlike some other states in its neighborhood, however, Georgia also enjoys a relatively good civil liability system. The one regulatory policy area where Georgia does somewhat poorly is occupational freedom. The extent of licensing grew most significantly in 2011 and 2014, and health care professions face generally tight scope-of-practice rules, though Georgia joined the Nurse Licensure Compact and gave dental hygienists some independent practice freedom in 2017. The state also maintains certificate-of-need laws for hospitals and moving companies.

On personal freedom, Georgia is about what one would expect from a conservative southern state. Its incarceration rates are very high, even adjusted for crime rates, although victimless crime arrests have fallen and are lower than average. Civil asset forfeiture is unreformed, though equitable sharing has declined in recent years, as in most other states. The burden of proof remains on innocent owners, all proceeds go to law enforcement, and some actions require only probable cause to show that the property is subject to forfeiture. It is one of the worst states for cannabis and gambling. Yet, it is one of the best states for educational freedom, scores well on gun rights, and lightly regulates tobacco use compared with most other states. It has the lowest cigarette taxes as of 2021. It was one of the worst states for marriage freedom, but the state has benefited from the *Obergefell* decision.

HAWAII

2019 RANK

49th

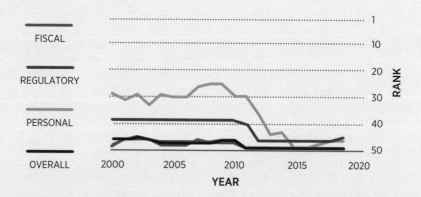

FISCAL

REGULATORY

PERSONAL

OVERALL

RANK

YEAR

PARTY CONTROL

		2021	2019	2017
■R ■D				
GOVERNOR		Ige	Ige	Ige
SENATE				
HOUSE OF REP.				

POLICY RECOMMENDATIONS

Fiscal: Local government looks quite inefficient. The state spends far more than the national average on air transportation, sanitation and sewerage, parks and recreation, public buildings, health and hospitals, and interest payments. Cut spending in these areas and cut local taxes.

Regulatory: Relax the state's extreme land-use regulations. Allow residential uses on land deemed "agricultural," and eliminate either state or county review, which are duplicative.

Personal: Legalize sale and possession of recreational marijuana.

ANALYSIS

Hawaii has long had one of the lowest levels of economic freedom in the country, but it has also slid behind on personal freedom. Thus, it isn't surprising that Hawaii is now the second least-free state in the Union. Even with its huge locational rents, Hawaii has experienced a net outflow of residents to the rest of the United States since at least the beginning of the past decade.

Hawaii's fiscal policy is decidedly tax and spend. State-level taxes rose from an already high estimated 8.3 percent of personal income in FY 2009 to 10.5 percent in FY 2020. Local government also taxes at a very high level given how little it has to do (state government runs schools). Government debt is much higher than the national average. Government employment is at about the national average, as is government GDP share.

Hawaii does poorly in almost every area of regulatory policy, but its two worst categories are land-use and labor-market freedom. It has among the strictest restrictions on residential building in the country. Eminent domain abuse is unchecked by law. Fortunately, the state doesn't have rent control, despite discussions in the legislature. It has a minimum wage that was fairly modest at $7.25 per hour as recently as 2014, but it has been raised on a schedule since then and now stands at $10.10 per hour in 2021. It has no right-to-work law, and it has strict workers' compensation mandates, a short-term disability insurance mandate, and a stricter-than-federal anti-discrimination law. Hawaii is about average for occupational freedom. It has a hospital certificate-of-need requirement, strict insurance regulations, a price-gouging law, and a general "unfair sales" law

(you are not allowed to sell at prices that are "too low"). We show a sustained and substantial improvement in the quality of Hawaii's civil liability system, which rose from about average in 2000 to well above average by 2017. This result came about because of increasing scores on the Chamber of Commerce survey of businesses and shrinkage in the size of the legal sector relative to the economy, whether measured by number of lawyers or legal services share of GDP.

Hawaii is now one of the worst states on personal freedom despite being one of the better states in the incarceration and victimless crimes category. It enjoys incarceration and drug enforcement rates that are well below average, while other victimless crime arrest rates have also improved. Hawaii has a worse-than-average civil asset forfeiture law. Tobacco freedom is among the lowest in the country, with extremely high cigarette taxes, draconian smoking bans on private property, and significant local e-cigarette regulation. The state has virtually no legal gambling, other than social home games. It has a long-standing and permissive medical cannabis law, but implementation was slow, with dispensary sales starting only in 2017 following a law passed in 2015. Possession was finally decriminalized in 2019. Alcohol freedom is better than average, especially with grocery store sales of wine and spirits and no state involvement in distribution, but beer taxes are high. The protection of gun rights is the worst in the country. It is virtually impossible to get a concealed-carry license, all Class III weapons are banned, there is comprehensive registration and purchase permitting of firearms, dealers are licensed, "assault weapons" are banned, large-capacity firearm magazines are banned, and so on. Hawaii does not require helmets for adult motorcycle riders.

IDAHO

2019 RANK
10th

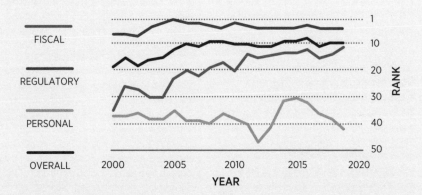

	FISCAL
	REGULATORY
	PERSONAL
	OVERALL

RANK
YEAR

PARTY CONTROL

■ R   ■ D

	2021	2019	2017
GOVERNOR	Little	Little	Otter
SENATE			
HOUSE OF REP.			

POLICY RECOMMENDATIONS

Fiscal: Comprehensively decentralize power by making it easy for new municipalities to incorporate and secede from existing ones, shifting responsibilities from counties to municipalities, freeing up local property tax–varying power, and reducing state aid to schools so that localities rely on their own tax base. The last move will also allow the state to cut taxes, particularly the general sales tax, which will give localities more tax room.

Regulatory: Make workers' compensation insurance voluntary and privatize the state fund.

Personal: Eliminate or reduce mandatory minimums for nonviolent offenses to reduce the incarceration rate. Allow currently imprisoned offenders to petition for release under the new guidelines.

ANALYSIS

Idaho is one of the most economically and socially conservative states in the country. As a result, it is perhaps unsurprising that it is a top-10 state for economic freedom and a bottom-10 state for personal freedom. The state continues to enjoy substantial in-migration, primarily from the less free West Coast. It is also one of the least cronyist states in the Union.

Idaho's fiscal policy has been improving over time, but it remains a weak spot in certain respects. State-level tax collections as a share of income have settled consistently below 6.0 percent in the 2010s, at least half a percentage point below where they averaged in the first decade of the century. Local taxes are well below the national average at 2.8 percent of adjusted personal income. Local governments are territorially large: Idaho has only about one effective competing jurisdiction per 400 square miles. Government debt is 2 standard deviations below the national average. Government GDP share has shrunk from 12.1 percent of income in 2000 to 9.8 percent in 2019. However, government employment is about average.

Idaho does well across the board on regulatory policy, earning its second-place ranking. It is one of the best states for occupational freedom, but since 2009, the state has begun to license more occupations. Nurse practitioner independence is protected, and physician assistants have full prescribing authority. It is one of the very best states for insurance freedom. There is no certificate-of-need requirement for hospitals or moving companies, and direct auto sales are legal under some conditions. In 2018, Idaho repealed its "sales below cost" laws. The state's civil liability system is one of the best, and the state also scores well above average on labor law, with a right-to-work law. Workers' compensation mandates, though, are strict. Despite its huge influx of new residents during the past two decades, Idaho held the line on land-use controls for a long time. But it is middling relative to other states, and we have seen evidence that new building restrictions have started to come into force since 2006. The state has done little to curb eminent domain abuse. Statewide video franchising was enacted in 2012, and telecommunications rate review was liberalized in 2005.

Idaho is among the worst states outside the Deep South on criminal justice policy. Crime-adjusted incarceration rates are nearly a standard deviation above the historical national average, and the drug enforcement rate is high and rising. Nondrug victimless crime arrests are better than average, suggesting that the state's biggest problem is sentencing. Idaho is also much less free than average for alcohol and gambling. Taxes on spirits are especially high. Tobacco freedom is much higher than average: cigarette taxes are low, and the state has no smoking ban for bars. Homeschooling and private schooling are almost unregulated, but the state has no private school choice programs. It has a religious freedom restoration act. Gun rights are much better than average, and they improved in 2015 when the state passed legislation allowing concealed carry without a permit for residents over 21 years of age and in 2018 when the legislature specified no duty to retreat when engaging in self-defense outside the home. The state does have a stricter-than-federal minimum age to possess firearms.

ILLINOIS

2019 RANK

37th

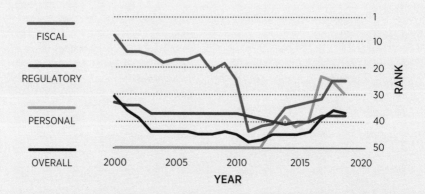

- FISCAL
- REGULATORY
- PERSONAL
- OVERALL

RANK

YEAR

PARTY CONTROL

■ R   ■ D

	2021	2019	2017
GOVERNOR	Pritzker	Pritzker	Rauner
SENATE			
HOUSE OF REP.			

POLICY RECOMMENDATIONS

Fiscal: Reform the retirement systems of localities to reduce local taxes, which are sky-high.

Regulatory: Reform the civil liability system by capping punitive damages, setting the standard for punitive damages at "beyond a reasonable doubt," and abolishing joint and several liability.

Personal: If serious about reducing smoking, preempt local flavored e-cigarette sales bans and vaping bans in bars and restaurants.

ANALYSIS

Illinois used to be a relatively decent state for economic freedom, although it almost always did much better on fiscal policy than on regulatory policy. But the state has lost some of that edge while also, not surprisingly, losing some of its economic vitality; its well-publicized woes with employee retirement spending threaten to drive local taxes and debt higher. It is also one of the most crony-ist states. Illinois did post one of the most dramatic improvements in personal freedom rankings we have ever seen between 2011 and 2017, and there is some sign that the fiscal situation has stabilized.

In FY 2020, Illinois's state-level taxes were about at 21st-century historic averages for the state, at 5.6 percent of adjusted personal income, and down from highs posted six and seven years before. The bigger problem is that local taxes are among the worst in the country, at 5.1 percent of income. However, residents have a good choice among local jurisdictions, with almost two effective competing governments per 100 square miles. The overall tax burden is 10.7 percent, much higher than average. Government GDP is quite a bit lower than the national average, but debt is quite high at 23.7 percent today, well above the average (although down from its height during the Great Recession), and cash and security assets are mediocre and have slid somewhat recently. Government employment, at 10.6 percent of private employment, remains significantly below the national average.

Regulatory policy has been a drag on Illinois's rankings throughout the time series. After California, it is the most cronyist state in America. It does reasonably well on land-use and insurance freedom but quite poorly on civil liability and occupational and labor free-dom. Illinois's land-use freedom, generally

a strength, has declined over time as it has pretty much everywhere else in the face of growing local zoning restrictions. The state's minimum wage at $11.00 an hour is now higher than it has ever been since 2000 as a percentage of the median wage. Unlike its neighbors, Illinois is not a right-to-work state. Renewable portfolio standards have been gradually tightened, raising electricity rates. In 2017, the state removed all telecom wireline regulatory authority. It had already enacted statewide video franchising. Licensing is extensive, but most of that growth occurred between 2002 and 2007. Nurse practitioners are highly constrained. Direct auto sales for Tesla were legalized in 2013/14. The state has been a fixture on the list of "judicial hellholes," with Madison and Cook Counties listed in 2017/18.[173] Illinois is one of the few states that have apparently not improved their tort sys-tems at all during the past two decades.

Illinois was long our bête noire on personal freedom, but that has dramatically changed with federal court decisions that have over-turned some extreme restrictions on gun rights, the legalization of same-sex marriage, marijuana reform, and the availability of driv-er's licenses to people without Social Security numbers. It is now comfortably in the middle of the pack. Illinois's new concealed-carry law, begrudgingly enacted by the legislature, is technically shall-issue but remains one of the country's strictest. The state still has local "assault weapon" and large-capacity firearm magazine bans, waiting periods for gun pur-chases, background checks for private sales, permitting of buyers for some weapons, local registration of some firearms, mandatory locking devices, and so on. Even fireworks are heavily regulated. Alcohol freedom is better than average, with no state role in distribu-tion and wine and spirits available in grocery stores. Beer and wine taxes are decent, but spirits taxes are high. Formerly one of the most restrictive states for cannabis, Illinois

---

173. Judicial Hellholes program website, www.judicialhellholes.org. Also see *Judicial Hellholes* 2017–2018 (Washington: American Tort Reform Foundation, 2017).

became the very first to legalize cultivation and sale through the legislative process (as opposed to ballot initiative) in 2019. Legal gambling is expansive, and the state is near the top in this category. Educational freedom is reasonably good, as virtually no restrictions are placed on homeschools or private schools. And the state has intradistrict school choice and expanded a tax deduction law for parents' educational expenses in 2017. Smoking bans are comprehensive, and cigarette taxes are among the very highest anywhere ($7.16 per pack in Chicago). Civil asset forfeiture was partially reformed in 2017. Illinois is in the middle of the pack on incarceration and arrests for the victimless crime category. Drug arrest rates are now below the national historical average after having been more than 5 standard deviations higher as recently as 2007.

INDIANA

2019 RANK

6th

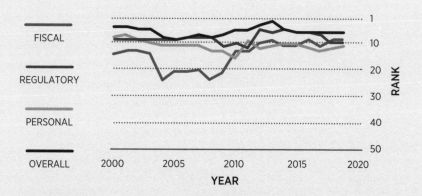

FISCAL

REGULATORY

PERSONAL

OVERALL

RANK

1

10

20

30

40

50

2000   2005   2010   2015   2020

YEAR

PARTY CONTROL

	R D	2021	2019	2017
GOVERNOR		Holcomb	Holcomb	Holcomb
SENATE				
HOUSE OF REP.				

POLICY RECOMMENDATIONS

Fiscal: Reduce debt and sales and income taxes by cutting spending on health and hospitals, housing, libraries, and interest on the debt, areas where Indiana spends more than average.

Regulatory: Allow independent nurse practitioner practice with full prescription authority.

Personal: Decriminalize marijuana possession.

ANALYSIS

Indiana has quietly built a record as one of America's freest states and the freest state in the Great Lakes region, though Michigan is now close. Hoosiers enjoy top scores on all three dimensions of freedom, with regulatory policy a particular area of excellence. Although it has still experienced small net outmigration to the rest of the country during the past 20 years, its record in that department has been better than that of any other of the eight Great Lakes states, and its economic growth has been better than all its neighbors' for at least a decade.

Although Indiana's fiscal policy deteriorated quite a bit between FY 2001 and FY 2005, it has made a good recovery since then. Local taxes have fallen from 4.6 percent of income in FY 2010 to 2.7 percent in FY 2020, and state taxes have edged down as well. Government debt, GDP, and employment have fallen during that period, but so have cash and security assets.

Although the PPACA disproportionately harmed the state because of its previously fairly free-market health insurance policies, Indiana has maintained the elements of a solid regulatory policy as far as it can. Land-use freedom is high overall, although one of our two proxies of local zoning restrictions shows substantial, unabated growth in stringency since 2000. The state also prohibits employers from banning guns on certain company property, and it could do more to reform eminent domain. The state passed right-to-work legislation in 2012 and has resisted increasing the minimum wage above the federal mark since 2010. It is a model state for telecommunications deregulation. Occupational freedom is extensive, though not for second-line health care professions. The state did legalize some autonomy for dental hygienists in 2018 and joined the Nurse Licensure Compact in 2019. Unfortunately, Indiana adopted a new certificate-of-need law for hospitals in 2018; it already had one for moving companies. Insurance freedom is above average. Direct auto sales, which were previously allowed under some circumstances, have now been completely banned. The civil liability system shows steady improvement during the past decade and is slightly better than average.

Indiana has more personal freedom than most other conservative states. It was forced to legalize same-sex marriage in 2014 but never had an oppressive super-DOMA. Gun rights are fairly secure, especially for concealed carry, but the state has stricter-than-federal minimum age limits for possession and dealer licensing. The ban on short-barreled shotguns was eliminated in 2015. Victimless crime arrests are fairly low, but the incarceration rate is higher than average, adjusted for crime rates. Educational freedom is excellent, and the state posted major gains in 2011 with a new statewide voucher law and a limited scholarship tax-credit law. The state's civil asset forfeiture law is fairly good, although it is sometimes circumvented through equitable sharing. Smoking bans have not gone quite as far as in other states. Marijuana freedom is virtually nonexistent, but alcohol freedom has been improving consistently in the past few years. The state now has direct-to-consumer wine shipments, and it legalized off-premises Sunday sales and happy hours in 2018, while alcohol taxes are low. Casino gambling has fallen off over time, perhaps reflecting regulatory barriers to innovation in this sector.

IOWA

2019 RANK

29th

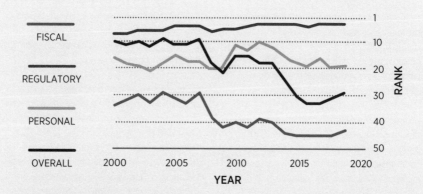

FISCAL

REGULATORY

PERSONAL

OVERALL

RANK

YEAR

PARTY CONTROL

■ R   ■ D

	2021	2019	2017
GOVERNOR	Reynolds	Reynolds	Reynolds
SENATE			
HOUSE OF REP.			

POLICY RECOMMENDATIONS

Fiscal: Trim spending in areas where the state spends more than the national average—education (especially higher education), hospitals, highways, parking lots, and sanitation—and use the savings to trim property, sales, income, and motor vehicle license taxes.

Regulatory: Repeal certificate-of-need requirements for new hospital construction and for moving companies.

Personal: Adopt constitutional carry and legalize Class III weapons.

ANALYSIS

Like other midwestern states, Iowa has long been a standout on regulatory freedom. Even though the state has moved right in recent years, it is one of just a few states whose fiscal situation has deteriorated during the past decade. As a result, its fiscal policy ranking has cratered. Not so long ago, Iowa was a top-10 state on overall freedom, but its competitive policy advantages have faded.

Both state and local tax burdens are above average in Iowa. Iowans pay 10.6 percent of adjusted personal income to government, similar to the figure in California. The state tax burden rose from 5.7 percent in FY 2011 to 6.4 percent in FY 2020. Government GDP share is higher now than in 2000 (12.0 percent versus 11.5 percent). Debt is quite low, however. Government employment is about average: 13.3 percent of private employment in 2016.

Iowa has consistently stood out as a leading state on regulatory policy. Land-use freedom is much better than average, although the state hasn't done as much as some others about eminent domain for private gain, and like everywhere else, local zoning has become tighter. It is a right-to-work state without a minimum wage, and workers' compensation–mandated coverages were liberalized slightly in 2008. Unlike most other states, Iowa doesn't mandate standing referrals or direct access to specialists in health plans. In 2017, telecom wireline regulatory authority was fully removed, and the state has statewide video franchising as well. Occupational freedom is about average and

has fallen over time because of the licensing of new occupations, especially between 2005 and 2009 and again in 2016. Iowa has certificate-of-need laws for hospital construction and moving companies. Insurance freedom rose with a switch back to "use and file" in 2018. The civil liability system is rated well above average and has generally improved.

On the personal freedom side, incarceration and victimless crime arrest rates are now about average, as other states have caught up with Iowa's previously relatively liberal approach. Iowa suspends driver's licenses for drug offenses unrelated to driving but has low prison collect call rates. Educational freedom is somewhat high because the state has a long-standing tax-credit scholarship program as well as interdistrict public school choice. Homeschooling was significantly liberalized in 2013. However, private schools are tightly regulated, with mandatory state approval, teacher licensure, and detailed curriculum control. Gambling freedom is high, and the state legalized some online betting in 2019. Marijuana freedom is sharply limited; a single marijuana offense not involving minors can carry up to 50 years of prison time. For a rural state, Iowa does not do very well on gun freedoms compared with most other states, but it has liberalized in recent years. Sound suppressors were legalized in 2016 and Stand Your Ground was enacted in 2017. Open carry requires a license, and the state has a stricter-than-federal minimum age to purchase a firearm. Iowa has no legal requirement for motorcyclists to wear a helmet. Alcohol freedom is mediocre because of state involvement in wholesaling and high distilled spirits taxes.

KANSAS

2019 RANK
27th

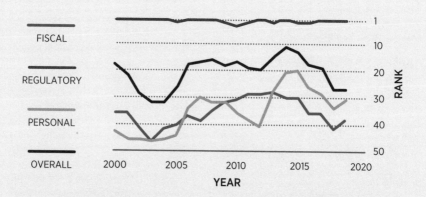

FISCAL

REGULATORY

PERSONAL

OVERALL

RANK

1

10

20

30

40

50

2000   2005   2010   2015   2020

YEAR

PARTY CONTROL

		2021	2019	2017
■R ■D				
GOVERNOR		Kelly	Kelly	Brownback
SENATE				
HOUSE OF REP.				

POLICY RECOMMENDATIONS

Fiscal: Cut spending on hospitals, where the state spends more than twice as much as the national average, as a percentage of income. Also cut spending on education, public buildings, libraries, and utilities, areas where the state spends a little more than the average. Cuts could be made in part through privatizations of hospitals and utilities. Reduce government employment to bring it closer to the national average.

Regulatory: Legalize independent nurse practitioner practice with full prescription authority, join the Nurse Licensure Compact, and enact a nursing consultation exception for interstate practice.

Personal: Follow the successful 2018 passage of transparency requirements with aggressive civil asset forfeiture reform consistent with the state's moderate criminal justice regime by mandating a criminal conviction before property can be forfeited.

ANALYSIS

Kansas has had a turbulent freedom record of late, bouncing around quite a bit year to year. Although the state tumbled 16 places on the overall freedom ranking between 2014 and 2019, the actual absolute loss in overall freedom was quite small. However, most other states gained significantly in freedom during this period. Whereas personal freedom and regulatory policy have been buoyant, fiscal policy has deteriorated since 2015.

Kansas made national news with its fiscal policy in 2013/14. The state's tax cuts were large and reduced the state tax burden from 5.5 percent of income to 5.1 percent, but the next year's tax hikes bumped that figure back up to 5.4 percent, just under the national average. Then, further tax increases in FY 2019 and FY 2020 boosted the tax burden to 6.2 percent of income, higher than the national average. Kansas's local tax burden (4.0 percent of income) is right at the national average. Thus, Kansas is today a high-tax state. Government employment is much higher than average (14.7 percent of private employment). Government consumption and investment is about average, at 10.7 percent of income, and hasn't changed much in a decade. Government debt peaked at 27.0 percent of income in FY 2010 and is now down around 18.0 percent, just under the national average.

Kansas is again our number one state on regulatory policy, as it has been through most of the past two decades. Land-use freedom is high, even though local zoning restrictions have grown. The state had enacted stricter-than-normal renewable portfolio standards in 2009, presumably as a sop to the wind industry, but those standards were made voluntary by legislation passed in 2015. Kansas has a right-to-work law and no state-level minimum wage, but it does have a law limiting employers from banning guns in company parking lots. The civil liability system is much better than average. In 2011, a major telecommunications deregulation bill passed. Occupational freedom is traditionally high,

except for nurses. By any measure, the extent of licensing is just about the lowest in the country. The state has no hospital certificate-of-need law. It has a price-gouging law, as well as a Depression-era law licensing moving companies. Kansas has none of the optional health insurance mandates we track in the PPACA era.

Kansas has been better than most other conservative states on criminal justice, but the incarceration rate has crept up a bit over time. Its victimless crime arrest rates, though, have edged down. The state doesn't suspend driver's licenses for drug offenses unrelated to driving, and its prison collect call rate is relatively affordable. Marijuana sentencing policies are actually milder than in most states, but the state has made no progress on more thoroughgoing reform. Social gambling is still illegal, but the state has casinos now. Kansas is still the best state in the country for gun rights. Permitless open carry was legalized in 2013, and permitless concealed carry was enacted in 2015. Educational freedom is about average after improving in 2013/14 with a new, albeit modest, tax-credit scholarship law. However, nonsectarian private schools are tightly regulated: they must get state approval and must hire only licensed teachers. Smoking bans are comprehensive, but cigarette taxes are not very high by today's standards. Localities haven't yet banned the sale of flavored e-liquids. Alcohol is much less regulated than it was in the days when Kansas banned bars, and taxes are low. But you still can't get wine or spirits in grocery stores, and there are local blue laws. The state liberalized the sale of stronger beer in grocery stores in 2017. Its civil asset forfeiture regime has improved, especially with the 2018 passage of sound transparency requirements, but it is still one of the worst in the country. The state takes in more than the average state in civil asset forfeiture equitable sharing funds. Kansas's personal freedom ranking benefited from having been forced to legalize same-sex marriage, a move that also overturned the state's oppressive super-DOMA law.

KENTUCKY

2019 RANK
25th

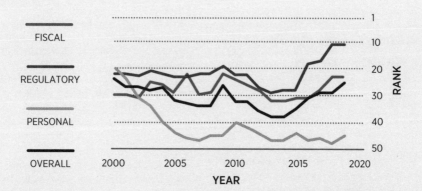

- FISCAL
- REGULATORY
- PERSONAL
- OVERALL

RANK

YEAR

PARTY CONTROL

		2021	2019	2017
R **D**				
GOVERNOR		Beshear	Bevin	Bevin
SENATE				
HOUSE OF REP.				

POLICY RECOMMENDATIONS

Fiscal: To reduce debt, tighten the rules for municipal bond issuance and cut spending, particularly on higher education, central staff, hospitals, highways, parking lots, and the Office of Unemployment Insurance.

Regulatory: Improve the health care system for consumers and practitioners alike by removing the certificate-of-need law for hospitals and by expanding independent practice freedom for nurse practitioners, dental hygienists, and physician assistants.

Personal: Reform sentencing for nonviolent offenders with an eye toward reducing the incarceration rate to the national average, while also enacting a medical marijuana law.

ANALYSIS

Kentucky has long been middling on economic freedom and low on personal freedom, but between 2015 and 2018 it made noticeable gains on economic freedom. As a result, Kentucky cracked the top half of the overall freedom ranking in 2019 for the first time since 2000.

Fiscal policy moved up strongly between 2013 and 2018. Local taxes have held steady at a low rate of 3.1 percent of adjusted income, and state taxes have also remained consistent at a high level of 6.2 percent of adjusted income since 2013. That means the state is very fiscally centralized. Government debt is also extremely high, at about 27.0 percent of adjusted personal income. It ranks second worst in the country after New York. The fiscal policy gains, therefore, have come almost entirely from a fall in government employment (from 13.5 percent to 12.3 percent of private employment since 2013) and in government GDP share (from 11.7 percent to 10.1 percent since 2013). The repeal of the prevailing wage law in 2017, which we recommended in the fifth edition, may have helped here.

Land-use freedom is relatively broad in Kentucky, although eminent domain for private gain remains mostly unreformed, and zoning restrictions have grown. The state has no minimum wage, and it enacted (as we suggested in the fourth edition) a right-to-work law at the beginning of 2017. The state has done more than most other low-income states to maintain reasonable standards for lawsuits, although punitive damages have not been reformed. Occupational freedoms are mediocre, and the state has a hospital certificate-of-need law. Property and casualty rate setting was liberalized substantially in 2018. A court struck down the state's anti-competitive regulations on moving companies in 2013/14. Telecom wireline regulatory authority was removed in 2017, but the state still has local cable franchising.

Kentucky has a lot of room for growth on personal freedom despite the bump from the *Obergefell* decision because the state had a super-DOMA in force. Otherwise, it has remained largely stagnant relative to other states. An exception is on gun rights, where constitutional carry (2019) substantially grew the state's score. Incarceration rates are very high and have actually risen a bit, although victimless crime arrest rates have moved down since the late aughts. Civil asset forfeiture is a big problem: state law is largely unreformed, and agencies participate enthusiastically in equitable sharing takings. Cigarette taxes were hiked in 2018, but otherwise tobacco (and vaping) freedom remains relatively good. Educational and alcohol freedom scores are low, whereas marijuana and gambling freedoms are extremely limited. With alcohol, Kentucky has local blue laws, very high beer and wine taxes, a total ban on direct wine shipment, and no wine or spirits in grocery stores. With education, the state has no private school choice programs, and it recently expanded mandatory schooling to 12 years. Some raw milk sales are allowed.

LOUISIANA

2019 RANK
32nd

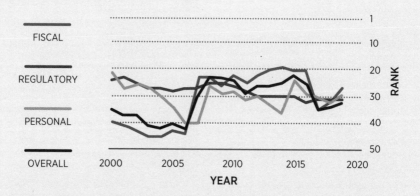

FISCAL

REGULATORY

PERSONAL

OVERALL

RANK

YEAR — 2000, 2005, 2010, 2015, 2020

RANK scale — 1, 10, 20, 30, 40, 50

PARTY CONTROL

	2021	2019	2017
GOVERNOR	Edwards	Edwards	Edwards
SENATE			
HOUSE OF REP.			

R ■   D ■

POLICY RECOMMENDATIONS

Fiscal: Cut spending in areas well above the national average: employee retirement, water transportation (the state spends five times as much as a share of personal income as Texas and more than twice as much as Mississippi), parks and recreation, public welfare operations, hospitals, employment security administration, fire protection, and general administration. Use the proceeds to cut the sales tax, one of the nation's highest.

Regulatory: Abolish judicial elections and enact punitive damages reforms.

Personal: Follow localities and decriminalize small-scale possession of marijuana at the state level.

ANALYSIS

Louisiana used to be one of the least economically free states in the South, but it has improved significantly on fiscal policy since 2008. The state is now in the middle of the pack on both economic freedom and personal freedom.

Louisiana's state-level tax burden stood at 5.0 percent of income in FY 2020, a bit below the national average and an increase over its 21st-century low of 4.1 percent in FY 2012. The major increase occurred in FY 2018. Meanwhile, local taxes have remained around the 21st-century historic average for the state, at 4.5 percent of income, a bit higher than the national average. Louisianans have little choice of local government, with only about one competing jurisdiction per 200 square miles of territory. Government debt is about average and has fallen slightly since recent peaks during the Great Recession. Government employment has fallen significantly, from 17.0 percent of private employment in 2000 to 12.3 percent today.

Louisiana is one of the better states for both land-use and labor-market freedom. Zoning is light but growing. The state has a right-to-work law and no minimum wage. A telecommunications deregulation bill was enacted in 2013/14, and the state has long had statewide video franchising. Then again, occupational freedom is notoriously bad in Louisiana (as of this writing, it is still the only state to license florists—out of a concern for public health and safety, no doubt). Nurses and dental hygienists have very little freedom of practice, but physician assistants gained additional prescription authority in 2018. The state has a hospital certificate-of-need law, but moving companies do not have to get a "certificate of public convenience and necessity" to open. An "unfair" pricing ban exists for prices that are too low, and a "price-gouging" ban exists for prices that are too high. Homeowner's insurance rates became more subject to regulatory control in 2018. Needless to say, Louisiana is one of the most cronyist states. Louisiana's court system has long been terrible no matter how you measure it (including enacted tort reforms, survey ratings, and the size of the legal sector).

On personal freedom, Louisiana hasn't seen the improvements enjoyed by other states, although it did receive a bump from the *Obergefell* decision. It was dragged down for this edition by being the second-worst state on criminal justice policy, but this represents an improvement over 2016, when it was the worst.[174] Crime-adjusted incarceration rates are extremely high despite getting better since 2016; the state is 1.6 standard deviations above the national mean for our entire data set. Drug arrests are also high and have not improved despite localities such as New Orleans decriminalizing low-level possession.[175] Louisiana remains subpar for marijuana freedom but did cautiously expand medical marijuana in 2019. The state's asset forfeiture law is worse than average. It remains a fairly good state for tobacco freedom, but smoking bans in bars were passed for the first time in 2013/14, and taxes went up in 2016. Louisiana is also a standout on educational freedom, with some public school choice, a very limited voucher law, and an expansive tax-credit scholarship program. However, private school teachers must be licensed. Gambling freedom is extensive. Alcohol freedom is high, with moderately taxed wine and spirits widely available, and the state has eliminated the restriction on direct wine shipping. Gun rights are about average, as the state makes it almost impossible to get a Class III weapon, concealed carry is weighed down with limitations, the permit cost for concealed carry is high, and a stricter-than-federal minimum age exists for possession.

174.   Julia O'Donaghue, "Here's How Louisiana Sentencing Laws Are Changing under Criminal Justice Reform," *Times-Picayune*, June 26, 2017.

175.   "New Orleans: Marijuana Arrests Plummet Post-Decriminalization," NORML, April 12, 2018.

MAINE

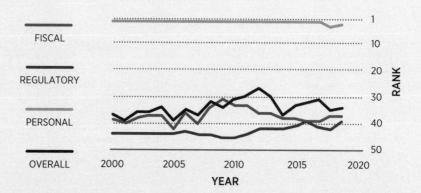

FISCAL

REGULATORY

PERSONAL

OVERALL

RANK

YEAR

PARTY CONTROL

	R	D	2021	2019	2017
GOVERNOR			Mills	Mills	LePage
SENATE					
HOUSE OF REP.					

POLICY RECOMMENDATIONS

Fiscal: Cut spending on public welfare, financial administration, the employment security administration, public buildings, and housing and community development. Maine is one of the most free-spending states on public welfare, financial administration, and employment security operations in the country, and it also spends much more than average on public buildings and housing and community development. Also cut individual and corporate income taxes.

Regulatory: Roll back exclusionary zoning and enact a housing appeals board like New Hampshire's to route regulatory disputes away from the slow court system.

Personal: Sell off the state liquor stores and replace the markup with a transparent ad valorem tax, as Washington has done. Maine could try to compete with New Hampshire on convenience, even if not on price.

ANALYSIS

Maine has long been one of the freest states in the country personally and one of the least free economically—the opposite of states such as Alabama and Idaho. Between 2009 and 2016, the state fell further behind on fiscal policy, which contributed to a relative decline in overall freedom. Since 2014, absolute freedom has risen in Maine, with the biggest gains occurring in 2015, 2016, and 2017.

Maine's taxes have long been high, crushing taxpayers overall at 11.4 percent of adjusted personal income and earning the state rankings in the bottom 10 for both state and local taxes. State taxes have fallen from their heights in the mid-2000s around 7.4 percent of adjusted personal income but are still painful for taxpayers at 6.6 percent today. Local taxes are 4.8 percent, again high relative to national norms. Mainers have slightly less choice of local government than other New Englanders, but more than most Americans. Government debt is very low, at 13.3 percent of income, but cash and security assets are also on the low side, at 14.0 percent of income. Government employment is down to 11.5 percent of private employment (from a peak of 12.9 percent in 2010), and government consumption plus investment is now just 9.3 percent of income, below the national average.

Maine was long a poor state on regulatory freedom, always staying in the bottom 10 until 2016. Since 2014, it has improved slightly. It is one of the most regulated states for land use. The court cases measure shows it as the worst in the country and getting worse all the time, whereas the Wharton Residential Land Use Regulation Index (WRLURI) suggests some improvement since 2005. Maine has one of the most extreme renewable portfolio standards in the country, by our measure (bested in 2019 by Vermont). Maine enacted a substantially higher minimum wage in 2018 (rising further to $12.15 in 2021) and has no right-to-work law. Telecom wireline regulatory authority has been removed (in 2016). Different measures of occupational freedoms give a conflicting picture of that policy, but there is no doubt that Maine allows more scope of practice to second-line health professions than just about any other state. Freedom from abusive lawsuits is above average and has improved steadily over time. The state has a certificate-of-need law for hospitals but not one for movers. It has a price-gouging law and a general law against sales below cost. So remember not to price your goods either higher or lower than the state legislature deems acceptable.

Maine is a leading state for criminal justice. It has very low incarceration rates—2 standard deviations better than the national average—and a better-than-average civil asset forfeiture law. Prison collect call rates, though, are high. Maine is a progressive state despite its sound gun laws (including concealed carry without a permit, enacted in 2015); it therefore allows marijuana rights (recreational possession became legal for adults over 21 years of age in 2016 and sale in 2019) and same-sex marriage (legalized by ballot initiative in 2012). It is, in brief, a very civil libertarian state. However, tobacco consumers will face punishingly high taxes ($2 a pack in 2021) and have been evicted from commercial private property by penalty of law. Educational freedom is also low despite having a limited voucher program. The state regulates private schools to the hilt: teacher licensing, detailed curriculum control, and state approval. However, some towns can "tuition out" to private schools, a form of voucher law that has been on the books for decades. Limited public school choice was enacted in 2011/12. We also show gambling freedom increasing over time, as the legal industry has expanded. Alcohol freedom is about average because of state monopolization of wine and spirits retailing, not to mention high beer taxes. Distilled spirits markups were raised substantially in 2018. But raw milk sales are legal.

MARYLAND

2019 RANK
45th

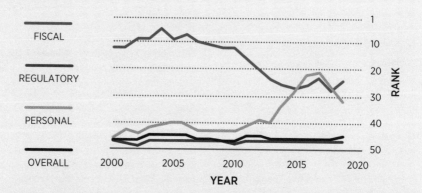

- FISCAL
- REGULATORY
- PERSONAL
- OVERALL

RANK

YEAR

PARTY CONTROL

		2021	2019	2017
■ R ■ D				
GOVERNOR		Hogan	Hogan	Hogan
SENATE				
HOUSE OF DELEGATES				

POLICY RECOMMENDATIONS

Fiscal: Trim spending in areas noticeably above national averages, such as housing and community development, fire protection, public buildings, parks and recreation, and sanitation. Cut local property taxes.

Regulatory: End rent control.

Personal: Allow sales of wine and spirits in grocery stores statewide.

ANALYSIS

Maryland is one of the least free states in the country, and it has had this status since the beginning of our time series in 2000. It performs especially poorly on regulatory policy and has also slipped considerably on fiscal policy since 2000. It does enjoy locational rents from its proximity to Washington, D.C. One bright spot for the state is that its personal freedom rank has gradually increased over time from its cellar-dwelling slot in 2000.

Maryland's overall tax burden is higher than average at 10.6 percent of income and has risen over time, especially in 2012 and 2016. Local taxes are much higher than average at 4.7 percent of adjusted personal income, while state taxes are a bit above at 5.9 percent. This situation would make for a favorable degree of fiscal decentralization, but Marylanders do not have much choice in local government, with only one competing jurisdiction per 200 square miles. It is less indebted than other states, though it also enjoys a lower cash and security balance and features lower government employment at 10.8 percent of private employment, as well as very low government GDP share at 8.5 percent of income. In general, the state's debt and asset position has deteriorated since the aughts, whereas government GDP and employment have improved a bit.

Maryland is the third-worst state on the most important component of regulatory policy, land-use freedom. Zoning restrictions are extensive, eminent domain abuse is mostly unchecked, and some local rent control exists. Its renewable portfolio standard has become consistently worse. At least it doesn't mandate free speech on private property. The state enacted a new minimum wage in 2013, and as a ratio to median wage it has risen most years since then (it is $11.75 per hour as of 2021). Maryland has no right-to-work law. Health insurance mandates are extensive.

Telecommunications regulation is unreformed. Occupational freedom is extremely low. By one measure (index of statutory mentions of regulatory keywords), Maryland has one of the highest figures for licensed occupations in the country, and it is one of the most cronyist states. However, nurse practitioners were freed for independent practice in 2015, and physician assistants and dental hygienists have some freedom as well. Maryland has a hospital certificate-of-need law but no such law for movers. Personal auto rates became more tightly regulated ("prior approval") in 2018. The state has both general and gasoline-focused laws against sales below cost. Its tort system is only about average, and unlike most states, it has shown no improvement since the early 2000s.

Reform efforts have helped improve Maryland's criminal justice score. The state passed the Justice Reinvestment Act in 2016, which eliminated mandatory minimums and reduced sentences for certain drug offenses. Crime-adjusted incarceration rates are now finally well below the 21st-century national average. The drug enforcement rate fell from 13.2 percent at its peak in 2007 to its to-date low of 4.0 percent in 2019. The state's asset forfeiture regime has traditionally been slightly above average, but it got significantly better in 2016 with reform that required government to provide "clear and convincing evidence" to seize property. Smoking bans are comprehensive, and cigarette taxes are high, encouraging smuggling. Tobacco prohibition was enacted for adults under 21 in 2019. Educational freedom is among the lowest in the country. Homeschools and private schools are tightly regulated, the latter more so (mandatory state approval and teacher licensing). The state raised the years of compulsory schooling from 11 to 12 in 2014 and then to 13 in 2017. However, it did enact a limited voucher law in 2016. Maryland raised its travel freedom score by allowing people without Social Security numbers to get driver's licenses in 2013/14. It also raised its marijuana freedom score substantially by enacting a "real" medical marijuana law and decriminalizing small-scale possession. Alcohol freedom is decent because of privatization and low taxes; however, beer taxes were hiked substantially during 2011–2014. Direct wine shipments are legal. The state has sharply limited firearms freedom, and it is now a bottom-five state in this category. It mandates locking devices, registers handgun owners, requires licensing with safety training for handgun purchasers, licenses dealers, bans possession for those under 21 years of age, bans certain types of guns and magazines, and makes it extremely difficult to get permission to carry in public. Gambling freedom is substantial, and the industry has grown in recent years.

MASSACHUSETTS

2019 RANK

30th

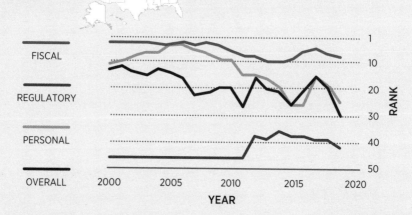

	FISCAL
	REGULATORY
	PERSONAL
	OVERALL

RANK

YEAR

PARTY CONTROL

■R ■D	2021	2019	2017
GOVERNOR	Baker	Baker	Baker
SENATE			
HOUSE OF REP.			

POLICY RECOMMENDATIONS

Fiscal: Massachusetts spends more than twice the national average on housing and community development. It also spends a great deal on public welfare operations, interest payments, and miscellaneous commercial activities. Cut these areas and pay down debt and build up cash assets.

Regulatory: Repeal outdated and cronyist regulations, such as the price-gouging law, the sales-below-cost laws, moving company licensure, and the certificate-of-need law for hospitals.

Personal: Make the civil asset forfeiture regime consistent with its top criminal justice score by requiring a criminal conviction before forfeiture and banning equitable sharing that does not comply with this standard.

ANALYSIS

Massachusetts has long had a better economic policy regime than one would expect given its strongly left-of-center electorate, and one of the better records on personal freedom, particularly for criminal justice. It suffers, though, from an onerous regulatory system and some relative decline on personal freedom that has harmed its overall ranking.

On fiscal policy, the nickname "Taxachusetts" is a bit of a misnomer. Massachusetts's overall tax burden is just slightly higher than average, although individual income taxes are among the highest in the country. Massachusetts residents have ample choice of local government, more than four every 100 square miles. Government debt is high, at about 20.5 percent of personal income, but has fallen 11 percentage points since FY 2009. Cash and security assets have fallen 8 percentage points of income, however, during that same period, wiping out most of those gains. Government employment is among the lowest in the country, at 9.0 percent of the private workforce, and government consumption is also low.

On the most important category of regulatory policy, land-use regulation, Massachusetts is worse than average, although our two indicators of zoning stringency give somewhat conflicting judgments. By one measure (court cases), zoning stringency has grown over time but is still better than average, but by the other (WRLURI-based imputation), it has fallen over time but is still worse than average. Renewable portfolio standards have grown rather high. Eminent domain for private gain is completely unrestrained. The state has consistently had a higher-than-federal minimum wage, and that rate is now one of the highest in the country, at $13.50 per hour in 2021. Workers' compensation coverage mandates are extreme, though employers have great freedom of choice in funding them, and there is no right-to-work law. A mandatory paid leave program was enacted in 2018. Telecommunications have not been deregulated. Occupational freedom is about average in Massachusetts, although nurses enjoy little freedom in the state. Property and casualty insurance remains tightly regulated, and the state has a certificate-of-need law for hospitals, as well as an anti-price-gouging law, licensure of moving companies, and both general and gasoline-focused sales-below-cost laws. The civil liability system is subpar but has improved over time, although not because of any particular statutory or institutional reforms.

Massachusetts is our top state for criminal justice. It has long locked up fewer of its residents than the vast majority of other states. It also arrests fewer people for drugs and other victimless crimes than most other places. Since 2016, it no longer suspends licenses for nondriving drug offenses, and prison phone call rates are low (and went down in 2016). However, its asset forfeiture law is among the worst in the country, putting the burden of proof on innocent owners, giving proceeds to law enforcement, and requiring only probable cause for showing the property is subject to forfeiture. Massachusetts scores highly for cannabis freedom, with a comparatively liberal medical marijuana law enacted in 2011/12 and a recreational use law enacted in 2016 (but implementation was delayed until 2018). The Second Amendment is nearly a dead letter in Massachusetts: the state tries to make guns as expensive as possible (locking mandates; dealer licensing; license to purchase any gun, with safety training) and virtually prohibits carry in public. It is the third-worst state for tobacco freedom, with comprehensive smoking bans and punishingly high cigarette taxes ($3.51 a pack after having been raised again in 2013/14). Educational freedom is low. Homeschooling parents have to jump through many hoops and must meet detailed curriculum guidelines. Private schools are subject to government approval. Casino gambling has expanded, and with it the state's gambling freedom score has risen. The state's alcohol freedom score improved in 2013 because of the repeal of the direct wine shipping ban, but wine in grocery stores remains subject to mind-numbingly complex rules undoubtedly designed for some obscure political purpose. Alcohol taxes are lower than average.

MICHIGAN

2019 RANK

7th

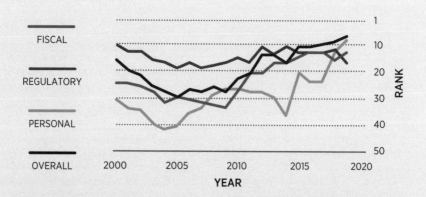

FISCAL

REGULATORY

PERSONAL

OVERALL

RANK

YEAR

PARTY CONTROL

	2021	2019	2017
GOVERNOR	Whitmer	Whitmer	Snyder
SENATE			
HOUSE OF REP.			

■ R   ■ D

POLICY RECOMMENDATIONS

Fiscal: Cut spending on higher education, health, and sewerage, which is much higher than average. Use the proceeds to reduce income and property taxes.

Regulatory: Allow full nurse practitioner independent practice and prescription authority, and join the Nurse Licensure Compact.

Personal: Enact a liberal tax-credit scholarship or educational savings account (ESA) program for private education.

ANALYSIS

Michigan has been hit hard by global economic conditions despite its relatively decent economic policies. Unfortunately, Great Lakes states cannot afford merely "decent" policies; they must be outstanding to overcome the headwinds they face in global markets and to compete with neighboring states, such as Indiana. Encouragingly, Michigan's fiscal policy has improved over time, and its personal freedom ranking has rocketed upward since 2014.

Michigan's local tax burden is relatively low, probably because of a school finance centralization accomplished by ballot initiative in the 1990s. The state tax burden has historically been higher than the national average, but it fell substantially in the late 2000s and now stands at 5.9 percent of adjusted personal income. Government debt has also fallen somewhat since 2008 and is now below average at 15.9 percent of income. Government employment fell from 13.3 percent of the private workforce in 2009 to 10.6 percent today. Government consumption plus investment divided by adjusted income has fallen from 12.1 percent in 2009 to 9.3 percent in 2019. Michiganders do have reasonable freedom of choice among local governments, with about one per 100 square miles, but the centralization of school finance has made this choice less significant.

Michigan's land-use and energy freedom is a little above average. It has little zoning restriction, but it has ratcheted up renewable portfolio standards since 2011. It also has a fairly high minimum wage for the local economy. A right-to-work law was enacted in 2012. Freedom from abusive lawsuits has been better than average in Michigan since 2000, and like most states it has improved over time. Occupational freedom is about average but has declined since 2008 because of new occupations being licensed. Regulations are fairly anti-nursing. Michigan deregulated telecommunications fully in 2014. Personal auto lines moved to prior approval of rates in 2019.

On criminal justice policy, Michigan arrests somewhat fewer than average for victimless crimes, but it has a slightly above-average incarceration rate. Those rates have been stable over time. The state passed criminal justice reform measures in 2017; incarceration rates did drop in 2018 and 2019, and the effects of the reform are likely to be long-term. The asset forfeiture law is better than average thanks to 2015 and 2019 reforms, but equitable sharing is still a significant end run around state law. Smoking bans are comprehensive, and cigarette taxes are fairly high. Educational freedom is among the lowest in the country. Although homeschools are scarcely regulated, private schools face many barriers. There are no private school choice programs, and compulsory schooling has extended to 12 years since 2009. The state does better than the median on gambling freedom, and aggravated gambling is no longer a felony as of 2016. A constitutional ban on all racial preferences in public services has been in effect since 2006. Travel freedom also grew a bit when the state repealed its motorcycle helmet law in 2012. Marijuana recreational sale and possession were legalized by ballot initiative in 2018. Alcohol and firearms freedoms are only about average, with spirits taxes a bit high and mandatory registration of some firearms.

MINNESOTA

2019 RANK

38th

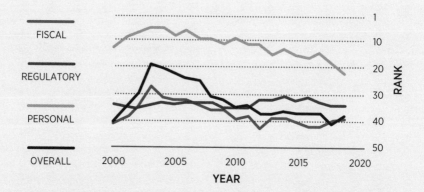

- FISCAL
- REGULATORY
- PERSONAL
- OVERALL

RANK: 1, 10, 20, 30, 40, 50

YEAR: 2000, 2005, 2010, 2015, 2020

PARTY CONTROL

■ R   ■ D

	2021	2019	2017
GOVERNOR	Walz	Walz	Dayton
SENATE			
HOUSE OF REP.			

POLICY RECOMMENDATIONS

Fiscal: Trim spending on public welfare, parking lots, natural resources, unemployment compensation, and parks and recreation, areas in which the state spends much more than average. Reduce taxes on individual income and selective sales, which are above national norms.

Regulatory: Deregulate telecommunications and cable entry and pricing.

Personal: Allow beer, wine, and spirits in grocery stores.

ANALYSIS

Minnesota is a classic "blue state" in that it scores well above average on personal freedom and below average on economic freedom. However, it has fallen relative to other states on personal freedom since 2006 as others have caught up and surpassed it.

Minnesota is fiscally centralized, with low local taxes (3.1 percent of adjusted personal income) and high state taxes (8.4 percent). Overall, the tax burden is high at 11.5 percent. On public employment and government consumption, the state performs better than average, while debt and liquid assets are right around average.

On the most important category in regulatory policy, land-use and environmental freedom, Minnesota is average. The state suffers from strict renewable portfolio standards that consistently got worse from 2010 to 2015. Zoning restrictions look about average, or slightly worse, but both of our measures suggest the state hasn't gotten much worse over time, unlike most other states. On labor policy, the state is below average, lacking a right-to-work law that all of its neighbors enjoy. Minnesota passed a minimum-wage law in 2014 that increased the rate every subsequent year until 2016 and then indexed it to inflation, though it remains not too high relative to the median wage. Workers' compensation funding was liberalized slightly in 2011/12. The state moved to partially deregulate telecommunications in 2015, as we recommended in previous editions of this study, but cable remains untouched. Occupational freedom is above average; the state passed an extensive nurse practitioner freedom-of-practice law in 2014, but we show big increases in statutory restrictive language

in 2015, 2016, and 2017, despite sunrise and sunset provisions. The state lacks a hospital certificate-of-need law and various other cronyist policies, but it does have sales-below-cost laws for gasoline and retailers generally. Its court system is highly rated, but in 2018 the state appeared on the list of "judicial hellholes" for the first time.

Minnesota scores above average on personal freedom largely because of its sound criminal justice policies, and it was helped in the past in relative terms by its marriage freedom (it enacted same-sex marriage in 2013). But the state performs poorly in a number of other categories. The incarceration rate is well below the national average but rose from 2000 to 2015, before falling back a bit. The drug arrest rate is lower than average and getting lower, while arrests for other victimless crimes have fallen even more rapidly. The state's asset forfeiture law was reformed in 2013, and equitable sharing participation has been low. The state, in bipartisan fashion, enacted limits on the use of license plate readers in 2015. Minnesota is mediocre on marijuana freedom, enacting a strictly limited medical marijuana program in 2014 and enjoying decriminalization. Tobacco freedom took a big hit in 2013 with a hike in the cigarette tax and an inflation indexing provision (that was ended by the legislature as of 2017). Educational freedom is slightly above average despite some private and home-school regulation, because of interdistrict public school choice, a modest tax-credit/deduction law, and compulsory schooling of only 10 years. Alcohol freedom is mediocre because of taxes and limits on grocery sales, but the state did finally repeal blue laws in 2017. Minnesota rose to average on gun policy by legalizing silencers in 2015.

MISSISSIPPI

2019 RANK
40th

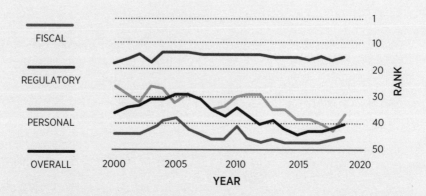

	FISCAL
	REGULATORY
	PERSONAL
	OVERALL

PARTY CONTROL

■ R   ■ D

	2021	2019	2017
GOVERNOR	Reeves	Bryant	Bryant
SENATE			
HOUSE OF REP.			

POLICY RECOMMENDATIONS

Fiscal: Cut spending on health and hospitals, where Mississippi is the third-most liberal-spending state, and also on education, natural resources, highways, and public welfare operations, where the state spends well more than the national average, as a share of the economy. Reduce government employment, and reduce state taxes, especially on sales and business income.

Regulatory: Liberalize insurance by moving to a "no-file" system like Wyoming's.

Personal: Enact a broad-eligibility ESA or tax-credit scholarship program.

ANALYSIS

Mississippi is a typical Deep South state in that its economic freedom far outstrips its personal freedom. But the state's worst dimension is actually fiscal policy, and its economic policies are worse than those of all its neighbors, including Alabama and Louisiana.

Mississippians' overall tax burden is a bit above average nationally at 10.0 percent, but local taxes are quite low. This fiscal centralization goes along with a lack of choice among local government (fewer than 0.4 per 100 square miles). Debt is much lower than average, but government employment and GDP share are far higher than average. State and local employment is 16.2 percent of private-sector employment.

Like most southern states, Mississippi does well on land-use and labor-market freedom. In 2011/12, it also finally enacted a limited eminent domain reform. However, local land-use restrictions have grown significantly over time. Mississippi has no minimum wage and has a right-to-work law. It also lacks stricter-than-federal anti-discrimination in employment protections. However, it does have an E-Verify mandate and restricts property owners from banning guns in parking lots. Health insurance mandates are modest. In 2011/12, a telecommunications deregulation bill was passed, but the state lacks statewide cable franchising. Occupational licensing is less extensive than average, but nurses and dental hygienists enjoy little practice freedom. The state strictly regulates insurance rates, hospital construction, moving companies, and pricing during disasters. Its civil liability system used to be much worse than average, but it is now actually quite better than average. The state reformed punitive damages and abolished joint and several liability in 2002 and 2004.

Personal freedom has gone up in Mississippi, even leaving aside the federalization of marriage policy. However, it suffers from a notoriously awful criminal justice system despite a dip in incarcerations after 2014. The state imprisons its population at a rate of 1.5 standard deviations above the national average, even adjusting for its high crime rate. Drug arrests are very high. Other victimless crime arrests are average or below, depending on measurement. The state asset forfeiture law is not terrible, but it doesn't matter because local law enforcement enthusiastically pursues adoptions from the Department of Justice (except in 2019, which might prove to be a blip). Marijuana law is illiberal. You can get a life sentence for a single marijuana offense not involving minors. Mandatory minimums exist for low-level cultivation, the "decriminalization law" is a ruse because local governments may criminalize possession, and the mostly harmless psychedelic *Salvia divinorum* is also banned. Gun laws used to be stricter than might be expected but are now some of the best in the country. Permitless open carry was reinstated in 2013/14, and permitless concealed carry was enacted in 2016. There is no duty to retreat, and silencers are now permitted. Alcohol freedom is below average. The state monopolizes liquor stores, wine direct shipping is banned, and wine and spirits are unavailable in grocery stores. Legal gambling is more open than in the average state. Educational freedom is about average. A very limited voucher law was enacted in 2011/12 and liberalized since, but public school choice is extremely thin. Tobacco freedom is above average, as smoking bans leave plenty of exceptions, and cigarette taxes are not too high. The state banned same-sex marriage at the end of 2014, but the *Obergefell* decision has since eliminated that restriction.

MISSOURI

2019 RANK
11th

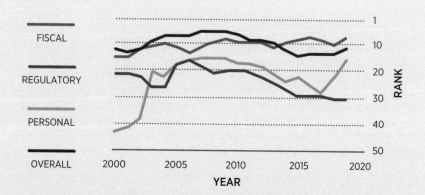

FISCAL

REGULATORY

PERSONAL

OVERALL

RANK

YEAR

1

10

20

30

40

50

2000   2005   2010   2015   2020

PARTY CONTROL

	R	D	2021	2019	2017
GOVERNOR			Parson	Parson	Greitens
SENATE					
HOUSE OF REP.					

POLICY RECOMMENDATIONS

Fiscal: Clamp down on the more than 1,000 special districts, which local governments form to get around tax and debt limitations and which local voters find hard to monitor. Dissolve as many as possible and make it difficult to form new ones.

Regulatory: Improve labor and occupational freedom by securing the right to work while promoting independent practice freedom for nurses, physician assistants, and dental hygienists.

Personal: Pass strict anti-circumvention reform to eliminate the equitable sharing loophole in the state's civil asset forfeiture laws that costs Missourians millions.[176]

176.   Nick Sibilla, "Loophole Lets Missouri Cops Keep Millions in Forfeiture Funds (and Away from Schools)," Institute for Justice website, March 2017, http://ij.org/loophole-lets-missouri-cops-keep-millions-forfeiture-funds/.

ANALYSIS

Missouri is one of the country's freer states, but in recent years it has run the risk of falling back into the middle of the pack. Its slide in regulatory policy is most worrisome, especially because it is not merely relative but is absolute as well, including and excluding federalized policies.

Missouri's local taxes are a bit above average (4.1 percent of adjusted personal income), but state taxes are well below average (4.4 percent of income), making for high fiscal decentralization. In addition, Missourians have some choice in local government, with more than one effective competing jurisdiction per 100 square miles. We show that state taxes have fallen since FY 2007 and overall taxes are less than average. Government consumption plus investment and employment is also below average, whereas debt and cash and security assets are about average.

We see good evidence of continued backsliding on regulatory policy. The state has adopted a modest renewable portfolio standard and has done little to limit eminent domain for private gain. But overall land-use policy is above average. Local zoning is quite loose compared with other states. The state adopted a right-to-work law in 2017, as we suggested in the fourth edition, but a statewide referendum then blocked it. Missouri's minimum wage was hiked in 2018. The state does above average on occupational licensing, although our two main measures of licensure extent point in very different directions. Freedom is limited for nurses, physician assistants, and dental hygienists. The civil liability system remains below average and went backward between 2013 and 2015. Insurance rate-setting freedom is fairly high. Cable and telecommunications are fully liberalized.

Missouri has a fairly strict approach to criminal justice, involving long sentences that lead to an incarceration rate that is well above average and a high level of arrests for drugs. It does better when it comes to other victimless crimes. It also has a low prison phone rate and wisely avoids suspending driver's licenses for nondriving drug offenders. The incarceration rate did notably fall between 2017 and 2019. The state's asset forfeiture law is one of the best in the country, but it is frequently circumvented through equitable sharing. An extensive medical marijuana law was adopted in 2018, but you can still get life in prison for a single marijuana offense not involving minors. Same-sex marriage was banned in 2014, but the *Obergefell* decision trumped that restriction. Missouri is a good state for gambling, alcohol, and tobacco freedoms. Cigarette and alcohol taxes are notably low, and smoking bans are more moderate than in other states, although several localities (including St. Louis city and county) did pass a minimum legal sale age increase to 21 for tobacco products in 2016. Gun rights were slightly better than average in 2015 and got better in 2016 after substantial reform (something we called for in the fourth edition of this study). The state secured the right not to retreat from attackers in public during 2016 and allowed for permitless concealed carry. Raw milk sales are legal, whereas seat belts and motorcycle helmets are required by law.

MONTANA

2019 RANK
18th

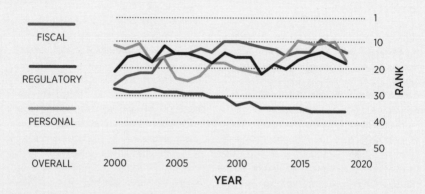

	RANK
FISCAL	1
	10
REGULATORY	20
	30
PERSONAL	40
	50
OVERALL	2000 2005 2010 2015 2020

YEAR

PARTY CONTROL

■ R   ■ D

	2021	2019	2017
GOVERNOR	Gianforte	Bullock	Bullock
SENATE			
HOUSE OF REP.			

POLICY RECOMMENDATIONS

Fiscal: Trim spending on public welfare operations, public buildings, health, employment security administration, central staff, and financial administration, which are all substantially above national averages.

Regulatory: Montana is surrounded by right-to-work states. Enact a similar law that does not violate freedom of association, like the one proposed in the "Labor-Market Freedom" section of this book (see page 46-47).

Personal: Abolish all mandatory minimum sentences for victimless crimes and reduce maximum sentences significantly.

ANALYSIS

Residents of Big Sky country enjoy ample personal freedom and good fiscal policy, but regulatory policy has seen a worrying, long-term decline in both absolute and relative terms. It will be welcome if a tiny turnup for the absolute score of regulatory freedom in 2019 was the beginning of a positive trend.

Montana's tax burden is well below the national average. State taxes have held steady during the past several years at about 5.0 percent of adjusted personal income. Local taxes spiked in FY 2009 but then settled down to about 3.1 percent of income shortly thereafter. They've trended up slightly during the past few years to nearly 3.2 percent after nearly hitting 3.0 in FY 2017. Montanans have virtually no choice in local government, as counties control half of local taxes. Montana's debt burden has fallen from 19.9 percent of income in FY 2007 to 11.5 percent now. Government employment and consumption have fallen since the Great Recession and are now slightly better than national historical averages. Overall, Montana posted consistent gains on fiscal policy up to 2017 but has fallen back slightly since in relative and absolute terms.

Land-use freedom and environmental policy have deteriorated since 2007. Building restrictions are now more onerous than average. Eminent domain reform has not gone far. The state's renewable portfolio standards are among the toughest in the country, raising the cost of electricity. The state has a fairly high minimum wage for its median wage level. Overall, Montana is one of the least free states when it comes to the labor market. Health insurance mandates are extremely expensive. Montana has among the most extensive occupational licensing regimes. However, nurses and physician assistants enjoy substantial practice freedom. Cable franchising is still local, but telecom wireline authority has been fully deregulated. Insurance freedom is middling, as the state imposes some restrictions on rating criteria but has gone to "file and use" for most lines. It joined the Interstate Insurance Product Regulation Compact in 2013/14. Montana has a general ban on sales below cost, and medical facilities and moving companies both face entry barriers. The state's lawsuit freedom is slightly above average (less vulnerable to abusive suits).

Montana is one of the best states for gun rights, but constitutional carry postdates our study. Montana also does well on gambling, where it has an unusual, competitive model for video terminals that does not involve casinos. On criminal justice, Montana is above average. Drug arrests are more than 1 standard deviation below the national average, but the incarceration rate is about average when adjusted for crime rates. The state is schizophrenic on cannabis, with a reasonably liberal medical marijuana program but also the possibility of a life sentence for a single cannabis offense not involving minors and a one-year mandatory minimum for any level of cultivation. Montana reformed its terrible asset forfeiture law in 2015 but has not touched the equitable sharing loophole. Tobacco and alcohol freedoms are subpar, with draconian smoking bans, higher-than-average cigarette taxes, and state monopoly of liquor stores. Educational freedom is slightly better than average, with fairly light regulation of private schools and home-schools and, since 2015, a strictly limited tax-credit scholarship law. The state was forced to legalize same-sex marriage in 2014, and its oppressive super-DOMA was, therefore, also overturned.

NEBRASKA

2019 RANK

33rd

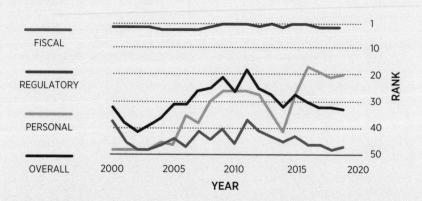

FISCAL

REGULATORY

PERSONAL

OVERALL

RANK

YEAR

PARTY CONTROL

		2021	2019	2017
■R ■D				
GOVERNOR		Ricketts	Ricketts	Ricketts
LEGISLATURE*		nonpartisan	nonpartisan	nonpartisan
n/a		n/a	n/a	n/a

*Nebraska has a unicameral legislature.

POLICY RECOMMENDATIONS

Fiscal: Cut spending on education, which is far higher than average, especially spending on salaries. Trim utilities, sales, and income taxes.

Regulatory: Repeal the certificate-of-need requirement for hospital construction.

Personal: Preempt local regulation of firearms sales, possession, and carrying.

ANALYSIS

Nebraska is a state of extremes within our economic freedom dimension. It is the second-best state on regulatory power but 47th on fiscal policy. Like other Great Plains states, Nebraska has usually had very good regulatory policy. Kansas is the only state in the country that outranks it on that margin. But Cornhuskers have long suffered from poor fiscal policy, and it's only worsened in the past few years. Fortunately for Nebraskans, the state has gone from 48th on personal freedom in 2000 to 20th today.

Nebraska is relatively fiscally decentralized but relatively highly taxed, with somewhat lower-than-average state tax revenues (about 5.4 percent of adjusted personal income, a drop from 6.0 percent in FY 2006) and much higher than average local tax revenues (5.2 percent of income). Nebraskans have little choice of local governments, limiting the benefits of this approach—the state has only 0.46 effective competing jurisdictions per 100 square miles. Debt is lower than average but so are assets. Public employment is just above average, whereas government GDP share is quite a bit higher than average at 12.5 percent.

Nebraska does very well on the most important regulatory policy category, land-use and environmental freedom. However, it has not done much to check eminent domain for private gain. On labor policy, it is above average because of a right-to-work law and flexible workers' compensation funding rules, but it enacted a high minimum wage in 2014. Health insurance freedom is extensive and tied for best in the nation, with few mandated benefits outside the PPACA essential benefits and with a light touch on managed care. Nebraska does better than average on occupational freedom but has slipped on keeping occupational licensing in check. In 2015, nurse practitioners gained full practice authority, while 2018 saw new sunrise legislation strengthening the prior law. The state has long had one of the best civil liability systems in the country. It has a certificate-of-need law for hospital construction. Telecommunications have been deregulated but cable has not.

Nebraska is only middling on criminal justice policy. Incarceration rates have generally been low, but they have increased over time, unlike in some other above-average states. Drug arrest rates have been high, but they have come down pretty steadily (with a one-year blip up in 2019). Victimless crime arrests have been moving in the right direction for a while and are now near countrywide averages. That is a far cry from the sky-high rates two decades ago. The legislature finally enacted a comprehensive asset forfeiture reform in 2016, one of the best in the country. Nebraska is fourth worst on educational freedom. Controls are high, including detailed annual reporting requirements and notifications for homeschoolers, and nonsectarian private schools are subject to mandatory approval and teacher licensing. The state has no private school choice programs. Gambling freedom is mediocre; even social gaming isn't allowed. Sports betting appeared to get the green light in 2020, but putting regulations in place around it has bogged down the process. Travel freedom is below average. Gun rights are woefully behind what you'd expect in a red state. There is no constitutional carry. Some of Nebraska's lower scores on firearms policies come from special provisions for Omaha or general lack of preemption. Marijuana policy is also well below average. You can still get life in prison as a maximum sentence for a single pot offense. There is no medical marijuana law. However, Nebraska is solidly above average on alcohol and tobacco freedom. Like other states with the ballot initiative, the nonsmoking majority of Nebraska has foisted on private business owners fully comprehensive smoking bans, but tobacco taxes are below average. Alcohol taxes are similarly low. Since 2008, the state has had a constitutionally entrenched ban on governmental racial discrimination, such as affirmative action. Raw milk sales are legal.

NEVADA

2019 RANK
3rd

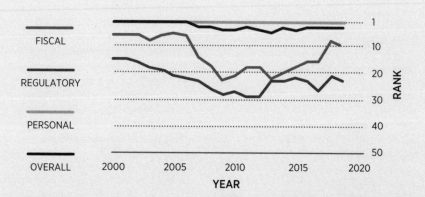

FISCAL

REGULATORY

PERSONAL

OVERALL

RANK

2000   2005   2010   2015   2020

YEAR

PARTY CONTROL

		2021	2019	2017
GOVERNOR		Sisolak	Sisolak	Sandoval
SENATE				
ASSEMBLY				

R   D

POLICY RECOMMENDATIONS

Fiscal: Cut spending on air transportation, employment security administration, public buildings, and parks and recreation. Use the proceeds to trim sales and miscellaneous minor taxes. Nevada spends far more than the national average on police, but that may be warranted given the nature of its social and economic model.

Regulatory: Deregulate occupations such as epidemiologists, environmental health specialists, title plant personnel, interior designers, sign language interpreters, clinical laboratory technologists, pharmacy technicians, veterinary technologists, opticians, athletic trainers, massage therapists, security guards, landscaping contractors, child-care workers, bill and account collectors, well drillers, alarm installers, taxi drivers, and crane operators.

Personal: Abolish private school teacher licensing, state approval of private schools, and detailed curriculum requirements.

ANALYSIS

Unsurprisingly, Nevada is consistently one of the top states for personal freedom. But it is a top-five freest state overall as well, coming in third. It does so through a top-10 score on overall economic freedom to go along with its No. 1 ranking on personal freedom. The Great Recession greatly damaged Nevada's fiscal position, so we should expect the COVID-19 pandemic to cause some dip for 2020–2021 despite a recent upswing in the state as the gambling sector rebounded.[177]

Nevada's fiscal policy worsened between the beginning of our data set in 2000 and 2014, a fact that might have something to do with a 2003 state supreme court decision setting aside the part of the state constitution that required a supermajority for tax increases.[178] But it's basically been improving overall since 2014, though still nowhere near where it was in the early 2000s. State-level taxes have gone up from a low of 5.2 percent of adjusted personal income in FY 2004, bouncing around in the middle to high fives since, and settling at almost 5.7 percent today. Local taxes were steady at between 3.3 percent and 3.5 percent of income for most of the past decade but are now at 3.1 percent. Nevadans have virtually no choice of local governments given the importance of territorially vast counties. Government employment is super low relative to the national average, and government consumption is also well below average. This remains true after both spiked during the Great Recession. Government debt peaked at nearly 30.0 percent at that point in 2009, but it has come down since and is now only 18.8 percent of income (unfortunately, still above the national average). Cash and security assets are below average.

After years of deterioration, Nevada's regulatory policy rebounded in 2013 because of a variety of factors. As one of the Sand States attracting huge net in-migration in the 1990s and early 2000s, Nevada retained some degree of land-use freedom. But it is getting steadily worse and now places 35th. Renewable portfolio standards are quite high and rising, affecting the cost of electricity. Nevada does have a right-to-work law but also has a minimum wage, which was hiked further in 2015 and again in 2019 (with scheduled bumps out to 2024). Cable and telecommunications have been liberalized. Occupational freedom declined dramatically between 2000 and 2006 because of the expansion of licensing. It has suffered another expansion during the past half decade. A bright spot is, in 2013, nurse practitioners' gaining the right of independent practice with full prescription authority. Insurance freedom expanded in 2018 due to reform of laws regarding prior approval of rates and forms. In 2011/12, the state had joined the Interstate Insurance Product Regulation Compact. Nevada has certificate-of-need requirements for hospitals and household goods movers. Direct auto sales were partially legalized in 2013. The court system is above average and has been improving since 2013 as the state gradually moved off the "judicial hellhole" list.

Nevada is No. 1 for gambling freedom (no surprise), and it is the only state with legal prostitution (local option). However, on criminal justice policy, Nevada is more of a mixed bag. Nondrug victimless crime arrests were high but have fallen over time, and it is possible that they are overstated because of Nevada's high tourist population. The incarceration rate is about average for its crime prevalence and has been trending in the right direction. Drug arrests are low. The civil asset forfeiture regime is mediocre following a small reform in 2015. Marijuana was legalized in 2016 by initiative, and now it is a top state for marijuana freedom. Gun rights are middling relative to other states. Extensive

177.   "Las Vegas Roars Back to Life with Record Gambling Win," Voice of America, August 29, 2021.

178.   Michael J. New, "Judicial Nonsense in Nevada," Cato Institute, August 8, 2003.

background checks were enacted in 2019. Open carry is extensive, but there is no permitless concealed carry. Nevada is one of the top states for alcohol freedom, with fully private wholesaling and retailing, low taxes, no blue laws, legal direct wine shipping, and wine and spirits in grocery stores. In 2013, the state enacted a law giving illegal immigrants access to driver's licenses, which outweighs its 2011 move to ban handheld cell phone use in increasing overall travel freedom. Nevada is a bit above average on educational freedom. Private schools are tightly regulated, facing mandatory state approval, mandatory teacher licensing, and detailed private school curriculum control. However, the state has a broad tax-credit scholarship, enacted in 2015. Even tobacco is not as tightly controlled as one would expect from a state with the ballot initiative, although taxes were raised significantly in 2015. Nevadans may still light up in bars with permission of the owner.

NEW HAMPSHIRE

2019 RANK

1st

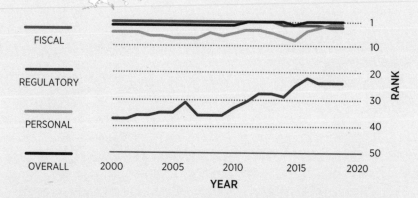

FISCAL

REGULATORY

PERSONAL

OVERALL

RANK

YEAR

PARTY CONTROL

	R	D	2021	2019	2017
GOVERNOR			Sununu	Sununu	Sununu
SENATE					
HOUSE OF REP.					

POLICY RECOMMENDATIONS

Fiscal: Local governments need to get a handle on school spending and taxes. State government may be able to help by moving town meetings and local elections to coincide with state elections, boosting turnout and diluting the political power of insiders.

Regulatory: Pass a right-to-work law that is consistent with free association, as described in the text.

Personal: Legalize more forms of private gambling that pay out at a higher ratio than the state lottery and therefore, even for anti-gambling advocates, should be considered less exploitative.

ANALYSIS

In the fifth edition of the index, Florida had overtaken New Hampshire as the freest state. This time, New Hampshire has regained the crown as the freest state in the Union. In the more distant past, New Hampshire had a huge lead over the rest of the country on fiscal policy, a lead that partly dissipated between 2000 and 2008 because of big increases in local property taxes, which were in turn driven by growth in education spending. It has rebounded quite a bit in absolute terms but has been eclipsed by Florida and Tennessee on the fiscal front. New Hampshire grabs the top spot overall because it does well in both economic freedom (third) and personal freedom (second), something that is also true of Florida but is not the case for Tennessee. It could be a challenge for rivals to catch New Hampshire next time because of policy changes in 2021 in a pro-freedom direction, including tax cuts and the passage of the education freedom accounts program. The "New Hampshire Advantage" could get even stronger within New England. The three states of northern New England pose a stark contrast in economic policies and, for most of the late 20th and early 21st centuries, economic outcomes.

New Hampshire's overall tax burden is well below the national average at 8.1 percent. The state government taxes less than any other state but Alaska. We show a decline in state taxes as a share of adjusted personal income from a high of 3.8 percent in FY 2002 to 3.0 percent today. Meanwhile, local taxes have risen from 3.7 percent of income in FY 2001 to 5.1 percent in FY 2019 (which is down from a high of 5.6 percent in FY 2012). New Hampshire is, therefore, a highly fiscally decentralized state. Granite Staters have quite a wide choice in local government, with 2.8 competing jurisdictions per every 100 square miles. Government debt (12.7 percent), consumption (7.9 percent), and employment (10.1 percent) are all much lower than average, and in all these categories we see improvements since 2010, especially on the debt side. However, cash and security assets are below average and have been dropping.

New Hampshire's regulatory outlook is not so sunny. However, it is still an above-average state and improving relative to its past when a decade ago it ranked in the mid-30s. The Granite State's primary sin is exclusionary zoning. Both measures suggest that New Hampshire is among the more regulated states, although one measure shows improvement since 2005 relative to other states. Part of the problem might be the absence of a regulatory takings law. However, the eminent domain law is strong. The state has a renewable portfolio standard. On labor-market freedom, New Hampshire is below average primarily because of the absence of a right-to-work law and of any exceptions to the workers' compensation mandate. New Hampshire has no state-level minimum wage. Health insurance mandates are low, but the state mandates direct access to specialists, hobbling managed care. A telecommunications deregulation bill was passed in 2011/12, but the state has not yet adopted statewide video franchising. The state is above average on occupational freedom solely because the health professions enjoy broad scope of practice; the extent of licensing grew significantly during the 2000s and continued in the past half decade. Insurance freedom is generally better than average, except for some rate classification prohibitions. The hospital certificate-of-need law was abolished in 2011/12, but that only became effective in 2016. Household goods movers are still licensed. There are no price-gouging or sales-below-cost laws. New Hampshire is one of the least cronyist states. The state's civil liability system is far above the national average; punitive damages were abolished long ago.

New Hampshire is quite personally free. Incarceration rates are low but rose significantly around 2011, only to get better again during the past few years. Drug arrest rates are also low but had moved up during 2011–2016 before falling again. Nondrug victimless crime arrests are down substantially after being only about average for years. The state enacted a significant asset forfeiture reform in 2016 and is among the top states. Tobacco freedom is below average, as taxes are fairly high, and smoking bans are extensive. The state now has a limited anti-vaping law. Educational freedom is extensive in the Granite State. A liberal tax-credit scholarship law was enacted in 2012 and a local-option voucher law in 2018, raising the state significantly above average on educational freedom even though compulsory schooling lasts 12 years, and private schools require state approval. A 2021 expanded ESA will help the state improve its ranking in this category. Because New Hampshire has only charitable gambling, it scores well below average in the gambling freedom category. Its ranking should improve because of the 2020 legalization of sports betting. Cannabis freedom is above average, helped by the 2017 decriminalization law but dragged down by an inability to fully legalize. Alcohol freedom is about average; the state monopolizes liquor retail and wine wholesale, but the effective tax rate is extremely low. Wine (but not spirits) is in grocery stores. It is one of the two best states in the country for gun rights. The constitutional carry bill enacted in 2017 helped here. New Hampshire has neither a seat belt law nor a motorcycle helmet law.

NEW JERSEY

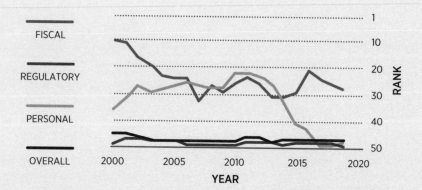

	FISCAL
	REGULATORY
	PERSONAL
	OVERALL

RANK

1 — 10 — 20 — 30 — 40 — 50

YEAR: 2000 · 2005 · 2010 · 2015 · 2020

PARTY CONTROL

■ R   ■ D

	2021	2019	2017
GOVERNOR	Murphy	Murphy	Christie
SENATE			
GENERAL ASSEMBLY			

POLICY RECOMMENDATIONS

Fiscal: Cut spending on the "miscellaneous" category and employee retirement, areas in which New Jersey spends a lot more than average. Income, utilities, and property taxes are abnormally high and could be cut.

Regulatory: End rent control, especially given its unintended consequences on housing quality and quantity.

Personal: Fully free wine sales from the currently arcane regulatory system.

ANALYSIS

About 60 years ago, New Jersey was considered a tax haven. It grew wealthy under that regime, but during the past decade it has dwelt in the bottom five for economic freedom. It still does relatively well on fiscal policy, but it is a regulatory nightmare and performs poorly on personal freedom as well. As long as it is better than New York on fiscal policy and not much worse than Connecticut, it will probably continue to get tax refugees from that state, but more New Yorkers now move to Florida than to New Jersey.

New Jersey's state-level taxes were basically average (5.7 percent of adjusted income) for many years but have crept up in the past two and are now above average at 6.3 percent. Local taxes have gone the other way, trending downward to 5.3 percent (but still well above the national average of 3.9 percent). The combined tax rate is quite high relative to the rest of the country but still lower than New York's. New Jerseyans have more choice of local government than residents of any other state, with 6.3 effective competing jurisdictions per 100 square miles, which may imply that many residents are content with high local taxes and services. Government debt has now fallen to a slightly below average level (16.4 percent of income), but cash and security assets are well below average too (11.2 percent of income). The government employment ratio and government GDP share have both improved significantly since the Great Recession and are better than average.

Land-use freedom is quite limited in New Jersey, with only Oregon faring worse. The state lets cities adopt rent control, and local zoning rules are often highly exclusionary, even though the state is no longer a destination. It has mandated speech on private property such as malls and community associations. Renewable portfolio standards are among the highest in the country, raising electric rates. In 2013, the state adopted a minimum wage that has suffered big hikes recently. Labor-market freedom was already bad because of strict workers' compensation rules, mandated short-term disability

insurance, mandated paid family leave, no right-to-work law, and a stricter-than-federal anti-discrimination law. Health insurance mandates are extensive. In 2018, New Jersey even legislated a state-level individual health insurance mandate. New Jersey has had no telecommunications deregulation, but it has statewide video franchising. Occupational licensing is more extensive than average, and it has worsened since 2017. In 2013, nurse practitioner freedom of independent practice was abolished despite more states going the other direction. Insurance rate regulation is strict, and the state has a price-gouging law, which Governor Chris Christie deployed after Hurricane Sandy to devastating effect.[179] The Tesla sales model was recently legalized. The civil liability system is somewhat better than average.

New Jersey personal freedom is limited, coming in third worst. Criminal justice has been a rare high point for the state, ranking 12th. Incarceration and victimless crime arrests, drug and nondrug, have all fallen since 2000, but drug arrests were spiking until a dip during the past two years. The state did slash prison collect phone call rates in 2015 and stopped suspending driver's licenses for non-driving drug offenses in 2019. Asset forfeiture, however, has been reformed little. New Jersey is a bad state for tobacco freedom, travel freedom, and gun rights, but is decent on gambling (perhaps not as good as might be expected). The state was a pioneer in sports betting. The picture on educational freedom is mixed. Homeschools and private schools are barely regulated, but Milton Friedman's home state has no public or private school choice programs. Cannabis freedom was mixed but will improve significantly with the passage (and fulfillment) of Question 1 in 2020 and follow-on legislation, which will legalize marijuana. Alcohol freedom is a bit above average, but the state interferes here too. Taxes are modest, but direct wine shipment is tightly regulated, and the rules on when a grocery store may sell wine are complicated—perhaps to create a "tollbooth" where state politicians can extract rents. Fireworks freedom improved in 2017, and physician-assisted suicide was legalized in 2019.

179.   Matthew Yglesias, "Miles-Long Gasoline Lines in New Jersey Show the Case for 'Price Gouging,'" *Slate*, November 1, 2012.

NEW MEXICO

2019 RANK

42nd

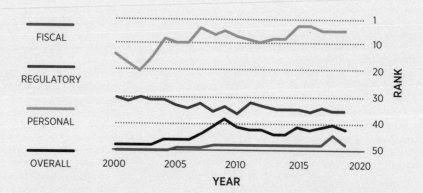

- FISCAL
- REGULATORY
- PERSONAL
- OVERALL

PARTY CONTROL

	2021	2019	2017
GOVERNOR	Lujan Grisham	Lujan Grisham	Martinez
SENATE			
HOUSE OF REP.			

R ■   D ■

POLICY RECOMMENDATIONS

Fiscal: Trim spending on police and fire, corrections, education, general administration, public buildings, hospitals, parks and recreation, public welfare, sanitation and sewerage, and employee retirement, which are all much higher than the national average, as a share of income. Cut the gross receipts tax.

Regulatory: Promote tort reform since the state performs poorly on lawsuit freedom, creating a drag on its economy.

Personal: Enact a generous private tax-credit scholarship program.

ANALYSIS

New Mexico has long had far more personal freedom than economic freedom, but it has never fully turned it around economically despite some movement in the right direction in absolute terms since 2000 on fiscal policy. Still, it remains mired at 48th place on fiscal policy, with a 35th-place ranking on regulatory policy. With a 43rd-best score on economic freedom as a whole, its 5th-best ranking on personal freedom can't keep it out of the bottom 10 states in overall freedom.

New Mexico's overall tax burden of 10.0 percent of adjusted personal income is just above the national average of 9.6 percent. State taxes came in at 6.3 percent, which was a recent high after the rate had dropped into the high fives for most of the past decade (with some bouncing around) and had come down to 5.1 percent in FY 2019. The big one-year jump in FY 2020 was due to a package of tax increases in 2019. Local taxes have risen from 2.7 percent of income in FY 2000 to 3.6 percent in FY 2019. That growing fiscal decentralization does little for choice in government, however, as the state has fewer than one competing jurisdiction per 100 square miles. Government debt and employment ballooned during the Great Recession and is still much higher than average. However, both have come down from those peaks. Cash and security assets are robust. New Mexico's big problems are government consumption and employment, each of which are approaching 2 standard deviations higher than national norms.

New Mexico has slid on land-use freedom and is now below average. Zoning regulations have significantly tightened over time, and the state has implemented relatively strict renewable portfolio standards. It long ago did eminent domain reform. The state has had a minimum wage for some time, but it was not extremely high until 2018. There is no general right-to-work law. Health insurance freedom is low because of costly mandates and bans on man-

aged care gatekeeping models. In 2013/14, the state passed a telecommunications deregulation bill, but it has not implemented statewide video franchising. The extent of occupational licensing skyrocketed between 2006 and 2009, then jumped again in 2016. Nurses enjoy broad scope-of-practice freedom. Insurance freedom has been fairly high since reforms enacted in 2009/10. There is no certificate-of-need law for hospital construction. Otherwise, cronyist regulation is limited, besides licensing for moving companies and a ban on direct-to-consumer auto sales. The civil liability system is much worse than average, and the state has done little to address the problem.

New Mexico's personal freedom is where it stands out from the pack. It has solid criminal justice policies, coming in at 13th. Victimless crime arrests, drug and nondrug, are low, as are incarceration rates. The state's asset forfeiture law is the best in the country, since putting limits on equitable sharing in 2015. Cannabis, alcohol, and travel freedoms are all strong suits for New Mexico, although the state isn't a leader in any of those areas. However, marijuana was legalized in 2021, so that should substantially help its ranking on marijuana policy. Gambling freedom is limited, but it's still a top-20 state. From 2013 to 2017, physician-assisted suicide was legalized, but that is a tiny part of our index. The state is one of just two to have both a broad religious freedom restoration act and a broad equal rights amendment (Connecticut is the other). Tobacco and educational freedoms are weak spots in a top state. Students are required to go to school for 13 years, the most in the country, and the state has no choice programs apart from public school open enrollment. Cigarette taxes are high, and smoking bans are extensive. New Mexico has avoided raising the minimum age. It also performs weakly on gun rights, coming in 33rd. The state does well on open carry, but still has no permitless concealed carry. The state has no motorcycle helmet law.

NEW YORK

50th

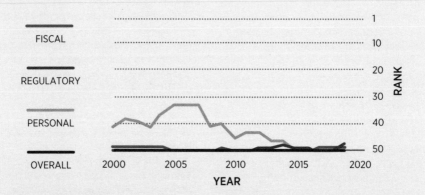

FISCAL

REGULATORY

PERSONAL

OVERALL

RANK

YEAR

PARTY CONTROL

	R D	2021	2019	2017
GOVERNOR		Cuomo	Cuomo	Cuomo
SENATE				
ASSEMBLY				

POLICY RECOMMENDATIONS

Fiscal: Cut spending on hospitals, highways, housing, public buildings, public welfare, education, corrections, fire, sanitation and sewerage, employee retirement, and "miscellaneous," which are all above national averages. Cut all taxes and pay down debt.

Regulatory: Abolish the housing anchor that is rent control.

Personal: Slash cigarette taxes, which are so high as to be almost tantamount to prohibition.

ANALYSIS

New York has been the least free state in the country for a long time. In fact, the Empire State has been the worst state for freedom in every year since our data set began in 2000. Economic freedom is the most significant weakness, but the state has not kept up with the rest of the country on personal freedom either. It belies the "blue" state stereotype in that it is No. 50 on economic freedom *and* personal freedom.

The only fiscal policy area where New York is not below average is the ratio of government to private employment, where the state has actually improved significantly since the early 2000s. It now stands at 11.7 percent, a smidge below the national average. The government GDP ratio has scarcely fallen during that same period, suggesting that New York pairs relatively low government employment with high salaries and benefits for public employees. New York's local tax burden has fallen recently but is twice that of the average state: 7.9 percent of income in FY 2019—a dramatic rise from the early 2000s, when it was less than 7.0 percent. However, New Yorkers have ample choice in local government: 4.1 competing jurisdictions per 100 square miles. The state tax burden—at a projected 6.6 percent of income in FY 2020—is also higher than the national average. Combined state and local taxes are crushing. Debt is down from years past but is still the highest in the country at 27.4 percent of income, and liquid assets are roughly half that, at 14.2 percent of income.

New York is no longer the worst state on regulatory policy as it has jumped all the way up to 48th—although it is still close to New Jersey and California as the worst regulatory environments. Land-use freedom is very low, primarily because of the economically devastating rent control law in New York City. Eminent domain remains unreformed. The state has an onerous renewable portfolio standard, though local zoning is fairly moder-

ate compared with surrounding states. The state enacted a minimum wage in 2013/14, and it has gotten worse since. New York also has a short-term disability insurance mandate and, as of 2016, paid family leave. Cable and telecommunications are unreformed. Occupational freedom is a bit subpar, but nurse practitioners did gain some independence in 2013/14 that has since disappeared. Insurance freedom is a mixed bag. The state has stayed out of the Interstate Insurance Product Regulation Compact, but freedom for property and casualty insurers to set rates was dumped after briefly gaining them in 2013/14. State rate classification prohibitions were newly created in 2018. The civil liability system looks poor, but we may underrate it slightly because of the state's large legal sector.

New York is the worst state on personal freedom, and yet its criminal justice policies are reasonably decent. While drug arrests are about average, nondrug victimless crime arrests are quite low. Incarceration rates are below average and declining. The state was one of only a few to impose the loss of a driver's license as a punishment for nondriving drug crimes, but that ended in 2019. Prison phone call rates have always been low. Local law enforcement enthusiastically participates in equitable sharing, even though the state law imposes only modest limits in the first place. Tobacco freedom is the second worst in the country because of smoking bans and stratospheric taxes ($5.85 a pack, only topped by Illinois's absurd $7.16 a pack rate). Since 2014, localities have enacted total prohibition of tobacco sales for 18- to 20-year-olds, followed by the state itself in 2019. Naturally, the state also has a vaping ban. New York is perhaps the worst state for homeschoolers, and it has no private school choice programs and only a meager public program. Sparklers were legalized in 2015, and mixed martial arts competitions in 2016. Gambling freedom is better than average; casinos were introduced in 2005, and sports

betting is now legal. Cannabis freedom
is slightly above average in this index, as
the state enacted a limited medical law in
2014, but marijuana was legalized in 2021.
Therefore, the state is certain to rise in the
next edition. Alcohol freedom is a bit above
average, with modest taxes, but grocery
stores can't sell wine. Gun rights are hedged
about with all kinds of restrictions, but it is
possible with some effort to get a concealed-
carry license in some parts of the state. Raw
milk sales are illegal, but driver's licenses
were made available to illegal immigrants in
2019, suggesting even New York paternalism
has its limits.

NORTH CAROLINA

2019 RANK

16th

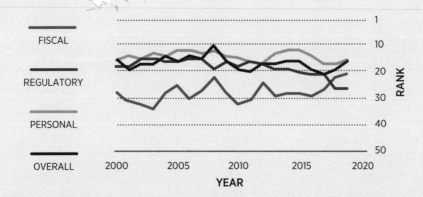

FISCAL

REGULATORY

PERSONAL

OVERALL

RANK

YEAR

PARTY CONTROL

■R ■D	2021	2019	2017
GOVERNOR	Cooper	Cooper	Cooper
SENATE			
HOUSE OF REP.			

POLICY RECOMMENDATIONS

Fiscal: Cut spending on hospitals, possibly through privatization, which is more than twice the national average as a percentage of income. Build up the rainy-day fund or trim individual income taxes further.

Regulatory: Eliminate all rate regulations on property and casualty insurance, and fully free direct-to-consumer auto dealerships while they are at it.

Personal: Allow fully legal internet sports betting.

ANALYSIS

North Carolina is a rapidly growing southern state with a reasonably good economic freedom profile and an even better record on personal freedom, especially when compared with its neighbors. Although it has improved of late on its fiscal policy scores, it has slipped a bit on regulatory policy.

North Carolina gradually improved its fiscal policies from FY 2011 to FY 2020. State taxes fell from 6.1 percent of adjusted personal income to 5.6 percent, right around the national average. Local taxes have also declined, moving from 3.5 percent of income to 3.2 percent, seven-tenths of a percentage point below the national average. Government consumption and employment fell, but they are still a bit above the national average. Government debt and financial assets are well below the national average at 10.2 percent and 9.5 percent, respectively.

Despite large in-migration, North Carolina has disdained excessive controls on the housing supply. Yet it has slowly declined on land-use freedom since 2000. It has never effectively reformed eminent domain and has a significant renewable portfolio standard. Labor law is good and has been fairly stable since the beginning of our time series. The state has no minimum wage, a right-to-work law, and relatively relaxed workers' compensation rules, but it enacted an E-Verify mandate in 2011. Regulation has killed off the managed care model for non-large-group health insurance, but mandates are low. Cable and telecommunications have been liberalized. Occupational freedom is a weak spot, especially for the health professions. A sunrise review requirement for occupational licensing proposals was scrapped in 2011, and licensing has grown consistently. North Carolina is one of the worst states for insurance freedom. It has a large residual market for personal automobile and homeowner's insurance because of strict price controls and rate classification prohibitions. It also has a price-gouging law and a minimum-markup law for gasoline. Entry is restricted for medical facilities and moving companies. North Carolina's civil liability system has improved over time and is now about average.

North Carolina has one of the best criminal justice regimes in the South, though nationally it is only 20th on this margin. Incarceration and both its victimless and drug crime arrest rates are all below average. The state has no state-level civil asset forfeiture, but local law enforcement frequently does an end run around the law through the Department of Justice's equitable sharing program. Revenues are down, though. Gun rights are more restricted than in many other southern states, with carry licenses somewhat costly to obtain yet hedged with limitations. Plus, buying a pistol requires a permit, local dealers must be licensed, background checks are required for private sales, and most Class III weapons are difficult to obtain (sound suppressors were legalized in 2014). Alcohol freedom is low because of state liquor stores and somewhat high markups and taxes. The state also introduced limited mandatory training for servers in 2018. Marijuana has not been liberalized apart from a 1970s-era decriminalization law. Gambling freedom is quite low. Not even social gaming is legal. The state is No. 6 on educational freedom because of a 2013 voucher law that survived the court and relatively light regulation. North Carolina is also—as might be expected—a top-five state for tobacco freedom, largely due to reasonable taxes and workplace freedom, but not freedom in bars or restaurants.

NORTH DAKOTA

2019 RANK
15th

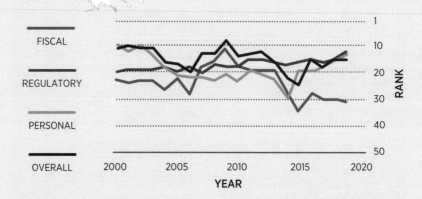

FISCAL

REGULATORY

PERSONAL

OVERALL

RANK

1
10
20
30
40
50

2000   2005   2010   2015   2020

YEAR

PARTY CONTROL

		2021	2019	2017
■R ■D				
GOVERNOR		Burgum	Burgum	Burgum
SENATE				
HOUSE OF REP.				

POLICY RECOMMENDATIONS

Fiscal: Enhance fiscal decentralization and choice among local governments with different policies by cutting state taxes and aid to local schools and allowing local towns to vary property tax to meet school funding needs. The state tax in greatest need of cutting is the sales tax.

Regulatory: Allow employers to purchase workers' compensation insurance from any willing seller, or to self-fund, and allow certain businesses to opt out entirely.

Personal: Eliminate teacher licensing, mandatory state approval, and detailed curriculum requirements for private schools, and reduce the notification and record-keeping burdens on homeschooling families.

ANALYSIS

After a stretch of years in which its relative overall freedom ranking declined from 12th to 25th, North Dakota has seen steady absolute gains during the past six years and is now at 15th nationally. There remains the most room for improvement on fiscal policy, where it is a middling 31st.

North Dakota's state-level tax burden fell to its lowest level in our time series, 4.6 percent of adjusted income, in FY 2018. But it has jumped up in the past two years to 5.3 percent. The local tax burden remained static for many years but has crept up significantly during the past three. It is now at 4.1 percent, above the national average and 1.3 percent above its low of 2.8 percent in FY 2014. Clearly, the trend is not heading in the right direction. North Dakotans do have substantial choice of local government: 1.7 per 100 square miles. State debts have risen lately after some years of decline; financial assets continue to be built up. Government consumption and employment have risen from their respective 2012 and 2014 lows, but they are still lower than they were in the early and mid-2000s. So far, there is little sign of the resource curse that has struck Alaska and Wyoming. But these numbers are still higher than the national averages and should be brought down.

Most Great Plains states have good regulatory policies, and North Dakota is no exception, although it falls behind its southern neighbor. Land use is lightly regulated, and the state ranks in the top 10 on this margin. North Dakotans can be proud that their state has one of the strongest limits on eminent domain abuse in the country. The state has a right-to-work law and no state-level minimum wage. However, North Dakota has a monopoly state fund for workers' compensation insurance and has long had an employment discrimination law. When it comes to health insurance regulation still under state control, North Dakota is tied with Idaho and Nebraska for No. 1 in the nation, with none of the most expensive mandates and with a light touch on managed care plans. Telecommunications was deregulated more fully in 2015, but cable remains unreformed. Occupational licensing in North Dakota has crept up, but nurses and physician assistants enjoy ample freedom of practice. There is no sunset review law. Insurance freedom is low because of prior approval of rates and lack of membership in the Interstate Insurance Product Regulation Compact. There is no certificate-of-need law for hospitals, but there is one for moving companies. The state has a general "unfair sales" act and a minimum markup for gasoline. The civil liability system is third best in the country.

North Dakota's criminal justice policies are generally good because of the low incarceration rate, though they aren't as good as they used to be. However, victimless crime arrests are high even though they have come down over the years. The drug arrest rate has risen substantially and steadily during the past 20 years. The state's civil asset forfeiture law was among the worst in the country until a 2019 reform, but local law enforcement rarely participates in equitable sharing. Prison phone call rates were curtailed radically in 2017. Smoking bans were intensified in 2012, but cigarette taxes are below average. Vaping bans started early here. With just a few exceptions, gun rights are strong in North Dakota. Those exceptions have mostly to do with Class III weapons. The state adopted constitutional carry in 2017. Alcohol freedom is generally good, but wine and spirits are available in grocery stores only when put into a separate enclosure. A reasonably effective medical marijuana law was enacted by initiative in 2016, and partial decriminalization was passed in 2019. Gambling freedom is low, but fireworks freedoms are decent. North Dakota remains the very worst state in the country for educational freedom. Private schools and homeschools are both more harshly regulated than anywhere else, and the state has no private or public school choice.

OHIO

2019 RANK
31st

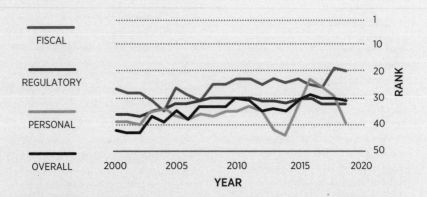

FISCAL

REGULATORY

PERSONAL

OVERALL

RANK

YEAR

PARTY CONTROL

		2021	2019	2017
■R ■D				
GOVERNOR		DeWine	DeWine	Kasich
SENATE				
HOUSE OF REP.				

POLICY RECOMMENDATIONS

Fiscal: Trim spending on housing and community development, sanitation and sewerage, education, and employee retirement, areas where Ohio spends more than the average state. Cut property taxes.

Regulatory: Look at Indiana as a model "Rust Belt" state with regard to regulatory policy, and reform Ohio's regulatory system according to that model. For instance, consider liberalizing the workers' compensation system and rolling back occupational licensing. Adopt a right-to-work law in line with Indiana and Michigan.

Personal: Abolish mandatory minimum sentences for nonviolent offenses, with an eye toward reducing the incarceration rate to a level more consistent with its crime rate.

ANALYSIS

Ohio is a thoroughly mediocre state when it comes to freedom. It is 20th on fiscal policy but really needs to do a lot better on both regulatory (32nd) and personal freedom (40th). It should trouble Buckeyes that their state's policy regime is significantly worse than that of other Great Lakes states that have been reforming, such as Indiana, Michigan, and Wisconsin.

Ohio's taxes are about at the national average overall. But it is more fiscally decentralized than the average state. Local taxes add up to about 4.7 percent of adjusted personal income, while state taxes sit at a projected 4.9 percent of income in FY 2020. The latter have been in decline since a high of 6.2 percent in FY 2005. The discovery of shale gas has allowed Ohio to raise severance taxes and essentially shift some of its tax burden to consumers of natural gas throughout North America. State and local debt, government consumption, and public employment are all lower than average and in long-term decline.

On the most important regulatory policy category, land-use and environmental freedom, Ohio does well, though it has slowly declined. Zoning has a light touch, but the trend is in the wrong direction according to at least one of our sources, and renewable portfolio standards exist but are very low. Labor-market freedom is a problem area for Ohio. Eminent domain reform could have gone further. The state has a minimum wage that is getting worse, no right-to-work law, and strict workers' compensation coverage and funding rules. Health insurance mandates are costly. Cable and telecommunications have been liberalized. The average of different

measures suggests that in Ohio, the extent of occupational licensing is greater than average and has been growing. Nursing scope of practice is the most restricted in the country, but at least dental hygienists and physician assistants have been freed. The state has a hospital certificate-of-need law, and household moving companies are restricted, but price regulation in most markets is limited. Insurance rating was liberalized somewhat in 2015 but then restricted again somewhat in 2018. The civil liability system has bounced around over time and is now below average.

Ohio has a higher-than-average crime-adjusted incarceration rate, and it has risen over time, albeit with some slight decline lately. Meanwhile, victimless crime arrest rates are lower than average and have fallen over time. A significant asset forfeiture reform was enacted in 2016; it could be improved even further, but right now Ohio is above average in this category. Driver's licenses stopped being suspended for non-driving drug offenses in 2016, and a year earlier, prison phone call rates were slashed dramatically. A limited medical marijuana law was enacted in 2015, and the state already enjoys limited decriminalization. Gun rights are better than average but still mediocre. Casinos were legalized in 2012, but sports betting wasn't as of December 1, 2021. Educational freedom is above average mostly because of a statewide voucher program, but private schools and homeschools are sharply regulated despite mandatory private school registration ending in 2016. Tobacco freedom is limited, with draconian smoking bans in place for a decade and an increased minimum age for purchase. Alcohol, gambling, and travel freedom are middling.

OKLAHOMA

2019 RANK

19th

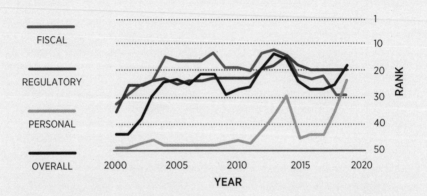

FISCAL

REGULATORY

PERSONAL

OVERALL

RANK

YEAR

PARTY CONTROL

■ R ■ D	2021	2019	2017
GOVERNOR	Stitt	Stitt	Fallin
SENATE			
HOUSE OF REP.			

POLICY RECOMMENDATIONS

Fiscal: Reduce the bloated government payroll. The proceeds could be applied to shaving the sales tax.

Regulatory: Legalize nurse practitioner independent practice with full prescription authority.

Personal: Eliminate mandatory minimum sentences for victimless offenses.

ANALYSIS

Oklahoma is among the most improved states for the 2000–2019 period, with some regression in 2015–2016 and then a return to the upswing more recently. It used to be a bottom-10 state for overall freedom and second worst for personal freedom. Now the Sooner State is about average on both because of rising personal freedom and declining relative economic freedom. It is now 19th in overall freedom.

Oklahoma is one of the lowest-taxed states in America. However, it is also fiscally centralized. Local taxation is about 3.3 percent of adjusted personal income, whereas state taxation is 4.7 percent. Yet Oklahomans should beware that both of the taxes have risen during the past few years. State and local debt is much lower than average (11.6 percent of adjusted income), but so are financial assets of state and local governments (16.1 percent of adjusted income). Government employment is much higher than average (15.2 percent of private employment), and government GDP share is also high (14.7 percent of income).

Land-use regulation is light in Oklahoma; in fact, it is a top-three state despite not restraining eminent domain for private gain and banning employers from prohibiting guns in their own parking lots. Labor law is average, with a right-to-work law and no state-level minimum wage. However, some backsliding took place in 2016 after a 2014 repeal of mandated workers' compensation coverage. Moreover, the state has an above-federal anti-discrimination law and a long-standing ban on noncompete agreements. Telecommunications and cable have gone unreformed. Occupational licensing has grown over time and is more extensive than average. Nurses' practice freedom is mixed, with nurses losing any autonomous practice in 2014, but the state did join the Nurse Licensure Compact in 2017. Physician assistants and dental hygienists are relatively free. Insurance freedom is high, with rate filing liberalized in 2010. However, rate classification prohibitions were reenacted in 2018 after being eliminated in 2013/14. The state does have both general and gasoline-focused prohibitions on sales below cost, a price-gouging law, a certificate-of-need law for both medical facilities and moving company licensing, and a ban on Tesla's direct-sales model. The court system is relatively good because of tort reforms in the 1990s and early 2000s.

Oklahoma is a mass-incarcerating state, and federal data show the situation worsened significantly in the 2013–2015 period. It is modestly better than this today, though still quite bad. Despite that, victimless crime arrests as a percentage of all arrests declined from about 2005 to 2012, then edged up again slightly to the present. The decline has been steady as a percentage of the population. Drug arrests have bounced around. Civil asset forfeiture reform has not gone far, but revenues are down. A life sentence is still possible for a single cannabis offense not involving minors. The mandatory minimum sentence is two years for even small-scale cultivation. The state enacted a medical marijuana reform in 2018. For a state without a government liquor monopoly, Oklahoma does average on alcohol freedom. It has a near-total ban on direct wine shipment, and a ban on all alcohol sales but wine in grocery stores. The state passed mandatory server training in 2018, but blue laws and happy hour bans were eliminated. Casino gambling was legalized in 2005, but social gambling is still illegal. Educational freedom has grown recently, with a very limited voucher law in 2010 and a modest tax benefit for contributions to private scholarship funds enacted in 2011/12. Homeschools and private schools are virtually unregulated, and a statute was enacted in 2016 codifying the existing homeschool legal regime. Tobacco freedom was relatively good but has declined to below average with a substantial tax increase in 2018. The state was forced to legalize same-sex marriage, suspending its super-DOMA, in 2014. Gun laws are a high point, with the state coming in 16th. Constitutional carry passed in 2019. Raw milk sales are legal, and there is an affirmative action ban in public services.

OREGON

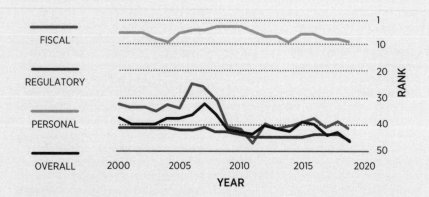

	FISCAL
	REGULATORY
	PERSONAL
	OVERALL

RANK

YEAR

PARTY CONTROL

■ R ■ D

	2021	2019	2017
GOVERNOR	Brown	Brown	Brown
SENATE			
HOUSE OF REP.			

POLICY RECOMMENDATIONS

Fiscal: Cut fire protection, financial control and general administration, employee retirement, health and hospitals, and public welfare current operations to levels consistent with national norms. Cut individual income and property taxes.

Regulatory: Eliminate occupational licensing for farm labor contractors, environmental science technicians, dietitians, pharmacy technicians, massage therapists, private detectives, landscaping contractors, well-drilling contractors, low-power installers, locksmiths, crane operators, and other occupations.

Personal: Follow Washington's lead and privatize the distilled spirits retail industry.

ANALYSIS

Oregon used to have some advantages compared with its less free southern neighbor, California. However, it has become more and more like the Golden State over time. That has not been good for the freedom of Oregonians. Oregon was ranked as high as 32nd back in 2007. Today, it is 46th. Oregon is among the worst states on economic freedom but despite a relative slide remains a top-10 state on person freedom.

Oregon's fiscal ranking has been roughly the same since the Great Recession, when it dropped significantly and entered the bottom 10 states. State taxes for FY 2020 come in at 6.1 percent of adjusted income, above the national average, and significantly higher than they were a decade ago. Local taxes have dropped during that time and are now near the national average at about 4.0 percent of income. Oregonians have little choice of local government, with just 0.43 effective competing jurisdictions per 100 square miles. Government debt has come down but is still higher than average. State and local employment is lower than average, whereas government GDP share is higher.

Land use has been a controversial issue in Oregon, and the Beaver State is indeed more regulated in this department than all other states. It's been quite onerous for years and continues to get worse. The state also ratcheted up its renewable portfolio standard in 2014. It does have both compensation and economic assessments for takings. And new to 2019 is local rent control. By contrast, the state legislature has recently taken steps to preempt single-family local zoning rules.[180] Oregon's labor policy is generally anti-employment, with one of the highest minimum wages in the country relative to the median wage, no right-to-work law, and comprehensive workers' compensation mandates. In 2019, the state added paid family leave. Telecommunications and cable remain unreformed. The managed care model of health insurance has been virtually banned since 2003, but mandated benefits are modest. Several independent measures show that Oregon licenses far more occupations than most other states. However, health professions' practice freedom is moderate. Insurance freedom grew years ago with an end to rating classification prohibitions and the joining of the Interstate Insurance Product Regulation Compact. The state has an anti-price-gouging law, household moving certification, and certificate-of-need requirements for hospitals. The civil liability system looks a bit better than the national average.

Oregon's criminal justice policy does not quite match the state's live-and-let-live reputation. It is only 18th on incarceration and arrests. Incarceration rates are pretty average, but drug and victimless crime arrests have come down substantially during the past decade to above average levels. Marijuana liberty is expansive, but that is not the case for freedom to buy distilled spirits, which are available only in extremely expensive government stores. Beer taxes, though, are low. Civil asset forfeiture has been fairly restricted since 2005, and law enforcement does not often circumvent state law through equitable sharing. Tobacco freedom is extremely limited, with extensive smoking bans that are comprehensive and airtight. The state also has new vaping bans and has increased the minimum age to purchase. But taxes haven't been terrible. Gun rights are better than one might expect from a left-of-center state, but in 2007 open carry was regulated. Illegal immigrants can now get driver's licenses again, but travel freedom remains low because of bans on handheld cell phones and open containers, seat belt and helmet laws, and mandatory underinsured driver coverage. Physician-assisted suicide is legal. Fireworks are highly regulated. Educational freedom is low because of a total lack of school choice policies (even public school open enrollment), but private schools and homeschools are regulated with a light touch. Oregonians are free to gamble using video slot machines and to bet on sports.

---

180.   Laurel Wamsley, "Oregon Legislature Votes to Essentially Ban Single-Family Zoning," NPR, July 1, 2019.

PENNSYLVANIA

2019 RANK

14th

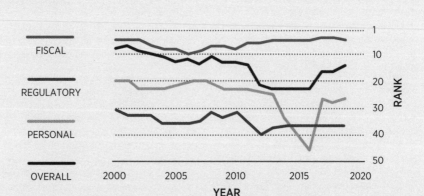

PARTY CONTROL

		2021	2019	2017
GOVERNOR		Wolf	Wolf	Wolf
SENATE				
HOUSE OF REP.				

Legend: ■ R ■ D

POLICY RECOMMENDATIONS

Fiscal: Reduce spending, especially on parking lots, public buildings, public welfare operations, and employee retirement benefits, which are high by national standards. Reduce numerous minor taxes that are relatively high by national standards.

Regulatory: Free nurses through increasing independent practice authority for nurse practitioners and joining the Nurse Licensure Compact.

Personal: Unburden private schools and homeschools from paternalistic regulations.

ANALYSIS

The Keystone State is freer than all its neighbors. At No. 14 in our ranking, it is also better than most states in the country. Pennsylvania does particularly well on fiscal policy, where it is a top-five state. Regulatory policy drags down the commonwealth's economic freedom score and is an area ripe for improvement.

Fiscal policy is the dimension where Pennsylvania has done best. Pennsylvania's tax burden is about average, but the state is a bit more fiscally decentralized than average, with local governments making up a larger share of the total tax take. The tax burden has declined slightly since 2000. Pennsylvanians have ample choice of local government, with more than 4.9 effective competing jurisdictions per 100 square miles. State and local debt is higher than average, and financial assets are lower, but public employment is much lower than average (9.0 percent of the private workforce), and so is government GDP (7.9 percent of adjusted income).

Pennsylvania ranks a woeful 37th on regulatory policy. It is mediocre on land-use freedom. However, it is better than most northeastern states, a fact that economist William Fischel attributes to the state supreme court's one-time willingness to strike down minimum lot sizes and other zoning regulations that have exclusionary intent.[181] One of our measures (WRLURI based) shows slight improvement in zoning over time, whereas the other (court cases) shows marked deterioration. The state is not as bad as most other northeastern states on labor-market regulation, but it lacks a right-to-work law and has avoided raising the minimum wage above federal minimums. Pennsylvania has banned managed care health coverage since the 1990s, but insurance mandates are relatively low. By most measures, occupational licensing is not very extensive in Pennsylvania, but nurses enjoy little practice freedom.

Insurance freedom is low, with prior approval of homeowner's insurance rates and rating classification prohibitions. In 2016, personal automobile insurance rates were slightly liberalized, but this reform was clawed back in 2018. The state has a general sales-below-cost law and an anti-price-gouging law. The civil liability system is much worse than the national average. The state has partisan judicial elections and has made only timid efforts at tort reform.

Pennsylvania's criminal justice policy is a mixed bag. Rising crime-adjusted incarceration rates bottomed out in 2009–2013 before getting slightly better since, whereas nonviolent victimless crime arrests have been down since 2004–2005. Drug arrests rates have also gotten better during the past decade. Civil asset forfeiture was reformed for 2017 and is now the 12th best in the country. Pennsylvania finally enacted a modest medical marijuana law in the 2015/16 session but has not decriminalized low-level possession. Gun rights are much better respected than in many other states, with carry licenses affordable and not terribly restricted, all Class III weapons legal, and a right to defend oneself in public legally recognized in 2011. Since legalizing casinos in 2007, Pennsylvania has risen to become one of the best states in the country for gambling liberty—except for home poker games. It has also legalized sports betting. Then again, Pennsylvania is one of the worst states for alcohol freedom. A notoriously inefficient state bureaucracy monopolizes wine and spirits. Wine markups are especially high, and even beer is prohibited in the physical space of grocery stores. However, direct wine shipments were legalized in 2016. On education, Pennsylvania has a long-standing and liberal tax-credit scholarship program, but private schools and homeschools are tightly regulated. Smoking bans have gone far but are not total. Cigarette taxes, though, are draconian at $2.60 a pack.

---

181.   William A. Fischel, *The Homevoter Hypothesis: How Home Values Influence Local Government Taxation, School Finance, and Land-Use Policies* (Cambridge, MA: Harvard University Press, 2001), p. 282.

RHODE ISLAND

2019 RANK
41st

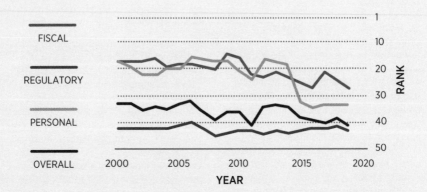

	FISCAL				RANK
	REGULATORY				
	PERSONAL				
	OVERALL	2000	2005	2010	2015	2020

YEAR

PARTY CONTROL

■ R   ■ D

	2021	2019	2017
GOVERNOR	McKee	Raimondo	Raimondo
SENATE			
HOUSE OF REP.			

POLICY RECOMMENDATIONS

Fiscal: Cut spending on public buildings, housing, public welfare operations, and employee retirement, all areas in which state and local governments spend abnormally high amounts. The savings could be applied to reductions in selective sales and individual income taxes.

Regulatory: Reform land-use regulations, perhaps through an Arizona-style regulatory takings compensation requirement combined with eminent domain reform.

Personal: Legalize cultivation, sale, and possession of recreational marijuana.

ANALYSIS

Rhode Island has long been a fairly typical deep-blue state with ample personal freedom and weak economic freedom, but that has changed lately, as Rhode Island has not kept up with the rest of the country's growing personal freedom. It is now only middling on personal freedom, coming in 33rd. Unfortunately for Rhode Islanders, the state's regulatory freedom weighs down their economic freedom ranking, where it comes in 40th. It is also one of the few states that has lost overall freedom since both 2000 and 2018.

Rhode Island's fiscal policy is slightly subpar. State and local taxes are high, coming in at a combined 10.9 percent compared with a national average of 9.6 percent. Local taxes are particularly problematic. Government debt is excessive, while financial assets are below the national average. The state does benefit from government consumption and employment that are well below the national average. With nearly four effective competing jurisdictions per 100 square miles, Rhode Island affords its residents quite a bit of choice among localities.

Rhode Island's regulatory policy score has been essentially static—and bad—during the past two decades, setting aside the effects of federal health law. Land-use freedom is low because of exclusionary zoning and eminent domain abuse, and at least one of our indicators suggests it has steadily worsened since the early 2000s (another suggests some mild improvement during the past few years). Renewable portfolio standards are high. Labor policy is also anti-employment, with a high minimum wage; no right-to-work law; a short-term disability insurance mandate; a stricter-than-federal anti-discrimination law; and, since 2013/14, a paid family leave mandate. Health insurance freedom is poor and even includes a state-level individual mandate. Cable and telecommunications have been liberalized. Occupational licensing extent is about average, but freedom of practice for health care paraprofessionals is quite high. A price-gouging law was enacted in 2011/12, and the state has long had a general ban on "unfair(ly low)" prices." Medical facilities and moving companies face entry restrictions. But a "Tesla law" was passed in 2018 allowing some direct-to-consumer auto sales. Freedom from abusive lawsuits is a bit below average but has improved slightly during the past two decades.

Rhode Island has the second-best criminal justice system in the country, only trailing Massachusetts. Incarceration rates are well below average, as are drug and nondrug victimless crime arrests. Unfortunately, the state has not sufficiently reformed civil asset forfeiture, and—although a big equitable sharing payout somewhat skews Rhode Island's scores on that variable—evidence suggests that local law enforcement participated eagerly in the program even before that payout and since. The state has a fairly extensive medical cannabis law, and low-level possession of cannabis was decriminalized in 2012. However, it is still possible to get life imprisonment for a single marijuana offense not involving minors. The state was working toward legalization in 2021, with some hope that a special session could see legislation pass this year. Gambling freedom is high, unless you want to play poker with friends in your own home. Internet gambling was liberalized in 2018. A tax-credit scholarship law and repeal of private school teacher licensing passed in 2011/12, bringing the state's educational freedom above average. The state would benefit from another burst of reform. Tobacco freedom is one of the lowest in the country because of sky-high cigarette taxes (well over $3 a pack) and comprehensive smoking bans. It now has vaping bans as well. Alcohol freedom is mediocre, with decent tax rates but bans on almost all direct wine sales. Gun laws are extremely restrictive but have not changed much since 2000.

SOUTH CAROLINA

28th

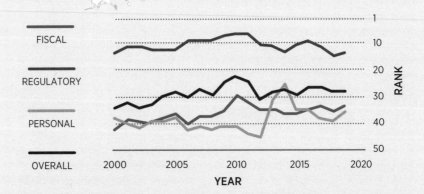

	FISCAL
	REGULATORY
	PERSONAL
	OVERALL

RANK

2000   2005   2010   2015   2020

YEAR

PARTY CONTROL

		2021	2019	2017
■ R	■ D			
GOVERNOR		McMaster	McMaster	McMaster
SENATE				
HOUSE OF REP.				

POLICY RECOMMENDATIONS

Fiscal: Hospital spending as a share of income is nearly three times the national average, and public employment is also abnormally high. These problems could be solved by privatization and cuts. Cut the sales tax.

Regulatory: South Carolina was one of the states where a certificate-of-need law for health care facilities was suspended in reaction to COVID-19.[182] Permanently abolish certificate-of-need laws and other barriers to meeting consumer needs.

Personal: Pass a medical marijuana bill similar to one that Republican legislators have proposed in the past.

182.   Angela C. Erickson, "States Are Suspending Certificate of Need Laws in the Wake of COVID-19 but the Damage Might Already Be Done," Pacific Legal Foundation, January 11, 2021.

ANALYSIS

South Carolina has traditionally done better on economic freedom than on personal freedom. The court-ordered legalization of same-sex marriage gave South Carolina a big spike on personal freedom in 2014, but other states quickly followed, and that relative advantage was undone (although obviously not the improvement in freedom in an absolute sense). The split between economic freedom and personal freedom rankings survives, but the difference isn't as great as one might expect. This factor is due to South Carolina's less-than-stellar fiscal policy, where it ranks 33rd. The state's overall freedom has grown since 2000 and during the past two years, in an absolute sense.

As one of the states more dependent on the federal government, the Palmetto State gets by with high government employment and consumption and a relatively low tax burden. Local taxes are average, but state taxes—at a projected 4.6 percent of adjusted personal income in FY 2020—are below the 5.7 percent national average for 2000–2019. South Carolina enjoyed big tax cuts in the mid- to late 2000s according to our measure. Government GDP share of income has fallen steadily from its 2009 high, as has government employment. But they are both still much too high. Debt remains above average but since FY 2010 has fallen a remarkable 12.1 percentage points of adjusted income, even though cash and security assets have fallen 2.0 points during that same period.

South Carolina's regulatory policy has improved noticeably over time, ignoring the PPACA impact. Much of that improvement is because of tort reforms in 2005 and 2011 and an improving civil liability system, in which confidence continues to increase according to the latest data. Land-use freedom is decent but steadily declining because of more restrictions. Fortunately, eminent domain reform has gone far, and the state has avoided a mandatory renewable portfolio standard. Labor law is generally good, with no state-level minimum wage and a right-to-work law,

but the state did enact an E-Verify mandate in 2008. Health insurance mandates are lower than average. Cable and telecommunications have been liberalized. Occupational licensing grew further and is starting to look like a real problem for the state, even in comparison with the rest of the country. Nurses enjoy only a little practice freedom. Insurance freedom is a bit subpar, and the state went backward to prior approval. South Carolina also regulates prices for gasoline, general retailers, and in emergencies. It has entry barriers to hospitals and moving companies.

South Carolina's criminal justice policies are not much like the Deep South. Incarceration and victimless crime arrest rates have been more or less average—and improving of late. Drug arrests have been a different story and remain worse than average. Asset forfeiture abuse has not been curbed, but participation in equitable sharing has declined with regard to revenue. Cannabis penalties are somewhat harsh, and South Carolina's inability to keep up with changes in other states places it in the bottom 10. For example, it doesn't have medical marijuana. Gun rights are reasonably broad but as of our data cutoff, they were below the level enjoyed in Pennsylvania or even blue Oregon. Recent changes should improve the situation, as 2021 saw the enactment of legislation that allows concealed-carry permit holders to open carry while also eliminating the cost of a concealed-carry permit.[183] However, the state resisted a constitutional carry amendment. Educational freedom is slightly above average. Private schools and homeschools are harshly regulated, and school choice programs have only a modest tax benefit. Tobacco freedom is above average, as smoking bans on private property contain exceptions, and cigarette taxes are low. The state was forced to legalize same-sex marriage in 2014, overturning its super-DOMA banning private contracts for gay couples. Alcohol freedom is middling, with beer taxes remarkably high. Automated license plate readers are totally unregulated, but raw milk sales are allowed. There is little legal gambling freedom, even for sports betting.

---

183. "South Carolina: Open Carry & Free CWP Bill to Go into Effect," Institute for Legislative Action, National Rifle Association, August 13, 2021.

SOUTH DAKOTA

2019 RANK
5th

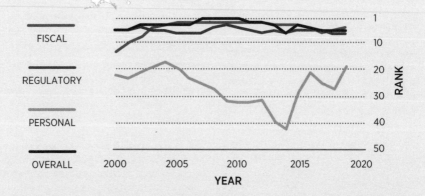

		RANK
FISCAL		1
		10
REGULATORY		20
PERSONAL		30
		40
OVERALL		50

YEAR: 2000 · 2005 · 2010 · 2015 · 2020

PARTY CONTROL

■ R   ■ D

	2021	2019	2017
GOVERNOR	Noem	Noem	Daugaard
SENATE			
HOUSE OF REP.			

POLICY RECOMMENDATIONS

Fiscal: Trim spending on employment security administration, natural resources, and parks and recreation, areas far above national averages. Eliminate the bank franchise tax.

Regulatory: Amend the constitution to require a supermajority (say, 60 percent) to pass any new regulatory infringement on the rights of private citizens through the initiative process. This change could help with both labor-market and tobacco freedom.

Personal: Reform asset forfeiture to place the burden of proof on the government, not on innocent owner claimants, and direct funds to the treasury, not to the seizing departments.

ANALYSIS

South Dakota was once the stereotypical deep-red state that performed really well on economic freedom but poorly on personal freedom. However, this isn't true today—and it wasn't always true anyway. In the early 2000s, it was in the middle of the pack and even rose all the way to 17th on personal freedom in 2004. But then it slid relative to other states all the way to 39th by 2013 and 42nd in 2014. However, South Dakota has been on the upswing since then, moving to 29th in 2015. It then went from 27th in 2018 to 18th in the most recent year. It is little wonder considering its consistently stellar across-the-board economic performance that South Dakota remains one of the top-five freest states.

South Dakota's fiscal policy is excellent. The state has one of the lowest tax burdens in the country, although it has risen slightly at both state and local levels since a decade ago. State taxation is extremely low at 3.6 percent, with local taxation at 4.2 percent. It is also relatively fiscally decentralized, and South Dakotans do have some choice among local jurisdictions (1.3 effective jurisdictions per 100 square miles). State and local debt is well below the national average, but cash and security assets are low. Public employment is now above the national average at 12.7 percent of private employment, but this has more to do with other states getting better; South Dakota's ratio of public to private employment has shrunk slightly since 2016. The government GDP share of income is low at 9.3 percent. We register a fairly significant reduction in debt since FY 2009, but assets have also fallen during that time.

South Dakota's regulatory policy is well above average, but it has actually declined a bit, even discounting the PPACA, since 2000. Land-use freedom is sound, with eminent domain reform passed long ago; the state has avoided renewable portfolio standards. However, the state has no compensation for regulatory takings, and land-use restrictions have gone up. Labor law is generally good because of right-to-work and other provisions, but a very high (for the local market) minimum wage was enacted by ballot initiative in 2014. South Dakota is one of the best states for health insurance freedom, with only a handful of the costliest mandates and few restrictions on the managed care model. Telecommunications has been liberalized, but statewide video franchising has not been enacted. Multiple indicators suggest that occupational licensing has grown, and the state is no longer better than average here. Nursing practice freedom is subpar but liberalized slightly in 2016. Insurance freedom is mediocre, as the state has held out against the Interstate Insurance Product Regulation Compact and has enacted a rate classification prohibition. However, the state is mercifully free of a variety of other cronyist entry and price regulations, including a certificate-of-need law. The state's civil liability system is above average and has improved over time.

South Dakota's criminal justice policies are excessively strict from our point of view. For its crime rate, it imprisons more than it should. Drug arrests are well above national norms. However, the victimless crime arrest rate dipped significantly from 2018 to 2019, no matter how it is measured, and is part of a longer trend in the right direction. Asset forfeiture is virtually unreformed, though local law enforcement does not participate much in equitable sharing. Prison phone call rates were more than halved in 2015/16. Cannabis law is harsher than in most states, though not the harshest. Medical marijuana was passed in 2020. Gambling freedom is extensive and will get more so now that sports betting was legalized in 2020 for in-person and internet betting. Private school and homeschool regulations are not as burdensome as those of the neighbor to the north, and the legislature enacted a limited private scholarship tax benefit in 2016. Smoking bans are extreme, with vaping bans added in 2019. South Dakota is one of the best states in the country for gun rights and has improved in absolute terms since the fifth edition, with the passage of constitutional carry in 2019. Alcohol freedom is also fairly extensive, and the ban on direct shipment of wine was repealed in 2015.

TENNESSEE

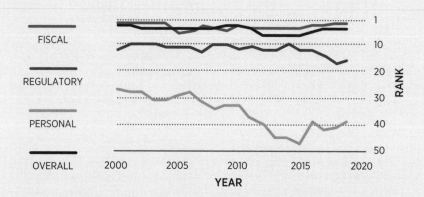

- FISCAL
- REGULATORY
- PERSONAL
- OVERALL

PARTY CONTROL

■ R   ■ D

	2021	2019	2017
GOVERNOR	Lee	Lee	Haslam
SENATE			
HOUSE OF REP.			

POLICY RECOMMENDATIONS

Fiscal: Separate spending and tax committees in the legislature, a reform shown to correspond to lower spending over time. Sales taxes are high and could be cut.

Regulatory: Repeal the price-gouging law and all minimum-markup laws.

Personal: Deregulate private schools and homeschools by removing mandatory approval and teacher licensing for private schools and relaxing annual notification requirements for homeschoolers.

ANALYSIS

Tennessee has long been one of the economically freest states, largely because of its outstanding fiscal policies, but it also used to be one of the personally freest states in the South. That edge disappeared as it became a more stereotypical red state. As a result, Tennessee fell from third in overall freedom in 2001 to seventh in 2012. It has recovered some ground since and is now fourth overall in this year's index.

The Volunteer State lacks an income tax, and both state and local tax collections fall well below the national average. We show state-level taxes falling from 5.1 percent of adjusted personal income in FY 2007 to 4.2 percent in FY 2014, then rising to 4.4 percent in FY 2017 and falling to a low of 4.1 percent in the latest data. This shift compares to a national average in FY 2020 of 5.7 percent. Local taxes were already below the national average of 3.7 percent in FY 2009, but they fell off a cliff to only 2.5 percent of income now. State and local debt is low at 14.3 percent of income. Government consumption and investment is low at 9.1 percent of income and has been falling for a decade. Government employment is only 10.2 percent of private employment, a big drop since 2010 as the job market has recovered.

Tennessee's land-use regulations are flexible, and the state has a regulatory takings law. However, eminent domain reform has not gone far. The state put into place a law preventing employers from banning guns on certain company property in 2015. Tennessee is in the top 10 for labor-market freedom, with a right-to-work law, no minimum wage, and relaxed workers' compensation rules. Unfortunately, E-Verify was mandated in 2011. The managed care model of health coverage has been effectively banned. Mandates are low. Cable and telecommunications have

been liberalized. On the downside, the extent of occupational licensure looks rather high, though different indicators give different pictures. Nurse practitioners lost whatever independent scope of practice they had in 2010, but dental hygienists gained some in 2013. The state marginally loosened insurance rate regulation in 2009/10 but restrictions came back in 2018. The state has general and gasoline-specific minimum-markup laws, as well as an anti-price-gouging law, household mover licensing, and a certificate-of-need law for medical facilities. The civil liability system improved to above average with reforms in 2011 to punitive damages.

Tennessee's criminal justice policies have been improving the past few years, though it still ranks outside the top 30. The crime-adjusted incarceration rate rose steadily from 2000 to 2011 but has been on a downward trend since. It is still above average, but the past two years have seen a good drop. Drug arrest rates and victimless crime arrest rates are also moving in the right direction. The latter is below average. Asset forfeiture is mostly unreformed, but equitable sharing revenue is going in the right direction. Cannabis laws are strict, though a very limited medical marijuana law was enacted in 2021. Tennessee is mediocre on gun rights in our index, but its passage of permitless handgun carry in 2021 has significantly expanded gun freedom in the state. The new Smith & Wesson presence will provide a positive interest group force in the state. Alcohol freedom is now above average because of blue law relaxation in 2017/18. Beer taxes remain excessive. The state has little gambling, though it now has sports betting as of 2019. Educational freedom is slightly below average, but a voucher program was passed in 2019. Private schools and home-schools face significant regulatory burdens. Tobacco freedom is a bit better than average, with relatively low taxes, but new regulations on internet purchase appeared in 2017.

TEXAS

2019 RANK

21st

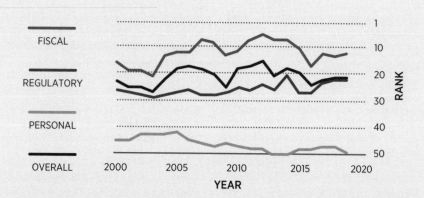

Legend:
- FISCAL
- REGULATORY
- PERSONAL
- OVERALL

RANK axis: 1, 10, 20, 30, 40, 50
YEAR axis: 2000, 2005, 2010, 2015, 2020

PARTY CONTROL

	2021	2019	2017
GOVERNOR	Abbott	Abbott	Abbott
SENATE			
HOUSE OF REP.			

■ R   ■ D

POLICY RECOMMENDATIONS

Fiscal: Tighten the rules for municipal annexation and make municipal secession easy to provide Texans with more choice in local government. Decentralize county responsibilities to the municipal level.

Regulatory: Pass a law allowing direct-to-consumer auto sales so that Texans can more easily take advantage of the new Tesla auto plant being built in Austin.[184]

Personal: Enact a general educational savings account plan similar to the one enacted in Nevada in 2015.[185]

184. Mitchell Clark, "Teslas Made in Texas Will Likely Have to Leave the State before Texans Can Buy Them," *The Verge* (blog), May 30, 2021.

185. See Kent Grusendorf and Nate Sherer, "How ESAs Can Keep Texas the Land of the Free and Home of the Brave," policy brief, Texas Public Policy Foundation, January 2016.

ANALYSIS

Texas talks a good game about freedom but could stand to deliver a more freedom-oriented policy regime. It comes in only at 21st in this edition, rescued largely by its top-10 economic freedom score, and it has never been higher than 15th overall. The problem is that Texas has always been a less free state for personal freedom and now is the second-worst state on that margin despite some absolute improvement over time. Its economic freedom is likely one reason it hasn't slipped out of the top half states and why it's been such a job-producing and population-attracting machine. It does especially well on fiscal policy where it ranks 12th. It is also a solidly above-average state on regulatory policy, but not as good as one might expect at 22nd.

Texas's fiscal policy is very good. It is a fiscally decentralized state, with local taxes at about 4.9 percent of adjusted personal income, above the national average, and state taxes at about 3.5 percent of income, quite far below the national average of 5.7 percent. However, Texans have little choice of local government, with only 0.39 jurisdictions per 100 square miles. State and local debt is above average at 21.2 percent of income, with the biggest problem being local debt burdens, but the overall debt burden has come down noticeably since FY 2010. Public employment has fallen to significantly below average, at 10.7 percent of private employment, and government share of GDP is only 9.7 percent, below the national average of 10.3 percent. If Texas could get a handle on local taxes and debt, it could improve on its top-10 economic freedom score and become an even greater economic powerhouse.

Texas's land-use freedom keeps housing abundant and affordable, but it has slipped a bit lately. The state has a renewable portfolio standard, but it has not been raised in years. Texas is our top state for labor-market freedom. Workers' compensation coverage is optional for employers; most employees are covered, but not all. The state has a right-to-work law, no minimum wage, and a federally consistent anti-discrimination law. Cable and telecommunications have been liberalized. However, health insurance mandates are way above average, and the gatekeeper model of managed care has been banned. The individual health insurance mandate was removed federally in 2019 and was not replaced at the state level. The extent of occupational licensing is high, but the state enacted a sunrise review requirement for new licensure proposals in 2013. Time will tell whether it is at all effective. Nurse practitioners enjoy no freedom of independent practice. Texas does not have many cronyist entry and price regulations, but it does have a price-gouging law, and Tesla's direct sales model is still illegal. Texas suffered a marked deterioration in homeowner's insurance regulation in 2015, resulting in a large residual market, but the state reformed it back to file and use in 2018. The civil liability system used to be terrible, but now it is merely below average. The state abolished joint and several liability in 2003, but it could do more to cap punitive damages and end political parties' role in judicial elections.

Personal freedom is abysmally low in Texas, especially given how we operationalize it. Criminal justice policies are generally aggressive, but reforms have been ongoing in the state for some time. Even controlling for crime rates, the incarceration rate is far above the national average but has been improving. Drug arrests have fallen over time and are now about average for the user base. Nondrug victimless crime arrests have also fallen over time and are now much below the national average. This change would seem to show the power of the criminal justice reform efforts. Asset forfeiture is mostly unreformed, but law enforcement participation in equitable sharing has declined with regard to revenues. Cannabis laws are harsh. A single offense not involving minors can carry a life sentence. Even cultivating a tiny amount carries a mandatory minimum of six months. In 2013/14, the state banned the mostly harmless psychedelic *Salvia divinorum*. Medical marijuana was further expanded in 2021. Travel freedom is low. The state takes a fingerprint for driver's licenses and does not regulate automated license plate readers. It has little legal gambling; sports betting remains illegal. Texas has no private school choice programs, but at least private schools and homeschools are basically unregulated. Tobacco freedom is moderate, as smoking bans have not gone as far as in other states. But the state did add a minimum age of purchase increase in 2019. Gun rights have been moderately above average, but the state wasn't even in the top half of the states despite Texas's reputation. Open carry was legalized in 2015. The big positive reform came in 2021 with the passage of constitutional carry. Alcohol freedom is above average, with taxes low. Texas has virtually no campaign finance regulations.

UTAH

20th

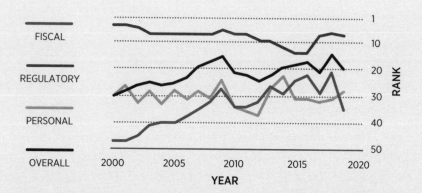

FISCAL

REGULATORY

PERSONAL

OVERALL

RANK

YEAR

PARTY CONTROL

		2021	2019	2017
■ R	■ D			
GOVERNOR		Cox	Herbert	Herbert
SENATE				
HOUSE OF REP.				

POLICY RECOMMENDATIONS

Fiscal: Build up cash reserves and retire state debt.

Regulatory: Eliminate occupational licensing for taxi drivers and chauffeurs, funeral attendants, occupational therapist assistants, recreational therapists, interpreters and translators, and other occupations. Enact mandatory sunrise review for new licensing proposals, ideally with consumer and professional economist representation.

Personal: Introduce "backpack funding" to free children and their caregivers to pursue their education as they see fit.

ANALYSIS

Utah is a top-10 state on regulatory freedom but has slipped in absolute and relative terms on fiscal policy, sinking back to where it was in 2014 after some years of improvement in terms of absolute scores. Personal freedoms are a mixed bag, consistent with the state's religious and ideological background.

Utah's overall tax burden is a bit above average. We show a dramatic drop in state revenues with the onset of the Great Recession, which haven't quite been replaced. In fact, further tax cuts were enacted in FY 2014. But state tax burden climbed a lot in FY 2020 compared with the previous year and decade, moving higher to 6.2 percent, above the national average. Local taxes, meanwhile, have remained generally steady at 3.7 percent, right below the national average rate of 3.9 percent of adjusted personal income. Utahans have little choice among local governments, just 0.38 jurisdictions per 100 square miles. Government GDP share was about average, but debt, government employment, and assets were all lower than average. Employment has been improving since 2011, moving from 13.0 percent to 11.5 percent.

Utah does well on regulatory policy overall, coming in eighth. It slipped a bit from 2012 to 2016, but it has improved slightly in absolute and relative terms since then. On land-use freedom, the Beehive State is much better than average, but it appears to be tightening zoning rules over time. Eminent domain reform was watered down in 2007. Labor law is solid but not at the very top. The state has a right-to-work law but no minimum wage. However, a new anti-discrimination law was passed in 2016, and the state has had mandated E-Verify for private hires since 2010. Utah changed workers' compensation for the better in 2017. Managed care is legally feasible, but the legislature enacted a costly mandated benefit for in vitro fertilization in 2014. The individual health insurance mandate was removed federally in 2019 and not replaced at the state level. As everywhere, occupational licensing has increased over time. Nursing freedom is better than average, and dental hygienists obtained a limited

right to initiate treatment without dentist authorization in 2015. Insurance freedom is among the best in the country, with "use and file" for most property and casualty lines, long-standing membership in the Interstate Insurance Product Regulation Compact, and no rating classification prohibitions. The state has a price-gouging law and a sales-below-cost law for gasoline on the books. However, its general sales-below-cost law was repealed in 2007/8, and direct auto sales were legalized in 2018. There is no hospital certificate-of-need law or moving company licensing. Utah's civil liability system is better than average and moving in the right direction. It also further deregulated telecommunications in 2017 by removing wireline regulatory authority.

On personal freedom, Utah does surprisingly well given its reputation for paternalism. Moreover, it has been improving over the years and is creeping up toward the top half of the country. The Beehive State does well on gun rights, travel freedom (where it is first in the nation), educational liberty (except for the school choice component of that category), and campaign finance freedom, but quite poorly on alcohol, gambling, and tobacco. The state was also very bad on marriage, but it was forced to legalize same-sex marriage in 2014, a move that also overturned its super-DOMA prohibiting gay partnership contracts. Alcohol and gambling controls are draconian, where the state is 50th in both categories (and causing lots of Utah license plates to be seen at border town casinos). The state has no motorcycle helmet law. It improved on marijuana policy in 2018 because of medical marijuana reform. Utah also does generally well on criminal justice policy. Its crime-adjusted incarceration rate is below the national average and has generally moved down since 2005. Nondrug victimless crime arrests used to be way above average but have come down below national norms, even as drug arrests have risen and hit highs. The state used to have an excellent asset forfeiture law, but it has been successively weakened, most recently in 2013/14. But it remains quite decent on this issue and should improve given a reform bill that passed in 2021.

VERMONT

2019 RANK
43rd

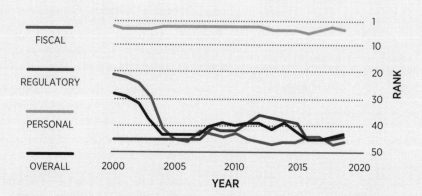

FISCAL

REGULATORY

PERSONAL

OVERALL

RANK

YEAR

PARTY CONTROL

		2021	2019	2017
■ R	■ D			
GOVERNOR		Scott	Scott	Scott
SENATE				
HOUSE OF REP.				

POLICY RECOMMENDATIONS

Fiscal: Undo the past two decades of centralization with a constitutional amendment limiting state government responsibility for education. Return property tax–varying power and school budgeting power fully to towns and reduce state aid to a low level. Use the proceeds to cut income taxes.

Regulatory: Enact regulatory takings compensation or other measures to deter excessively restrictive local zoning.

Personal: Move to a pro-choice and pro-competition position on alcohol sales while stopping the slide left on gun rights.

ANALYSIS

Vermont's economic policies are much worse than its social policies. Indeed, it is a stereotypical blue state. It is among the worst states on economic freedom, doing poorly on both fiscal and regulatory aspects, but among the best on personal freedom.

Vermont is one of the highest-tax states in the country. It also looks extremely fiscally centralized, with state government taking 9.8 percent of adjusted personal income and local government taking just 2.1 percent. However, this statistic is overstated, because Vermont counts the property tax as a state tax, even though towns have some discretion over the rate at which it is set locally. Vermonters would benefit from decentralization of tax and spending authority, as they have 3.3 effective competing jurisdictions per 100 square miles, well above the national average. Government debt is below average, but so are cash and security assets. Government share of GDP and public employment are slightly above average.

Vermont had a moment from about 2007 to about 2011 when it was doing better on regulatory policy. However, it fell consistently after that until 2018 when it bottomed out at 45th. It is among the worst states on land-use and energy freedom, and one measure of local building restrictions based on the prevalence of the term "land use" in appellate court decisions shows a dramatic escalation in restrictiveness since 2000. The other measure—using the WRLURI survey and imputation forward and backward with cost-of-living data—shows improvement since 2005. The state has done little to restrain eminent domain for private gain. One of the toughest renewable portfolio standards in the country was enacted in 2016. On labor policy, the state has a very high minimum wage compared with local market wages, and

it has been rising since 2010. Vermont does not have a right-to-work law. Health insurance mandated benefits are low, but managed care has been hobbled by several measures. The state legislature authorized single-payer health insurance, but the executive branch declined to implement the law, so we do not code this law in our index. Cable has been liberalized. Occupational freedom is one of the bright spots for Vermont for this dimension. It is better than the national average and comes in fifth. For instance, Vermont is one of only four states that do not license massage therapists. Vermont has sunrise review for new licensing proposals, and it is one of the few states with such a requirement to have taken it seriously, as evidenced by the review reports posted online.[186] Nurse practitioners gained full independent practice authority in 2011/12. Insurance freedom is excellent, with a "use and file" system for most property and casualty lines, long-standing membership in the Interstate Insurance Product Regulation Compact, and no rating classification prohibitions. In general, Vermont is one of the least cronyist states. However, the state has a hospital certificate-of-need law, and in 2013/14, it enacted an anti-science and anti-consumer GMO (genetically modified organism) labeling law, since preempted by Congress. Its civil liability system is mediocre; the state has passed no tort reforms.

Vermont ranks fifth for gun rights—but it has slid in the rankings since the fifth edition of the freedom index. It has passed a large-capacity ammunition magazine ban, increased the minimum age to purchase a firearm, and expanded background checks. Silencers were legalized in 2015. Vermont is one of the lowest states for alcohol freedom, with a state monopoly over wine and spirits retail and beer wholesaling. It is one of the better noninitiative states for cannabis, with decriminalization and a reasonably broad medical law. Legalization of personal pos-

---

186. "Sunrise Review," Office of Vermont Secretary of State, https://sos.vermont.gov/opr/regulatory/regulatory-review/.

session and cultivation has only made it freer (and the legalization of commercial sales occurred after our data cutoff). However, maximum penalties are rather high, high-level possession is a felony, and salvia was banned in 2011. Vermont took some travel freedom with one hand and gave back more with the other in 2013/14, enacting a primary handheld cell phone ban, which research has shown to be useless, but also letting illegal immigrants get driver's licenses and placing some limits on automated license plate readers (which sunset in 2015 and were then reenacted in 2016). Vermont has almost no legal gambling. Physician-assisted suicide was enacted in 2013. The state does well on educational freedom because some towns are allowed to "tuition out" students, a century-old practice approximating a voucher law. Homeschool regulations are fairly tough. Tobacco freedom is extremely low, with airtight smoking bans, vending machine and internet purchase restrictions, and high cigarette taxes. In 2019, it became stricter by moving up the minimum age of purchase to 21. The incarceration rate is below average for its crime rate, and victimless crime arrests are very low. Prison phone rates dropped by half in 2016 and then nearly half again in 2018. Vermont has one of the better asset forfeiture laws, but it was weakened in 2015, and equitable sharing provides an easy path to circumvention. Still, the state continues to perform well on this margin. Vermont has always been a legislative leader in marriage freedom and today retains its place with no waiting periods, blood tests, or ban on cousin marriage.

VIRGINIA

2019 RANK

13th

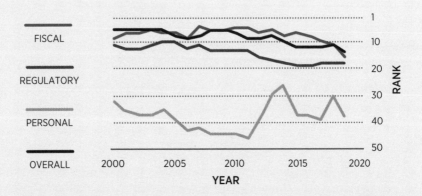

FISCAL

REGULATORY

PERSONAL

OVERALL

RANK

YEAR

PARTY CONTROL

R D	2021	2019	2017
GOVERNOR	Northam	Northam	McAuliffe
SENATE			
HOUSE OF DELEGATES			

POLICY RECOMMENDATIONS

Fiscal: Transfer spending responsibilities and taxation authority from counties to municipalities.

Regulatory: Legalize independent practice with full prescriptive authority for nurse practitioners, adopt a nursing consultation exception for interstate practice, and allow dental hygienists to clean teeth without dentist supervision.

Personal: Reform sentencing for nonviolent offenses with an eye toward reducing the incarceration rate to the national average in the long term.

ANALYSIS

Virginia has historically been a conservative southern state. However, one would be hard-pressed to call it that today despite some lingering policy advantages on the economic side. For the first time since 1993, Democrats won unified control of the state government in 2019 when they took the House and Senate to go along with a Democratic governor. And that Democratic Party is a very different one today than it was then when more conservative southern Democrats were still around.

Virginia has usually done much better on economic freedom than on personal freedom. That remains the case. However, we record slight relative declines in the rankings on both margins. Some significant improvement in personal freedom has taken place over time since its nadir a bit more than a decade ago. But it remains a low-ranking state as other states have liberalized more. It slid considerably in 2019 on fiscal policy, a worrying trend given the possibility of continued unified government in Richmond.

Virginia is a somewhat fiscally decentralized state with an average local tax burden (about 4.0 percent of adjusted income) and a below-average—but rising in FY 2020—state tax burden (5.0 percent of income). Virginians' choice in local government is subpar, with just 0.5 competing jurisdictions per 100 square miles; the reason for this is that counties raise much more in taxes than municipalities. Government debt is low, but so are cash and security assets. Government employment is a bit higher than average, and government share of GDP is much lower than average. Those policies do not show much change over time.

Virginia's land-use freedom is generally good. Indeed, it ranks fourth despite local zoning rules tightening slightly in recent years, reportedly especially in the northern part of the state. Eminent domain reform has been effective. Labor law is well above average,

and the state comes in as our second best in the country, with right to work, no minimum wage, fairly relaxed workers' compensation rules, a federally consistent anti-discrimination law, no E-Verify, no paid family leave or short-term disability mandate, and enforcement of noncompete agreements. Health insurance mandates have long been much higher than the national average. Cable and telecommunications have been liberalized. Occupational licensing is more extensive than in the average state. Nurses and dental hygienists enjoy little practice freedom. Insurance freedom is below average, and Virginia has a certificate-of-need law, a price-gouging law, and mover licensing. Some direct-to-consumer automobile sales were legalized in 2015/16. The civil liability system is about average.

Virginia's criminal justice policies are subpar but at least are no longer worsening. Victimless crime arrest rates are below average, but incarceration rates are still high. Asset forfeiture was slightly reformed in 2016. The state's approach to cannabis producers and consumers has been draconian, but things have changed since our data cutoff. Medical marijuana laws were reformed in 2020, and adult marijuana possession and personal cultivation were legalized in 2021. Sales will follow in 2024. Virginia is average for gun rights but passed a slate of restrictions in 2020, including universal background checks. As Virginia turns more solidly Democratic, this could augur a further slide. Alcohol freedom is subpar but improved in the early 2000s as some regulations were withdrawn. State liquor store markups are still huge, and spirits taxes are high. The state has not had much legal gambling. But there was some liberalization of slot/video games in 2018, online sports betting became legal in 2021, and new casinos are on the way with expanded gaming in the state. Educational freedom is a bright spot for Virginia, growing substantially in 2011/12 with a tax-credit scholarship law. There is still room for cutting regulations on private schoolers and homeschoolers. For a state with Virginia's history, it might be surprising that tobacco freedom is not very strong—the state only ranks 31st. Cigarette taxes are average, but respect for the property rights of private workplaces still exists. It recently increased the minimum age of sale to 21. The state was forced to legalize same-sex marriage in 2014, which also overturned the state's oppressive super-DOMA banning all relationship-style contracts between two gay people. The state allows cousin marriage but does not have covenant marriages.

WASHINGTON

2019 RANK
39th

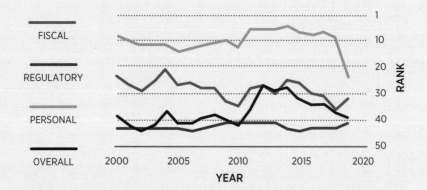

FISCAL

REGULATORY

PERSONAL

OVERALL

RANK

YEAR

PARTY CONTROL

	R	D	2021	2019	2017
GOVERNOR			Inslee	Inslee	Inslee
SENATE					
HOUSE OF REP.					

POLICY RECOMMENDATIONS

Fiscal: Enact strict, *ex post* balanced budget requirements to bring state debt down over time. Build up the rainy-day fund.

Regulatory: Better protect property rights by enacting further-reaching eminent domain reform and reducing centralized land-use planning by repealing or amending the Growth Management Act and the Shoreline Management Act.

Personal: Repeal teacher licensing and mandatory state approval and registration for private schools, ease the annual testing requirement for homeschoolers, and require homeschooling parents to keep only a record of attendance, not teaching materials.

ANALYSIS

Washington doesn't perform well on any dimension of freedom but managed to avoid the bottom 10 states overall in 2019 after dipping to 10th worst in 2017. Although Washington has had one of the more regulated economies in the United States for a long time, it has benefited from the fact that California and Oregon have had the same. However, it is a far cry from comparative regulatory heaven in neighboring Idaho. Washington is barely a top-half state in personal freedom.

Washington lacks an income tax; as a result, its fiscal policy is fairly good. Localities raise just below the national average in taxes, 3.8 percent of adjusted income. State government, meanwhile, raises 5.3 percent of income, also a little below the national average. Washingtonians enjoy little choice in local government, just 0.37 jurisdictions per 100 square miles. Government debt is higher than the national average but has come down recently. Cash and security assets are lower than average. Public employment and government share of GDP have come down substantially since 2009, partly because of economic growth rather than policy change.

Washingtonians do not enjoy much freedom to use their own land. Local and regional zoning and planning rules have become quite strict. Eminent domain abuse is almost unchecked. Renewable portfolio standards have been tightened. Washington is one of the worst states on labor-market freedom. It lacks a right-to-work law, limits choices for workers' compensation programs, and has extremely high minimum wages relative to its wage base. It added paid family leave in 2017. Managed care is hobbled by standing referral and direct access mandates. Cable and telecommunications have not been liberalized. Occupational licensing has become much more extensive than the national average. The state's sunrise commission law has proved useless. However, nurse practitioners, dental hygienists, and physician assistants enjoy broad scope of practice. Insurance freedom is quite poor because of prior approval of rates and rating classification prohibitions. Washington did rescind its rate classification prohibitions for some classes of insurance in 2019. The civil liability system is mediocre.

Washington's criminal justice policies are among the best in the nation. Incarceration and victimless crime arrest rates are far below national averages and fell substantially even before marijuana legalization. The state also reduced the cost of prison phone calls by nearly half in 2016. It is a top state for marijuana freedom. However, the state has done virtually nothing about civil asset forfeiture abuse. Marriage freedom is low because of a waiting period and lack of cousin and covenant marriage. Gun laws aren't terrible for a left-leaning state. The state has legalized some Class III weapons in recent years. However, in 2018, it did reimpose a firearms waiting period on some guns. Years ago, Washington increased its alcohol freedom to average from well below by privatizing state liquor stores and allowing spirits in grocery stores. However, taxes on distilled spirits are the highest in the country. Illegal immigrants have been able to get driver's licenses for a long time. The state is fairly mediocre on gambling freedom and prohibits online gaming. Physician-assisted suicide and raw milk sales are legal. Educational freedom is substandard, with some of the toughest licensing, approval, testing, and recordkeeping requirements for private schools and homeschools in the country. Smoking bans are comprehensive, and tobacco taxes are extremely high. New restrictions on electronic cigarettes and an increase in minimum age for legal sale to 21 occurred in 2019.

WEST VIRGINIA

2019 RANK

35th

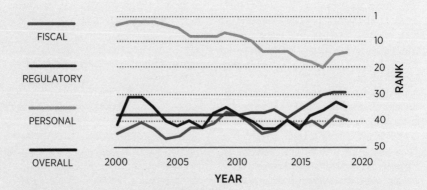

FISCAL

REGULATORY

PERSONAL

OVERALL

PARTY CONTROL

	2021	2019	2017
R ■ D ■			
GOVERNOR	Justice	Justice	Justice
SENATE			
HOUSE OF DELEGATES			

POLICY RECOMMENDATIONS

Fiscal: Reduce state employment, especially in general administration, highways, and public welfare. Further reduce the business income tax.

Regulatory: Return nurse practitioner scope of practice freedom.

Personal: Reform sentencing by abolishing mandatory minimums for nonviolent offenses, with an eye toward reducing the incarceration rate to its 2000 level.

ANALYSIS

West Virginia has usually done better on personal freedom than on economic freedom, but we show the lines converging as the state's public opinion has grown more conservative and Republican. In short, West Virginia is improving its relative ranking on fiscal and regulatory policy while declining on relative personal freedom (it was 4th in 2000, but is 14th today). However, the state is still lagging mightily on fiscal policy. Still, it has seen an above-average overall growth of freedom since 2000.

The Mountaineer State's overall tax burden is right about average, but it is centralized at the state level. The state takes about 6.7 percent of adjusted income, a significant decline since FY 2006, when it peaked at 7.9 percent, while local governments take 3.0 percent, a figure that has risen a touch during the same period. There are 0.7 effective competing jurisdictions per 100 square miles. State and local debt and financial assets are both low and have fallen somewhat over time, which we show as a slight net gain for freedom. Government employment is way above average, at 16.3 percent of private employment. Government share of GDP is also high (11.5 percent of income) but has fallen during the past decade.

Land-use freedom is broad in West Virginia. Eminent domain was partially reformed in 2006, and a takings law is on the books. Labor-market freedom is better than average despite a minimum wage. West Virginia became a right-to-work state in 2016. West Virginia is one of the very worst states for health insurance regulation and has virtually made the managed care model illegal. Mandates are especially plentiful. Neither telecommunications nor cable has been liberalized. Occupational freedom is a bit below average, both in extent of licensure and in scope of practice for second-line health professions. In an unusual reversal, nurse practitioners lost scope of practice in 2015. But the state became a member of the Nurse Licensure Compact in 2017. Insurance rate-setting freedom is restricted because of prior approval requirements. The state has a hospital certificate-of-need law, a price-gouging law, and a general unfair-sales law. Household goods moving companies were freed from needing a certificate of convenience and necessity in 2017. The civil liability system is still worse than average, but a significant tort reform in 2015 has improved the situation.

West Virginia used to lock up fewer of its residents than most other states, but that is no longer the case. It has gotten consistently worse during the past two decades until a recent two-year move in the right direction. Drug arrests have also risen over time as a share of the user base, but a significant decline took place from 2017 to 2019. Arrests for victimless crimes have been falling for some time. Asset forfeiture is essentially unreformed but, like most states, equitable sharing got significantly better since the fifth edition. Prison phone call rates were dramatically reduced in 2015. Cannabis laws improved in 2017 with passage of a medical marijuana bill. But laws are still harsh. Even low-level cultivation or sale carries a mandatory minimum of two years in prison. West Virginia is one of the best states for gun rights, buttressed by a constitutional carry law in 2016. And despite state involvement in alcohol distribution, it is also better than average for alcohol freedom. The seat belt law was upgraded to primary in 2013, and an open-container law was enacted in 2015, reducing travel freedom. The state has ample opportunities to gamble, including authorization for internet gambling, which came in 2018. Indeed, it is the third-best state for gambling freedom. Yet, social gambling remains illegal. West Virginia doesn't do well on educational freedom in this index, but it enacted a broad eligibility education savings account bill that will significantly help the state in the next edition. Private schools and homeschools are fairly heavily regulated. Tobacco freedom is only average after a big cigarette tax hike in 2016.

WISCONSIN

2019 RANK
17th

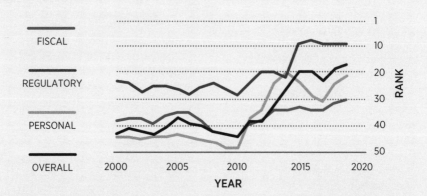

FISCAL

REGULATORY

PERSONAL

OVERALL

RANK

YEAR

PARTY CONTROL

■ R ■ D	2021	2019	2017
GOVERNOR	Evers	Evers	Walker
SENATE			
ASSEMBLY			

POLICY RECOMMENDATIONS

Fiscal: Reduce the income tax burden while continuing to cut spending on employee retirement and government employment.

Regulatory: Abolish price controls.

Personal: Reform the state's marijuana laws consistent with reforms carried out across the nation, including decriminalizing possession.

ANALYSIS

Wisconsin is one of the most improved states since 2000, and a great deal of the credit for that goes to a rise in personal freedom, not just economic freedom. The Badger State was 48th in the country in personal freedom as recently as 2010 but has steamed all the way to 21st since then.

In economic freedom, Wisconsin performs better on regulatory policy—where it is a top-10 state—than fiscal policy. It still has higher-than-average taxes, but they have fallen gradually since 2012, more at the local level than the state level. State taxes are projected to be 6.3 percent of adjusted personal income in FY 2020, whereas local taxes stood at 3.7 percent of income in FY 2020, slightly below the national average. Wisconsinites have ample choice among local governments, with more than two effective competing jurisdictions per 100 square miles. State and local debt has fallen almost continuously since FY 2007, but state and local financial assets have also fallen. Government employment is below average at 11.8 percent after peaking in FY 2010 at nearly 13.0 percent. Government share of GDP is 10.4 percent of adjusted income, essentially at the national average but lower than it has been every year except 2018. Wisconsin has generally seen definite improvement on fiscal policy since 2010, partly because of economic growth and partly because of policy changes. In 2018, Wisconsin's fiscal policy score was at its highest level in our whole time series, but it slipped slightly in 2019, absolutely but not relatively.

On regulatory policy, we do not see much change in recent years. Regulatory freedom grew in 2015 because of a right-to-work law, but the policy environment at the state level has been fairly stable since. The state ranks right in the middle of the pack on land-use freedom; local zoning has not gotten out of hand, though it has grown some since 2000. The state has a renewable portfolio standard, which was toughened in 2015. Apart from a right-to-work law, Wisconsin was already reasonably good on labor-market policy. Health insurance regulation is a bit better than average because of low mandates. Cable and telecommunications have been liberalized. Occupational licensing increased dramatically between 2000 and 2006 and has been relatively stable since; still, the state is about average overall on extent of licensure. Nurse practitioners enjoy no independent practice freedom. Insurance freedom is generally good, at least for property and casualty lines. The state has no certificate-of-need law for hospitals. It has a price-gouging law, and it also has controversial, strictly enforced minimum-markup laws for gasoline and general retailers. The civil liability system is above average and improved significantly since 2010 because of a punitive damages cap.

Wisconsin is a below-average-ranking state on criminal justice policies at 36th. The incarceration rate is right where it was 20 years ago, after getting better about 10 years ago and then worsening. Nondrug victimless crime arrests have dropped. The state's asset forfeiture regime is among the best in the country. Equitable sharing revenues are significantly lower than average. Tobacco freedom is low because of airtight smoking bans and high taxes. The state even has local vaping bans. Educational freedom grew significantly in 2013/14 with the expansion of vouchers. However, private schools are relatively tightly regulated. There is little legal gambling, even in social contexts. Cannabis law is unreformed. Wisconsin remains the best state for alcohol freedom, with no state role in distribution, no keg registration, low taxes (especially on beer—imagine that), no blue laws, legal happy hours, legal direct wine shipment, and both wine and spirits in grocery stores. The state is now better than average on gun rights after the legislature passed a shall-issue concealed-carry license a year ago (one of the last states in the country to legalize concealed carry) and repealed a waiting period in 2015. There is no duty to retreat.

WYOMING

2019 RANK
26th

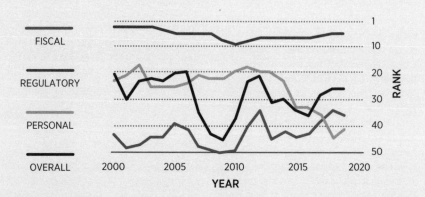

FISCAL

REGULATORY

PERSONAL

OVERALL

RANK

YEAR

PARTY CONTROL

	2021	2019	2017
GOVERNOR	Gordon	Gordon	Mead
SENATE			
HOUSE OF REP.			

■ R   ■ D

POLICY RECOMMENDATIONS

Fiscal: Privatize hospitals and cut health spending to reduce government employment and consumption and allow sales taxes to be cut. Wyoming spends far more on health and hospitals as a share of its economy than any other state.

Regulatory: Let employers buy workers' compensation coverage from any willing seller. Consider privatizing the state fund.

Personal: Adopt individualism in education by adopting a "backpack funding" model.

ANALYSIS

As a highly resource-dependent state, Wyoming's fiscal situation can fluctuate greatly from year to year, causing some volatility in its freedom scores over time. However, its overall freedom ranking has stayed relatively stable during the past three years, ending up in the middle of the pack each year. The Equality State is in the bottom third on fiscal policy and the bottom 10 on personal freedom, but its overall ranking is salvaged by a top-five showing on regulatory policy.

With favorable trust and corporate privacy laws and no income taxes of any kind, Wyoming is as good a place to park your wealth as any other state. Cowboy Staters derive a much larger share of their gross income from capital gains than the average American. Wyoming is a relatively fiscally decentralized state, especially for its small population. Excluding mineral severance, motor fuel, alcohol, and tobacco revenues, state taxes come to a projected 3.6 percent of adjusted income in FY 2020, well below the national average of 5.7 percent and a big decline from FY 2009, when Wyoming state taxes peaked at 5.9 percent. Local taxes stand at about 3.2 percent of income, slightly below the national average of 3.9 percent. However, Wyomingites have little choice in local government as counties are the locus of most taxation, thus squandering the advantages of fiscal decentralization. Government debt is the lowest in the country (a mere 5.6 percent of income), and liquid assets are huge (73.6 percent of income), but state and local employment is enormous (18.25 percent of private employment—a significant dip over its high of 19.6 in 2010 but still an increase over 2008, when it was 17.7 percent), and so is government share of income (14.4 percent). Like Alaska, then, Wyoming personifies the blessings and curses of abundant energy and mineral wealth: low taxes, extremely high reserves, and bloated budgets and public payrolls.

Wyoming does above average on land-use freedom but hasn't reformed eminent domain much. Labor law is generally good, with no minimum wage, a right-to-work law, and enforcement of noncompete agreements, but employers must obtain workers' compensation coverage from a monopoly state fund, and anti-discrimination law goes beyond the federal minimum. Health insurance mandates are lower than most states post-PPACA, and the managed care model is still viable. A telecommunications deregulation bill was passed in 2013/14, but there is no statewide video franchising. Occupational licensing has grown over time but is still well below the national average. Nurse practitioners and physician assistants enjoy broad scope of practice, but dental hygienists only enjoy the right to practice with a collaborative agreement with a dentist, enacted in 2017. Wyoming is the best state for insurance freedom, lacking price controls on property and casualty lines. Its price-gouging law was repealed many years ago, but it still has a Depression-era "unfair sales act" on the books. Its civil liability system is good, even though the state has not reformed punitive damages at all.

Wyoming's criminal justice policies are similar to those of Louisiana or Mississippi. Incarceration and drug arrest rates are high and have generally risen over time, but nondrug victimless crime arrests have fallen over time and are now only slightly higher than average. A timid asset forfeiture reform was enacted in 2016, but state law is still worse than average. However, Wyoming is better than average on equitable sharing. Cannabis laws are predictably bad, though not among the very harshest. However, unlike many other states across the country, Wyoming hasn't seen fit to liberalize in any meaningful way. Wyoming is one of the very best states for gun rights, having passed constitutional carry in 2010. Now that the state in 2018 passed a no duty to retreat in public law, not just in the home as it was, the only areas where it could improve involve removing location restrictions for carrying. Alcohol freedom is a bit above average despite state liquor stores because taxes are so low. Gambling freedom is below average, but the state does have pari-mutuel wagering, social gambling, and charitable games. It legalized sports betting in 2021. Education freedom is below average, which might be surprising given its individualistic sensibilities. Nonsectarian private schools are strictly regulated, and there are no private school choice programs. One upside is that homeschooling is explicitly permitted by statute. Tobacco freedom is above average, as smoking bans admit some exceptions. Cigarettes can be purchased on the internet, and vaping is only locally banned in restaurants, bars, and workplaces. Retail raw milk sales were legalized in 2015. Cousin marriage is illegal, but blood tests and waiting periods are not required for marriage.

APPENDIX A

DIMENSION, CATEGORY, AND VARIABLE WEIGHTS

Key:
Dimension
    Category
        Policy Variable

FISCAL POLICY: 30.4%
    State taxation: 11.7%
    Local taxation: 6.6%–8.7%
    Government consumption and investment: 8.2%
    Government employment: 2.0%
    Government debt: 0.3%
    Cash and security assets: 0.2%

REGULATORY POLICY: 34.9%
    Land-use freedom: 11.6%
        Local rent control: 5.3%
        "Land use" court mentions: 2.5%
        Wharton Residential Land Use Regulatory Index: 2.5%
        Renewable portfolio standards: 1.0%
        Regulatory takings compensation: 0.1%
        Eminent domain reform index: 0.1%
        Parking lot gun mandate: 0.01%
        Mandated free speech on private property: <0.01%

    Health insurance freedom: 8.9%
        Individual health insurance mandate: 2.4%
        Community rating, small groups: 2.3%
        Health insurance mandates index: 2.3%
        Individual guaranteed issue: 0.6%
        Small group rate review: 0.5%
        Community rating, individuals: 0.4%
        Direct access to specialists mandated: 0.3%
        Individual rate review: 0.1%
        Standing referrals mandated: 0.03%
        Individual policies, elimination riders banned: 0.02%
        Mandated external grievance review: 0.02%
        Financial incentives to providers banned: 0.01%

    Labor-market freedom: 4.8%
        General right-to-work law: 2.5%
        Short-term disability insurance: 0.9%
        Noncompete agreements permitted: 0.8%
        Minimum wage: 0.6%

Workers' compensation funding regulations: 0.5%
Workers' compensation coverage regulations: 0.2%
Employer verification of legal status: 0.1%
Employee anti-discrimination law: 0.01%
Paid family leave: <0.01%

Lawsuit freedom: 3.2%

Occupational freedom: 2.6%
Nurse practitioner independence index: 0.8%
Employment-weighted licensure: 0.8%
Regulatory keywords in statutes: 0.8%
Dental hygienist scope of practice: 0.1%
Sunrise commissions: 0.1%
Physician assistant prescribing authority: 0.04%
Nurse Licensure Compact membership: 0.03%
Sunset review: 0.02%

Miscellaneous regulatory freedom: 2.5%
Certificate-of-need requirements for hospitals: 0.7%
Rate filing requirements, personal auto insurance: 0.5%
Rate filing requirements, homeowner's insurance: 0.3%
Anti-price-gouging laws: 0.2%
General sales-below-cost laws: 0.2%
Rate classification prohibitions: 0.2%
Interstate Insurance Product Regulation Compact: 0.1%
Sales-below-cost law for gasoline: 0.1%
Direct auto sales: 0.1%
Moving company entry regulation: 0.02%
Mandatory labeling law: 0.01%

Cable and telecommunications: 1.1%
Telecommunications deregulation: 0.7%
Statewide cable franchising: 0.3%

PERSONAL FREEDOM: 33.2%
Incarceration and arrests: 6.7%
Crime-adjusted incarceration rate: 3.6%
Drug enforcement rate: 1.9%
Arrests for nondrug victimless crimes, % of population: 0.6%
Arrests for nondrug victimless crimes, % of all arrests: 0.6%
Driver's license suspensions for drug offenses: 0.04%
Prison collect phone call rate: 0.01%

Gambling: 4.2%
Casino and racino win (revenue): 2.7%
Slot/video games outside casinos: 1.3%
Pari-mutuel wagering: 0.03%
Aggravated gambling felony: 0.02%
Social gambling allowed: 0.02%

Charitable gambling: 0.01%
Express prohibition on internet gambling: <0.01%

Guns: 4.1%
Concealed-carry index: 1.9%
Initial permit cost: 0.5%
Local gun ban: 0.4%
Firearms licensing index: 0.3%
Waiting period for purchases: 0.3%
Initial permit term: 0.2%
Open-carry index: 0.1%
Training or testing requirement: 0.1%
Stricter minimum age: 0.1%
Assault weapons ban: 0.05%
No duty to retreat: 0.04%
Registration of firearms: 0.03%
Dealer licensing: 0.02%
Built-in locking devices: 0.02%
Restrictions on multiple purchases: 0.02%
Background checks for private sales: 0.02%
Design safety standards: 0.01%
Machine guns: 0.01%
Ballistic identification: 0.01%
Retention of sales records: 0.01%
Short-barreled shotguns: 0.01%
Short-barreled rifles: 0.01%
Large-capacity firearm magazine bans: <0.01%
Sound suppressor: <0.01%
.50 caliber ban: <0.01%

Marriage: 3.2%
Same-sex partnership index: 1.8%
Super-DOMAs: 0.8%
Sodomy laws: 0.3%
Cousin marriage: 0.2%
Covenant marriage: 0.1%
Blood test required: 0.01%
Waiting period: 0.01%

Education: 3.0%
Tax credit/deduction law for scholarships/expenses: 1.1%
Publicly funded voucher law: 0.7%
Mandatory licensure, private school teachers: 0.5%
Mandatory state approval, private schools: 0.2%
Compulsory school years: 0.2%
Curriculum control, private schools: 0.1%
Public school choice: 0.1%
Curriculum control, homeschools: 0.04%
Record-keeping requirements, homeschools: 0.03%
Standardized testing requirements, homeschools: 0.03%

Notification requirements, homeschools: 0.02%
Teacher qualifications, homeschools: 0.01%
Mandatory registration, private schools: <0.01%
Homeschooling statute: <0.01%

Tobacco: 2.7%
Cigarette tax: 1.8%
Minimum legal sale age 21: 0.5%
Smoking ban, bars: 0.2%
Internet purchase regulations: 0.05%
Flavored vape ban: 0.04%*
Smoking ban, private workplaces: 0.02%
Smoking ban, restaurants: 0.02%
Vending machine regulations: 0.02%
Vaping ban on private property: <0.01%*

Alcohol: 2.6%
Alcohol distribution control: 1.0%
Off-premises sales in grocery stores: 0.4%
Blue law index: 0.4%
Spirits taxes: 0.3%
Wine taxes: 0.2%
Beer taxes: 0.2%
Direct wine shipment ban: 0.1%
Keg registration/ban: 0.1%
Happy hour ban: 0.02%
Mandatory server training: <0.01%

Marijuana: 2.4%
Medical marijuana index: 1.0%
Possession decriminalization/legalization: 0.6%
Maximum marijuana penalty: 0.3%
Sales legalization: 0.2%
Marijuana misdemeanor index: 0.2%
Mandatory minimums: 0.1%
Salvia ban: 0.1%

Asset forfeiture: 2.0%
State asset forfeiture law, aggregate score: 1.0%
Moving average of equitable sharing revenue: 1.0%

Mala prohibita and civil liberties: 1.2%
Affirmative action ban: 0.7%
Prostitution legal: 0.2%
Trans-fat bans: 0.1%
Raw milk legal: 0.1%
Mixed martial arts legal: 0.05%
Fireworks laws: 0.04%
Equal Rights Amendment: 0.03%

* Indicates average weight for time-varying weights.

Physician-assisted suicide legal: 0.03%
DNA database index: 0.01%
Religious freedom restoration act: 0.01%

Travel: 1.1%
Automated license plate readers: 0.3%
Driver's licenses for illegal immigrants: 0.3%
Seat belt laws: 0.1%
Fingerprint for driver's license: 0.1%
Sobriety checkpoints: 0.1%
Motorcycle helmet law: 0.1%
Uninsured/underinsured motorist coverage mandate: 0.1%
Handheld cell phone ban: 0.01%

Campaign finance: 0.1%
Individual contributions to candidates: 0.03%
Individual contributions to parties: 0.02%
Grassroots political action committee contributions to candidates: 0.01%
Grassroots political action committee contributions to parties: 0.01%
Public financing: <0.01%

Note: Because of rounding, percentages listed do not sum to exactly 100. Because of how we weight the local taxation variable, the weights for the fiscal policy dimension range from 29.0 (New Jersey) to 31.1 (Hawaii). For more on this, see "Local Taxation" under "Fiscal Policy" in Part 1.

APPENDIX B

ALTERNATIVE INDEXES

This appendix gives alternative freedom indexes based on the exclusion of right-to-work laws and the inclusion of various positions on abortion policy.

LABOR-MARKET FREEDOM—ALTERNATIVE INDICES

The first set of alternative indexes excludes right-to-work laws. Consequently, new rankings are generated for labor policy, regulatory freedom, economic freedom, and overall freedom.

Rank	State	Labor-Market Freedom without Right-to-Work Laws, 2019		Rank	State	Labor-Market Freedom without Right-to-Work Laws, 2019
1.	Texas	0.022		26.	Illinois	−0.001
2.	Virginia	0.015		27.	Montana	−0.002
3.	Indiana	0.013		28.	Alaska	−0.002
4.	Iowa	0.013		29.	New Mexico	−0.003
5.	Kansas	0.013		30.	Missouri	−0.003
6.	Wisconsin	0.013		31.	Arkansas	−0.003
7.	New Hampshire	0.013		32.	West Virginia	−0.003
8.	Alabama	0.012		33.	Vermont	−0.007
9.	Mississippi	0.012		34.	Wyoming	−0.008
10.	Tennessee	0.012		35.	Ohio	−0.010
11.	Georgia	0.010		36.	Connecticut	−0.010
12.	North Carolina	0.010		37.	Maryland	−0.012
13.	Utah	0.008		38.	Massachusetts	−0.013
14.	Florida	0.008		39.	Maine	−0.014
15.	Kentucky	0.006		40.	Colorado	−0.017
16.	Pennsylvania	0.006		41.	Arizona	−0.021
17.	Idaho	0.006		42.	Oregon	−0.021
18.	Minnesota	0.004		43.	Oklahoma	−0.028
19.	South Carolina	0.004		44.	Washington	−0.032
20.	Louisiana	0.004		45.	New Jersey	−0.034
21.	Nebraska	0.003		46.	Hawaii	−0.039
22.	Nevada	0.002		47.	North Dakota	−0.042
23.	Delaware	0.002		48.	Rhode Island	−0.046
24.	South Dakota	0.001		49.	New York	−0.047
25.	Michigan	0.000		50.	California	−0.083

Note: States with the same rank are tied. States with different scores may appear identical due to rounding.

TABLE B2

Rank	State	Regulatory Policy without Right-to-Work Laws, 2019	Rank	State	Regulatory Policy without Right-to-Work Laws, 2019
1.	Kansas	0.100	26.	Texas	−0.013
2.	Nebraska	0.094	27.	Nevada	−0.014
3.	Iowa	0.084	28.	Alabama	−0.017
4.	Idaho	0.076	29.	North Carolina	−0.019
5.	Wyoming	0.054	30.	Ohio	−0.033
6.	South Dakota	0.043	31.	Delaware	−0.041
7.	Georgia	0.040	32.	Minnesota	−0.045
8.	Utah	0.040	33.	New Mexico	−0.045
9.	Wisconsin	0.038	34.	West Virginia	−0.049
10.	Indiana	0.038	35.	Montana	−0.070
11.	New Hampshire	0.034	36.	Louisiana	−0.075
12.	Kentucky	0.032	37.	Pennsylvania	−0.097
13.	North Dakota	0.024	38.	Illinois	−0.103
14.	South Carolina	0.024	39.	Maine	−0.120
15.	Arkansas	0.023	40.	Connecticut	−0.122
16.	Mississippi	0.022	41.	Washington	−0.132
17.	Alaska	0.021	42.	Massachusetts	−0.158
18.	Tennessee	0.021	43.	Rhode Island	−0.174
19.	Michigan	0.018	44.	Vermont	−0.184
20.	Virginia	0.015	45.	Hawaii	−0.209
21.	Arizona	0.011	46.	Oregon	−0.345
22.	Oklahoma	0.005	47.	Maryland	−0.372
23.	Colorado	0.004	48.	New York	−0.427
24.	Florida	−0.008	49.	New Jersey	−0.459
25.	Missouri	−0.011	50.	California	−0.463

Note: States with the same rank are tied. States with different scores may appear identical due to rounding.

Rank	State	Economic Freedom without Right-to-Work Laws, 2019		Rank	State	
1.	Florida	0.423		26.	South Carolina	0.062
2.	Tennessee	0.391		27.	Oklahoma	0.059
3.	New Hampshire	0.390		28.	Alaska	0.057
4.	South Dakota	0.306		29.	Kansas	0.053
5.	Idaho	0.272		30.	Massachusetts	0.048
6.	Georgia	0.262		31.	Connecticut	0.033
7.	Indiana	0.236		32.	Louisiana	−0.015
8.	Michigan	0.201		33.	Iowa	−0.022
9.	Missouri	0.197		34.	Illinois	−0.040
10.	Nevada	0.184		35.	Nebraska	−0.048
11.	Texas	0.174		36.	Washington	−0.093
12.	Virginia	0.174		37.	Minnesota	−0.094
13.	Colorado	0.162		38.	West Virginia	−0.104
14.	Pennsylvania	0.154		39.	Mississippi	−0.112
15.	Arizona	0.139		40.	Rhode Island	−0.115
16.	Arkansas	0.111		41.	Maine	−0.135
17.	Kentucky	0.111		42.	Delaware	−0.172
18.	Montana	0.104		43.	New Mexico	−0.259
19.	Alabama	0.099		44.	Maryland	−0.304
20.	Wisconsin	0.084		45.	Vermont	−0.320
21.	Wyoming	0.082		46.	New Jersey	−0.401
22.	Ohio	0.081		47.	Oregon	−0.405
23.	Utah	0.074		48.	California	−0.520
24.	North Carolina	0.070		49.	Hawaii	−0.578
25.	North Dakota	0.065		50.	New York	−0.734

Note: States with the same rank are tied. States with different scores may appear identical due to rounding.

TABLE B4

Rank	State	Overall Freedom without Right-to-Work Laws, 2019		Rank	State	Overall Freedom without Right-to-Work Laws, 2019
1.	New Hampshire	0.615		26.	Kentucky	0.110
2.	Florida	0.526		27.	Ohio	0.103
3.	Nevada	0.485		28.	Wyoming	0.102
4.	Tennessee	0.414		29.	Kansas	0.101
5.	South Dakota	0.399		30.	South Carolina	0.099
6.	Indiana	0.342		31.	Iowa	0.068
7.	Michigan	0.323		32.	Maine	0.055
8.	Georgia	0.304		33.	Louisiana	0.040
9.	Missouri	0.297		34.	Connecticut	0.040
10.	Arizona	0.296		35.	Nebraska	0.032
11.	Idaho	0.287		36.	Illinois	0.010
12.	Colorado	0.284		37.	West Virginia	−0.004
13.	Pennsylvania	0.223		38.	Minnesota	−0.018
14.	Montana	0.200		39.	Washington	−0.020
15.	Virginia	0.200		40.	Rhode Island	−0.070
16.	North Dakota	0.169		41.	Mississippi	−0.083
17.	North Carolina	0.166		42.	New Mexico	−0.100
18.	Alaska	0.164		43.	Vermont	−0.153
19.	Wisconsin	0.164		44.	Delaware	−0.180
20.	Oklahoma	0.134		45.	Maryland	−0.259
21.	Utah	0.130		46.	Oregon	−0.288
22.	Texas	0.129		47.	New Jersey	−0.437
23.	Alabama	0.126		48.	California	−0.451
24.	Massachusetts	0.117		49.	Hawaii	−0.580
25.	Arkansas	0.117		50.	New York	−0.790

Note: States with the same rank are tied. States with different scores may appear identical due to rounding.

ABORTION POLICY—ALTERNATIVE INDEXES

In this edition of the freedom index, abortion remains excluded from the main scores and rankings, given our discussion at the beginning of the book. However, we have again developed alternative abortion policy indexes here, which feed into personal freedom and overall freedom, should readers wish to personalize their results according to their view of the relation between abortion policy and freedom. The first alternative index is a pro-life abortion policy ("freedom from abortion") index. For this alternative index, more state restrictions on abortion are always pro-freedom, as is the lack of state subsidies for abortion through Medicaid.

The second alternative index is a moderately pro-choice abortion policy index. For this index, restrictions on late-term abortions and lack of subsidies for abortion are pro-freedom, although for a different reason from pro-lifers in the latter case (respect for conscience), whereas restrictions on early-term abortions are anti-freedom. For the moderately pro-choice index, restrictions on abortion that apply mostly but not entirely to late-term abortions and parental involvement laws for minors' abortions do not count at all.

Finally, the third alternative index is a strong pro-choice abortion policy index. For this alternative index, all limits on abortion are anti-freedom, and subsidies for abortion do not count.

We devised weights for policies on the assumption that for a pro-lifer, the estimated, measurable value of an aborted fetus's life is $3 million (caveat: this is an actuarial-type estimate, but we consider the moral value of life—whenever life begins—to be truly unmeasurable and view policies relating to unjust killings to be an insoluble problem for any index, including those of human rights and civil liberties internationally). The $3 million figure derives from a rough estimate of $5 million to $7 million for the statistical value of an adult life. Many or most fetuses are aborted naturally by the mother's body, so the value of a fetus's life should be about half that of an adult.

For pro-choicers, the value of the freedom to abort depends on the "consumer surplus" (in economic jargon, this term means the difference between what consumers would have paid and what they actually paid) derived from the observed price elasticity of demand for abortion, multiplied by the "constitutional weight" of 10, consistent with our methodology for the rest of the index. We derive the estimate of $5 million from a high-end estimate of the statistical value of an average human life ($7.5 million), multiplied by two-thirds because young fetuses of the age when abortion typically occurs are naturally aborted by the mother's body roughly one-third of the time.[187] This is, obviously, merely a

---

187.   Binyamin Appelbaum, "As U.S. Agencies Put More Value on a Life, Businesses Fret," *New York Times*, February 16, 2011; Mayo Clinic, "Diseases and Conditions: Miscarriage" web page, www.mayoclinic.org/diseases-conditions/pregnancy-loss-miscarriage/basics/definition/con-20033827; WebMD, "Pregnancy and Miscarriage" web page, www.webmd.com/baby/guide/pregnancy-miscarriage.

ballpark figure based on actuarial-type estimates. Moreover, we admit that this type of economic language and reasoning can be difficult, sterile, limiting, and perhaps even less accurate than we'd like (though it is hard to calculate in other ways consistent with the overarching methodology of the index).

The policies included in these alternative indexes are as follows: requirement that abortions be performed by a licensed physician (1.3 percent of overall pro-life freedom, 0.01 percent of overall moderate pro-choice freedom, 0.01 percent of strong pro-choice freedom); requirement that some abortions be performed in hospitals (0.01 percent pro-life, 0 percent moderate, 0.01 percent strong pro-choice); requirement that some abortions involve a second physician (0.01 percent pro-life, 0 percent moderate, 0.01 percent strong pro-choice); gestational limit on abortions (0.3 percent pro-life, 0.4 percent moderate, 0.02 percent strong pro-choice); partial-birth abortion ban (0.03 percent pro-life, 0.04 percent moderate, <0.01 percent strong pro-choice); public funding of abortion (4.4 percent pro-life, 0.1 percent moderate, 0.2 percent strong pro-choice); restrictions on private insurance coverage of abortion (14.4 percent pro-life, 0.1 percent moderate, 0.1 percent strong pro-choice); state-mandated waiting periods (4.7 percent pro-life, 0.1 percent moderate, 0.1 percent strong pro-choice); and parental notification and consent laws (2.0 percent pro-life, 0 percent moderate, 0.02 percent strong pro-choice).

Interestingly, for a pro-lifer who relies on these parameters, abortion policy is worth a full 27.2 percent of overall freedom. If you believe that the life of the marginal (in the economic sense) aborted fetus is worth (again, statistically, not morally) about half that of any other human being, then you must think of abortion as by far the most important policy states can control. You should be close to a single-issue voter. By contrast, moderate and strong pro-choicers should be far less interested in abortion policy. For moderates, abortion policy is worth 0.7 percent of overall freedom, whereas for strong pro-choicers, abortion policy should be worth only about 0.3 percent of overall freedom. Why is the freedom to abort worth so little? The evidence suggests that abortion demand in economic terms may be quite price-elastic, implying that the consumer surplus is low. We offer these alternative indexes of this very difficult moral, political, and methodological issue as a preliminary attempt rather than the definitive word on this issue and hope they will be treated in that light.

Rank	State	Freedom from Abortion (Pro-Life Index), 2019		Rank	State	Freedom from Abortion (Pro-Life Index), 2019
1.	Indiana	0.473		26.	West Virginia	−0.009
1.	Missouri	0.473		27.	Rhode Island	−0.044
1.	Oklahoma	0.473		27.	Wyoming	−0.044
4.	Kansas	0.473		29.	Florida	−0.067
5.	Michigan	0.473		29.	Minnesota	−0.067
5.	North Dakota	0.473		31.	Delaware	−0.068
5.	Texas	0.473		31.	Iowa	−0.068
5.	Utah	0.473		33.	Colorado	−0.075
9.	Idaho	0.473		34.	Nevada	−0.092
10.	Kentucky	0.472		35.	New Hampshire	−0.109
11.	Nebraska	0.472		36.	Massachusetts	−0.137
12.	Arizona	0.051		37.	Maryland	−0.162
12.	Ohio	0.051		38.	Hawaii	−0.186
12.	South Carolina	0.051		38.	New York	−0.186
12.	Tennessee	0.051		38.	Washington	−0.186
12.	Virginia	0.051		41.	New Mexico	−0.192
17.	Arkansas	0.051		42.	New Jersey	−0.192
17.	Louisiana	0.051		43.	Alaska	−0.193
19.	Mississippi	0.051		44.	Illinois	−0.197
20.	Alabama	0.051		45.	Montana	−0.220
20.	Pennsylvania	0.051		46.	Connecticut	−0.220
22.	North Carolina	0.050		47.	California	−0.221
22.	Wisconsin	0.050		47.	Maine	−0.221
24.	South Dakota	0.027		49.	Oregon	−0.228
25.	Georgia	0.027		49.	Vermont	−0.228

Note: States with the same rank are tied. States with different scores may appear identical due to rounding.

Rank	State	Moderate Pro-Choice Abortion Policy Index, 2019		Rank	State	
1.	Delaware	0.004		23.	Wisconsin	0.002
1.	Florida	0.004		27.	Hawaii	0.001
1.	Iowa	0.004		27.	Maryland	0.001
1.	Nevada	0.004		27.	Massachusetts	0.001
1.	Rhode Island	0.004		27.	New York	0.001
1.	Wyoming	0.004		27.	Washington	0.001
7.	Montana	0.003		32.	Indiana	0.000
8.	Arizona	0.002		32.	Kansas	0.000
8.	Arkansas	0.002		32.	Michigan	0.000
8.	Georgia	0.002		32.	Missouri	0.000
8.	Louisiana	0.002		32.	North Dakota	0.000
8.	Mississippi	0.002		32.	Oklahoma	0.000
8.	Ohio	0.002		32.	Texas	0.000
8.	South Carolina	0.002		32.	Utah	0.000
8.	South Dakota	0.002		40.	Minnesota	−0.001
8.	Tennessee	0.002		41.	Idaho	−0.001
8.	Virginia	0.002		41.	Kentucky	−0.001
18.	West Virginia	0.002		41.	Nebraska	−0.001
19.	California	0.002		44.	New Hampshire	−0.005
19.	Connecticut	0.002		45.	Colorado	−0.006
19.	Illinois	0.002		46.	New Mexico	−0.007
19.	Maine	0.002		47.	Oregon	−0.008
23.	Alabama	0.002		47.	Vermont	−0.008
23.	North Carolina	0.002		49.	Alaska	−0.008
23.	Pennsylvania	0.002		49.	New Jersey	−0.008

Note: States with the same rank are tied. States with different scores may appear identical due to rounding.

Rank	State	Strong Pro-Choice Abortion Policy Index, 2019		Rank	State	Strong Pro-Choice Abortion Policy Index, 2019
1.	Oregon	0.002		26.	Georgia	−0.001
1.	Vermont	0.002		27.	South Dakota	−0.001
3.	Alaska	0.002		28.	North Carolina	−0.001
4.	New Jersey	0.002		28.	Wisconsin	−0.001
5.	New Mexico	0.002		30.	Alabama	−0.001
6.	New Hampshire	0.002		30.	Pennsylvania	−0.001
7.	Colorado	0.002		32.	Mississippi	−0.001
8.	California	0.002		33.	Arkansas	−0.001
8.	Maine	0.002		33.	Louisiana	−0.001
10.	Connecticut	0.002		35.	Arizona	−0.001
11.	Montana	0.002		35.	Ohio	−0.001
12.	Hawaii	0.002		35.	South Carolina	−0.001
12.	New York	0.002		35.	Tennessee	−0.001
12.	Washington	0.002		35.	Virginia	−0.001
15.	Nevada	0.002		40.	Nebraska	−0.004
16.	Illinois	0.002		41.	Kentucky	−0.004
17.	Delaware	0.001		42.	Idaho	−0.004
17.	Iowa	0.001		43.	Michigan	−0.004
17.	Maryland	0.001		43.	North Dakota	−0.004
20.	Florida	0.001		43.	Texas	−0.004
21.	Rhode Island	0.001		43.	Utah	−0.004
21.	Wyoming	0.001		47.	Kansas	−0.004
23.	Massachusetts	0.001		48.	Indiana	−0.004
24.	West Virginia	−0.001		48.	Missouri	−0.004
25.	Minnesota	−0.001		48.	Oklahoma	−0.004

Note: States with the same rank are tied. States with different scores may appear identical due to rounding.

TABLE B8

Rank	State	Pro-Life Personal Freedom, 2019	Rank	State	Pro-Life Personal Freedom, 2019
1.	Michigan	0.595	26.	Ohio	0.074
2.	Indiana	0.579	27.	Georgia	0.069
3.	North Dakota	0.576	28.	Arkansas	0.056
4.	Missouri	0.573	29.	Colorado	0.048
5.	Nebraska	0.553	30.	Florida	0.037
6.	Oklahoma	0.548	31.	Iowa	0.022
7.	Utah	0.529	32.	Minnesota	0.009
8.	Kansas	0.520	33.	Rhode Island	0.001
9.	Idaho	0.488	34.	Wyoming	−0.024
10.	Kentucky	0.471	35.	Maine	−0.031
11.	Texas	0.427	36.	New Mexico	−0.033
12.	Nevada	0.210	37.	Vermont	−0.061
13.	Arizona	0.208	38.	Massachusetts	−0.068
14.	North Carolina	0.147	39.	Delaware	−0.076
15.	Wisconsin	0.131	40.	Alaska	−0.085
16.	South Dakota	0.120	41.	Oregon	−0.110
17.	Pennsylvania	0.119	42.	Washington	−0.113
18.	New Hampshire	0.115	43.	Maryland	−0.117
19.	Louisiana	0.106	44.	Montana	−0.124
20.	West Virginia	0.091	45.	Illinois	−0.148
21.	South Carolina	0.088	46.	California	−0.152
22.	Mississippi	0.080	47.	Hawaii	−0.188
23.	Alabama	0.078	48.	Connecticut	−0.214
24.	Virginia	0.077	49.	New Jersey	−0.229
25.	Tennessee	0.075	50.	New York	−0.242

Note: States with the same rank are tied. States with different scores may appear identical due to rounding.

Rank	State	Moderate Pro-Choice Personal Freedom, 2019		Rank	State	Moderate Pro-Choice Personal Freedom, 2019
1.	Nevada	0.306		26.	Massachusetts	0.071
2.	New Hampshire	0.220		27.	Pennsylvania	0.070
3.	Maine	0.192		28.	Louisiana	0.057
4.	Arizona	0.159		29.	Utah	0.056
5.	Vermont	0.159		30.	Illinois	0.051
6.	New Mexico	0.152		31.	Rhode Island	0.048
7.	Michigan	0.122		32.	Kansas	0.047
8.	Colorado	0.117		33.	Maryland	0.047
9.	Oregon	0.110		34.	Georgia	0.045
10.	Florida	0.108		35.	South Carolina	0.039
11.	Indiana	0.105		36.	Mississippi	0.032
12.	North Dakota	0.103		37.	Alabama	0.029
13.	West Virginia	0.102		38.	Virginia	0.029
14.	Missouri	0.100		39.	Tennessee	0.026
15.	Alaska	0.099		40.	Ohio	0.025
16.	Montana	0.098		41.	Wyoming	0.024
17.	North Carolina	0.098		42.	Idaho	0.014
18.	South Dakota	0.096		43.	Connecticut	0.008
19.	Iowa	0.094		44.	Arkansas	0.008
20.	Wisconsin	0.082		45.	Hawaii	−0.001
21.	Nebraska	0.080		46.	Kentucky	−0.003
22.	Minnesota	0.075		47.	Delaware	−0.004
23.	Oklahoma	0.075		48.	New Jersey	−0.044
24.	Washington	0.075		49.	Texas	−0.046
25.	California	0.071		50.	New York	−0.055

Note: States with the same rank are tied. States with different scores may appear identical due to rounding.

Rank	State	Strong Pro-Choice Personal Freedom, 2019	Rank	State	Strong Pro-Choice Personal Freedom, 2019
1.	Nevada	0.303	26.	Massachusetts	0.071
2.	New Hampshire	0.227	27.	Pennsylvania	0.067
3.	Maine	0.192	28.	Louisiana	0.054
4.	Vermont	0.169	29.	Utah	0.052
5.	New Mexico	0.161	30.	Illinois	0.051
6.	Arizona	0.156	31.	Maryland	0.046
7.	Colorado	0.125	32.	Rhode Island	0.046
8.	Oregon	0.120	33.	Kansas	0.044
9.	Michigan	0.118	34.	Georgia	0.042
10.	Alaska	0.110	35.	South Carolina	0.036
11.	Florida	0.105	36.	Mississippi	0.028
12.	Indiana	0.101	37.	Alabama	0.027
13.	West Virginia	0.100	38.	Virginia	0.025
14.	North Dakota	0.100	39.	Tennessee	0.023
15.	Montana	0.097	40.	Ohio	0.021
16.	Missouri	0.096	41.	Wyoming	0.021
17.	North Carolina	0.096	42.	Idaho	0.012
18.	South Dakota	0.092	43.	Connecticut	0.008
19.	Iowa	0.092	44.	Arkansas	0.004
20.	Wisconsin	0.079	45.	Hawaii	−0.001
21.	Nebraska	0.077	46.	Kentucky	−0.005
22.	Minnesota	0.075	47.	Delaware	−0.007
23.	Washington	0.075	48.	New Jersey	−0.034
24.	Oklahoma	0.071	49.	Texas	−0.050
25.	California	0.071	50.	New York	−0.055

Note: States with the same rank are tied. States with different scores may appear identical due to rounding.

Rank	State	Pro-Life Overall Freedom, 2019		Rank	State	Pro-Life Overall Freedom, 2019
1.	Indiana	0.841		26.	South Carolina	0.176
2.	Michigan	0.821		27.	Ohio	0.132
3.	Idaho	0.786		28.	Louisiana	0.117
4.	Missouri	0.747		29.	Wyoming	0.084
5.	North Dakota	0.668		30.	Iowa	0.027
6.	Oklahoma	0.634		31.	West Virginia	0.013
7.	Utah	0.629		32.	Mississippi	−0.006
8.	Texas	0.627		33.	Montana	−0.043
9.	Kentucky	0.608		34.	Massachusetts	−0.043
10.	Kansas	0.600		35.	Alaska	−0.051
11.	Nebraska	0.531		36.	Minnesota	−0.108
12.	Tennessee	0.492		37.	Rhode Island	−0.137
13.	Florida	0.485		38.	Maine	−0.189
14.	New Hampshire	0.483		39.	Connecticut	−0.204
15.	South Dakota	0.452		40.	Illinois	−0.210
16.	Nevada	0.420		41.	Washington	−0.228
17.	Arizona	0.373		42.	Delaware	−0.271
18.	Georgia	0.357		43.	New Mexico	−0.315
19.	Virginia	0.277		44.	Vermont	−0.404
20.	Pennsylvania	0.250		45.	Maryland	−0.443
21.	North Carolina	0.243		46.	Oregon	−0.538
22.	Wisconsin	0.241		47.	New Jersey	−0.652
23.	Alabama	0.203		48.	California	−0.694
24.	Arkansas	0.194		49.	Hawaii	−0.788
25.	Colorado	0.187		50.	New York	−0.999

Note: States with the same rank are tied. States with different scores may appear identical due to rounding.

Rank	State	Pro-Life Overall Freedom, No Right-to-Work Laws, 2019	Rank	State	Pro-Life Overall Freedom, No Right-to-Work Laws, 2019
1.	Indiana	0.815	26.	Ohio	0.155
2.	Michigan	0.795	27.	South Carolina	0.150
3.	Missouri	0.770	28.	Louisiana	0.091
4.	Idaho	0.760	29.	Wyoming	0.058
5.	North Dakota	0.641	30.	Iowa	0.000
6.	Oklahoma	0.608	31.	West Virginia	−0.013
7.	Utah	0.603	32.	Montana	−0.020
8.	Texas	0.601	33.	Massachusetts	−0.020
9.	Kentucky	0.582	34.	Alaska	−0.028
10.	Kansas	0.573	35.	Mississippi	−0.032
11.	New Hampshire	0.506	36.	Minnesota	−0.085
12.	Nebraska	0.504	37.	Rhode Island	−0.114
13.	Tennessee	0.466	38.	Maine	−0.166
14.	Florida	0.459	39.	Connecticut	−0.181
15.	South Dakota	0.426	40.	Illinois	−0.187
16.	Nevada	0.394	41.	Washington	−0.205
17.	Arizona	0.347	42.	Delaware	−0.248
18.	Georgia	0.331	43.	New Mexico	−0.292
19.	Pennsylvania	0.273	44.	Vermont	−0.381
20.	Virginia	0.251	45.	Maryland	−0.420
21.	North Carolina	0.217	46.	Oregon	−0.515
22.	Wisconsin	0.215	47.	New Jersey	−0.629
23.	Colorado	0.210	48.	California	−0.671
24.	Alabama	0.177	49.	Hawaii	−0.765
25.	Arkansas	0.168	50.	New York	−0.976

Note: States with the same rank are tied. States with different scores may appear identical due to rounding.

Rank	State	Moderate Pro-Choice Overall Freedom, 2019		Rank	State	
1.	New Hampshire	0.587		26.	Wyoming	0.132
2.	Florida	0.556		27.	South Carolina	0.127
3.	Nevada	0.515		28.	Kansas	0.126
4.	Tennessee	0.443		29.	Iowa	0.098
5.	South Dakota	0.428		30.	Massachusetts	0.096
6.	Indiana	0.368		31.	Ohio	0.083
7.	Michigan	0.348		32.	Louisiana	0.068
8.	Georgia	0.333		33.	Nebraska	0.057
9.	Arizona	0.325		34.	Maine	0.034
10.	Idaho	0.312		35.	West Virginia	0.024
11.	Missouri	0.274		36.	Connecticut	0.018
12.	Colorado	0.256		37.	Illinois	−0.012
13.	Virginia	0.228		38.	Washington	−0.041
14.	Pennsylvania	0.201		39.	Minnesota	−0.042
15.	North Dakota	0.195		40.	Mississippi	−0.054
16.	North Carolina	0.194		41.	Rhode Island	−0.089
17.	Wisconsin	0.192		42.	New Mexico	−0.130
18.	Montana	0.180		43.	Vermont	−0.184
19.	Oklahoma	0.160		44.	Delaware	−0.199
20.	Utah	0.156		45.	Maryland	−0.280
21.	Texas	0.154		46.	Oregon	−0.319
22.	Alabama	0.154		47.	New Jersey	−0.468
23.	Arkansas	0.145		48.	California	−0.472
24.	Kentucky	0.135		49.	Hawaii	−0.601
25.	Alaska	0.133		50.	New York	−0.812

Note: States with the same rank are tied. States with different scores may appear identical due to rounding.

TABLE B14

Moderate Pro-Choice Overall Freedom, No Right-to-Work Laws, 2019

Rank	State		Rank	State	
1.	New Hampshire	0.610	26.	Kentucky	0.109
2.	Florida	0.530	27.	Ohio	0.106
3.	Nevada	0.489	28.	Wyoming	0.106
4.	Tennessee	0.417	29.	South Carolina	0.101
5.	South Dakota	0.401	30.	Kansas	0.100
6.	Indiana	0.342	31.	Iowa	0.072
7.	Michigan	0.322	32.	Maine	0.057
8.	Georgia	0.307	33.	Louisiana	0.042
9.	Arizona	0.299	34.	Connecticut	0.041
10.	Missouri	0.297	35.	Nebraska	0.031
11.	Idaho	0.286	36.	Illinois	0.011
12.	Colorado	0.279	37.	West Virginia	−0.002
13.	Pennsylvania	0.224	38.	Washington	−0.018
14.	Montana	0.203	39.	Minnesota	−0.019
15.	Virginia	0.202	40.	Rhode Island	−0.066
16.	North Dakota	0.169	41.	Mississippi	−0.080
17.	North Carolina	0.168	42.	New Mexico	−0.107
18.	Wisconsin	0.166	43.	Vermont	−0.161
19.	Alaska	0.156	44.	Delaware	−0.176
20.	Oklahoma	0.134	45.	Maryland	−0.257
21.	Utah	0.130	46.	Oregon	−0.296
22.	Texas	0.128	47.	New Jersey	−0.445
23.	Alabama	0.128	48.	California	−0.449
24.	Arkansas	0.119	49.	Hawaii	−0.578
25.	Massachusetts	0.119	50.	New York	−0.789

Note: States with the same rank are tied. States with different scores may appear identical due to rounding.

Rank	State	Strong Pro-Choice Overall Freedom, 2019		Rank	State	Strong Pro-Choice Overall Freedom, 2019
1.	New Hampshire	0.594		26.	Wyoming	0.129
2.	Florida	0.554		27.	South Carolina	0.124
3.	Nevada	0.513		28.	Kansas	0.123
4.	Tennessee	0.439		29.	Iowa	0.096
5.	South Dakota	0.424		30.	Massachusetts	0.095
6.	Indiana	0.364		31.	Ohio	0.079
7.	Michigan	0.345		32.	Louisiana	0.065
8.	Georgia	0.329		33.	Nebraska	0.055
9.	Arizona	0.321		34.	Maine	0.034
10.	Idaho	0.309		35.	West Virginia	0.021
11.	Missouri	0.270		36.	Connecticut	0.018
12.	Colorado	0.264		37.	Illinois	−0.012
13.	Virginia	0.225		38.	Washington	−0.041
14.	Pennsylvania	0.199		39.	Minnesota	−0.042
15.	North Carolina	0.191		40.	Mississippi	−0.058
16.	North Dakota	0.191		41.	Rhode Island	−0.092
17.	Wisconsin	0.189		42.	New Mexico	−0.121
18.	Montana	0.179		43.	Vermont	−0.174
19.	Oklahoma	0.157		44.	Delaware	−0.201
20.	Utah	0.153		45.	Maryland	−0.280
21.	Alabama	0.151		46.	Oregon	−0.308
22.	Texas	0.151		47.	New Jersey	−0.458
23.	Alaska	0.144		48.	California	−0.472
24.	Arkansas	0.142		49.	Hawaii	−0.601
25.	Kentucky	0.132		50.	New York	−0.812

Note: States with the same rank are tied. States with different scores may appear identical due to rounding.

TABLE B16

Strong Pro-Choice Overall Freedom, No Right-to-Work Laws, 2019

Rank	State		Rank	State	
1.	New Hampshire	0.617	26.	Kentucky	0.106
2.	Florida	0.528	27.	Wyoming	0.103
3.	Nevada	0.487	28.	Ohio	0.102
4.	Tennessee	0.413	29.	South Carolina	0.097
5.	South Dakota	0.398	30.	Kansas	0.097
6.	Indiana	0.338	31.	Iowa	0.070
7.	Michigan	0.319	32.	Maine	0.057
8.	Georgia	0.303	33.	Connecticut	0.041
9.	Arizona	0.295	34.	Louisiana	0.039
10.	Missouri	0.293	35.	Nebraska	0.029
11.	Colorado	0.287	36.	Illinois	0.011
12.	Idaho	0.283	37.	West Virginia	−0.005
13.	Pennsylvania	0.222	38.	Washington	−0.018
14.	Montana	0.202	39.	Minnesota	−0.019
15.	Virginia	0.199	40.	Rhode Island	−0.069
16.	Alaska	0.167	41.	Mississippi	−0.084
17.	North Carolina	0.165	42.	New Mexico	−0.098
18.	North Dakota	0.165	43.	Vermont	−0.151
19.	Wisconsin	0.163	44.	Delaware	−0.178
20.	Oklahoma	0.130	45.	Maryland	−0.257
21.	Utah	0.126	46.	Oregon	−0.285
22.	Alabama	0.125	47.	New Jersey	−0.435
23.	Texas	0.125	48.	California	−0.449
24.	Massachusetts	0.118	49.	Hawaii	−0.578
25.	Arkansas	0.115	50.	New York	−0.789

Note: States with the same rank are tied. States with different scores may appear identical due to rounding.

FURTHER READING

FEDERALISM AND DECENTRALIZATION

Buchanan, James M. "Federalism as an Ideal Political Order and an Objective for Constitutional Reform." *Publius* 25 (Spring 1995): 19–27. Reprinted in *The Collected Works of James M. Buchanan*. Vol. 18, pp. 67–78. Indianapolis: Liberty Fund, 2001.

Fischel, William A. *The Homevoter Hypothesis: How Home Values Influence Local Government Taxation, School Finance, and Land-Use Policies*. Cambridge, MA: Harvard University Press, 2001.

Nozick, Robert. "Utopia." Part III of *Anarchy, State, and Utopia*. New York: Basic Books, 1974.

Somin, Ilya. "Foot Voting, Federalism, and Political Freedom." In *NOMOS LV: Federalism and Subsidiarity*, edited by James E. Fleming and Jacob T. Levy. New York: New York University Press, 2014.

Storing, Herbert J., and Murray Dry, eds. *The Anti-Federalist: Writings by the Opponents of the Constitution*. Chicago: University of Chicago Press, 1985.

Tabarrok, Alexander. "Arguments for Federalism." Speech given at the Hastings Law School, University of California, San Francisco. September 20, 2001.

Tiebout, Charles. "A Pure Theory of Local Expenditures." *Journal of Political Economy* 64 (1956): 416–24.

Weingast, Barry R. "The Economic Role of Political Institutions: Market-Preserving Federalism and Economic Development." *Journal of Law, Economics, and Organization* 11, no. 1 (Spring 1995): 1–31.

STATE POLITICS AND POLICY

Enns, Peter K., and Julianna Koch. "Public Opinion in the U.S. States: 1956–2010." *State Politics and Policy Quarterly* 13, no. 3 (2013): 349–72.

Erikson, Robert S., Gerald C. Wright, and John P. McIver. *Statehouse Democracy: Public Opinion and Policy in the American States*. Cambridge: Cambridge University Press, 1993.

Gelman, Andrew. *Red State, Blue State, Rich State, Poor State: Why Americans Vote the Way They Do*. Princeton, NJ: Princeton University Press, 2008.

Sorens, Jason, Fait Muedini, and William Ruger. "U.S. State and Local Public Policies in 2006: A New Database." *State Politics and Policy Quarterly* 8, no. 3 (2008): 309–26.

Tausanovitch, Chris, and Christopher Warshaw. "Measuring Constituent Policy Preferences in Congress, State Legislatures, and Cities." *Journal of Politics* 75, no. 2 (2013): 330–42.

THE RELATIONSHIP BETWEEN LIBERTY AND VIRTUE

Block, Walter. "Libertarianism and Libertinism." *Journal of Libertarian Studies* 11, no. 1 (Fall 1994): 117–28.

Meyer, Frank S. "The Locus of Virtue." In *In Defense of Freedom and Related Essays*. Indianapolis: Liberty Fund, 1996, pp. 128–48.

Nock, Albert Jay. "On Doing the Right Thing." *American Mercury*, November 1924. Reprinted in *The State of the Union: Essays in Social Criticism*, ed. Charles H. Hamilton. Indianapolis: Liberty Press, 1991.

Gillespie, Nick, William Ruger, Jason Sorens, Steven Horowitz, Deirdre McCloskey, and Katherine Mangu-Ward. "Libertarianism, Yes! But *What Kind* of Libertarianism? Virtue vs. Libertinism, or a Reason Debate on Liberty, License, Coercion, and Responsibility." *Reason.com*, June 9, 2016.

Smith, Adam. *The Theory of Moral Sentiments*. 1759.

RENT SEEKING

Krueger, Anne O. "The Political Economy of the Rent-Seeking Society." *American Economic Review* 64, no. 3 (June 1974): 291–303.

Olson, Mancur. *The Rise and Decline of Nations: Economic Growth, Stagflation, and Social Rigidities*. New Haven, CT: Yale University Press, 1982.

Tullock, Gordon. "The Welfare Costs of Tariffs, Monopolies and Theft." *Western Economic Journal* 5, no. 3 (June 1967): 224–32.

PERSONAL FREEDOM

Locke, John. "A Letter Concerning Toleration." 1689. http://oll.libertyfund.org/?option=com
_staticxt&staticfile=show.php%3Ftitle=764&chapter=80887&layout=html&Itemid=27.

Mill, John Stuart. "Of the Liberty of Thought and Discussion." Chapter 2 in *On Liberty*. 1859.

Ruger, William. "Why Tolerance Is Different than Acceptance: Let Ideas, Debate, and Freedom Bloom." *The Federalist*, August 18, 2015. http://thefederalist.com/2015/08/18/why
-tolerance-is-different-than-acceptance/.

FREEDOM AND JUSTICE

Boaz, David. *The Libertarian Mind: A Manifesto for Freedom*. New York: Simon & Schuster, 2015.

Buchanan. James M. "Classical Liberalism and the Perfectibility of Man." In *Why I, Too, Am Not a Conservative: The Normative Vision of Classical Liberalism*, pp. 11–21. Cheltenham, UK: Elgar, 2005.

Friedman, Milton. *Capitalism and Freedom*. Chicago: University of Chicago Press, 1962.

Kant, Immanuel. "On the Common Saying: 'This May Be True in Theory, but It Does Not Apply in Practice.'" 1793.

Locke, John. *Second Treatise of Civil Government*. 1690.

Madison, James. "Property." *National Gazette*, March 29, 1792. http://teachingamericanhistory
.org/library/index.asp?document=600.

Nozick, Robert. "State-of-Nature Theory, or How to Back into a State without Really Trying" and "Beyond the Minimal State?" Parts I and II of *Anarchy, State, and Utopia*. New York: Basic Books, 1974.

Spencer, Herbert. *Social Statics, or the Conditions Essential to Happiness Specified, and the First of Them Developed*. London: John Chapman, 1851.

ACKNOWLEDGMENTS

We wish to acknowledge our sincere gratitude to all those who have read, commented on, and helped improve our study in past years. A partial list of those to whom we owe a particular debt of thanks includes David Boaz, Jacob Levy, Dylan McLean, Claire Morgan, Fait Muedini, John Samples, Ilya Somin, Dean Stansel, Varrin Swearingen, Alison Winters, Ken Zuver, everyone at the Mercatus Center at George Mason University who did such an excellent job producing and promoting the first three editions of this index, and everyone at the Cato Institute who has helped us put out this and the previous two editions, along with countless, unnamable readers and listeners who have approached us at events or emailed us their questions and comments.

ABOUT THE AUTHORS

William Ruger is Vice President for Research and Policy at the Charles Koch Institute and Vice President for Foreign Policy at Stand Together. He was previously an Associate Professor in the Department of Political Science at Texas State University. Ruger earned his PhD in politics from Brandeis University and an AB from the College of William and Mary. His scholarship has appeared in a number of academic journals, including *International Studies Quarterly, Civil Wars,* and *Armed Forces and Society*. He is the author of the biography *Milton Friedman* and a coauthor of two books on state politics, including *Freedom in the 50 States*. Ruger has written op-eds for a number of outlets, such as the *New York Times,* the *Washington Post,* and *Foreign Affairs,* and he has been interviewed frequently for television and radio, appearing on MSNBC, CNN, and Fox News. Ruger is a veteran of the war in Afghanistan and an officer in the U.S. Navy (Reserve Component). Ruger was nominated by President Donald Trump to serve as the U.S. Ambassador to the Islamic Republic of Afghanistan, and was appointed by the president to the Fulbright Foreign Scholarship Board in 2020. He lives with his wife and two sons in Virginia.

Jason Sorens is Director of the Center for Ethics in Society at Saint Anselm College and received his PhD in political science from Yale University in 2003. He has researched and written more than 20 peer-reviewed journal articles and a book, *Secessionism* (McGill–Queen's University Press). His research has focused on independence movements around the world, the theory and practice of fiscal federalism, and subnational economic policymaking. He has founded two non-profits, the Free State Project (www.fsp.org) and Ethics and Economics Education (www.e3ne.org). He lives with his wife and daughters in New Hampshire.

ABOUT THE CATO INSTITUTE

The Cato Institute is a public policy research organization—a think tank—dedicated to the principles of individual liberty, limited government, free markets and peace. Its scholars and analysts conduct independent, non-partisan research on a wide range of policy issues.

Founded in 1977, Cato owes its name to *Cato's Letters,* a series of essays published in 18th- century England that presented a vision of society free from excessive government power. Those essays inspired the architects of the American Revolution. And the simple, timeless principles of that revolution—individual liberty, limited government, and free markets— turn out to be even more powerful in today's world of global markets and unprecedented access to information than Jefferson or Madison could have imagined. Social and economic freedom is not just the best policy for a free people, it is the indispensable framework for the future.